Keywords in News
and Journalism Studies

Keywords in News and Journalism Studies

Barbie Zelizer and Stuart Allan

Open University Press

Open University Press
McGraw-Hill Education
McGraw-Hill House
Shoppenhangers Road
Maidenhead
Berkshire
England
SL6 2QL

email: enquiries@openup.co.uk
world wide web: www.openup.co.uk

and Two Penn Plaza, New York, NY 10121—2289, USA

First published 2010

A catalogue record of this book is available from the British Library

ISBN-13: 9780335221837 (pb) 9780335221844 (hb)
ISBN-10: 0335221831 (pb) 033522184X (hb)

Typeset by Kerrypress, Luton, Bedfordshire
Printed and bound in the UK by Bell and Bain Ltd, Glasgow

Table of Contents

Preface

Keywords are building-blocks to inquiry, and writing a book about them felt at times as though we had been thrown back to the building-block stage of our development as academics. Crafting definitions for words we had been using for years without appreciating every nuance of their meaning or their precise origins was a humbling – and enriching – experience. Writing *Keywords in News and Journalism Studies* has thus enhanced our regard for the broad field of academic literature on news and journalism which we necessarily scoured to produce this book, much of it literature we already knew but which required careful rereading for this project.

We followed a few simple principles in setting up the criteria for what we felt merited attention as a keyword. Our keywords needed to be clear enough to be used by both academics and practitioners, durable enough to have withstood time, relevant enough to clarify the evolving state of journalism – as well as news and journalism studies – and general enough to warrant recognition beyond a local setting. We eschewed the inclusion of individual figures and news organizations, gravitated largely towards the national contexts we knew best (the United States and United Kingdom), strived to avoid jargon but remained sensitive to how journalese operates, and tried to project not only our sense of the field today but an anticipatory view of where it is going. These are, of course, principles of degree rather than kind, and our hope is that the resulting list, by no means exhaustive, will engage its readers in thinking anew about the organizing tenets of the study of news and journalism. There is a certain foolhardiness in attempting to delineate the conceptual vocabulary of any field, but doing so may lead us one step closer to its formalization.

Raymond Williams's *Keywords* project showed us that the preferred terms of scholarship only become meaningful when they are used, and it is to their varied, frequently complicated, uses in the existing literature that we pay homage. Various sources helped us, wittingly or not, craft this set of key terms. They include the *Encyclopedia of American Journalism, Encyclopedia of Journalism, International Encyclopedia of Communication, Key Concepts in Journalism Studies, Oxford English Dictionary, Project for Excellence in Journalism, The Routledge Companion to News and Journalism* and a plethora of web-based sources. On a personal level, we thank Angela Lee, Joel Penney, Michael Serazio, Piotr Szpunar and Lokman Tsui for locating some of the materials and

Richard Cardona and Sharon Black for technical assistance. Finally, we would like to thank everyone at Open University Press, as well as Cornelia Turpin for her stellar efforts checking the proofs.

A

Above-the-fold: a news item deemed sufficiently important to warrant placement on the top half of the front page of a **broadsheet** newspaper. Given the prestige associated with this most prominent of spaces, being positioned above-the-fold is highly prized by journalists.

Accuracy: the state of being precise and exact. Accuracy is a long-standing ideal associated with **neutral** or **objective** norms of journalistic practice. It is particularly associated with **professionalism**, by which journalists are expected to provide fact-based, value-free accounts of the events and issues on which they report. Accuracy stretches across all aspects of a news story – the spelling of names and places, correct grammar, the sequencing of events, and the veracity of the claims being made. Accuracy does not come into existence at any one point in time but rather involves a series of journalistic practices, including verifying facts, questioning the judgement calls of others, contextualizing and assessing details, eradicating mistakes and ensuring that the most widely supported perspective gets represented. Even when journalists have good intentions about being accurate, they are not always easily able to achieve it. Errant **eyewitnesses**, a source's slanted perspective, even the technical limitations of the medium can all get in the way of a reporter providing an accurate account.

Ace: abbreviation for assistant city **editor**. The term is also used more generally to refer to an on-call reporter.

Actuality: the sound of an event being recorded as it unfolds on location. Most strongly associated with radio journalism and also called natsot (short for 'natural sound on tape'), actuality produces audio clips – recording, for instance, the sound of a parade, **press conference**, **interview** with a sports fan – that may be inserted into a news item to further enhance its claim to have captured an aspect of reality. In **documentary** film, the notion of actuality similarly revolves around the use of recorded material from actual events – so-called 'actuality footage'. Early formative examples from **radio news** include the famous 'This is London' eyewitness broadcasts of Edward R. Murrow for CBS News during the Second World War. His reports furnished the listener with 'pictures in sound', engendering at times a breathtaking quality of **immediacy**. Experimental use of actuality material followed with the development of 'on the spot' battlefield reporting, a new mode of war journalism on radio with extraordinary appeal for audiences demanding 'authentic' news. The BBC's *War Report*, for example, promised to deliver the 'latest and fullest picture of the war' to the listener. It 'took the microphone to places where things were happening, and let it listen – as one would one's self like to listen – to the sounds of battle, to the voices of men just returned from the fighting line, to observers who spent that day touring the scene of action' (cited in Briggs 1970: 662).

Ad/ed ratio: the ratio of advertising to **editorial** content appearing on a specific page or within a section of **newspapers** and **magazines**. Typically, the ad/ed ratio ranges from 25/75 to 40/60.

Adversarial journalism: a type of journalism which displays a consistently hostile perspective in its treatment of government and politics. Thought to be a long tradition in liberal democracies and an outgrowth of the notion of journalism as a **fourth estate**, adversarial journalism is often seen as **participant** or **advocacy journalism** taken to an extreme, where reporters engage with political events, issues and figures in a rude, arrogant or cynical fashion. Current forms of adversarial journalism are increasingly thought to have tipped the balance in the direction of too much negativity. Said to be on the rise in the United States since the 1970s (when the **Watergate** scandal generated renewed interest in **investigative** techniques of newsgathering), adversarial journalism reflects a heightened degree of scepticism among journalists toward politicians and political institutions. Critics point to increasing levels of hostile content, brasher assertiveness and lessened deference in interactions with officials, an undue emphasis on political scandal, and a preoccupation with political strategy over political substance as evidence. They contend too that adversarial journalism is contributing to rising public distrust towards both government and the news media, and to cynicism about the optimum functioning of large-scale public institutions (Patterson 1994; Cappella and Jamieson 1997).

Advertorial: an advertisement presented in a blended format with the news or **editorial** copy surrounding it. Blurring two otherwise distinct genres of text in presentational and stylistic terms, the advertorial can be of either a commercial or political nature. Often advertorials alert the readers of more reputable newspapers and magazines to their status as a paid advertisement via a printed disclaimer on the same page or a section heading such as 'special advertising section', but sometimes no disclaimers are made and the similarities in writing style and typography render them indistinct from surrounding **copy**. Advertorials have been attempted in media other than **newspapers** and **magazines**, such as 'infomercials' for broadcasting, but they remain particularly prevalent in the print media. Critics maintain that presenting advertising as editorial content is irresponsible and risks violating the relationship of trust with the audience.

Advocacy journalism: a type of journalism that eschews principles of **neutrality**, **impartiality** and **objectivity**, and thereby the separation of news from opinion, in order to intentionally take a strategic position on events and issues in the news, usually for some larger social or political purpose. Traditionally allied with **muckrakers, whistleblowers, participant journalism** and **alternative journalism** and seen as the norm in various evolutions of journalistic practice such as the US colonial press or the **partisan** press of the 1800s, advocacy journalists believe that good journalism is accomplished by taking a stand, and in that light they declare their **bias** in an open and transparent fashion. Meaningful primarily when contrasted with norms of **objectivity** or models of **neutral journalism**, advocacy journalism aligns with political **partisanship** in many locations around the world. For instance, in newly independent developing nations, journalism was often associated with freedom movements that supported liberation from colonialism. Moreover, even as advocacy journalism seemed to be displaced by various forms of ostensibly value-free reporting, advocacy could still be found in **editorials**, **columns** and broadcast commentary, where journalists were expected to address the news from a point of view. Today, as **citizen journalism** and **blogs** have become more prevalent and certain news organizations – like Fox News or conservative papers in the United States – explicitly frame news events through an articulated perspective, advocacy journalism has experienced a resurgence. Organizations like the US National Conference for Media Reform or the Center for Independent Media now regularly debate the blending of straight fact and opinion as a recognizable aspect of journalism, lending support to the increasingly prevalent claim that it is impossible to separate the two.

Agenda setting: the focusing of public attention on a particular issue. Described as being less a matter of 'telling people what to think' and more about 'telling people what to think about', the extent of power associated with agenda setting is debatable. In assigning relative importance to a specific topic, news reporting selectively emphasizes certain concerns over and above others. Early formulations of agenda setting as a concept frequently credit Lippmann's (1922) *Public Opinion* which, in a chapter entitled 'The world outside and the pictures in our heads', argued that citizens' perceptions of public affairs are decisively shaped by what the media recurrently attach significance to, as well as by what is ignored or trivialized, over a period of time. Agenda setting today still draws considerable attention as an **effect of news**, especially where the analysis of election reporting is concerned. The ranking of salient issues on the 'news agenda' can be set in relation to their standing on the 'public agenda' (whether local, national or international) so as to ascertain the relative degree of correlation between the two agendas. Some researchers conclude that the greater the amount of coverage an issue warrants by news organizations (performing a **gatekeeping** role), the more likely it will be regarded as significant by members of the news audience.

Agony aunt/uncle: a newspaper or magazine columnist who answers readers' letters requesting advice about personal concerns or problems, often with regard to the travails of family life, careers and affairs of the heart. Letters are typically chosen for publication when they are perceived to be of interest to the general readership.

Alternative journalism: a type of journalism best defined as distinct from the mainstream. Alternative journalism typically positions itself against governmental and economic excess so as to be aligned with the individual, **labour**, the marginalized and the disempowered. It can also extend to splashy entertainment weeklies, new age pamphlets and 'amateur' efforts to report on everyday events.

Though the term 'alternative journalism' has most often been used in reference to a counter-culture **literary** press that emerged during the 1960s (which came to be known as one instance of '**new journalism**'), in fact some form of alternative newsmaking inhabited the journalistic landscape in its multiple geographic locations significantly earlier. Associated with **advocacy journalism**, **partisan journalism** and **participant journalism**, it has ranged across the underground printing presses of eighteenth-century France and the black American Abolitionist press of the 1800s to I.F. Stone's crusades against McCarthyism during the 1950s, the circulation of the mimeographed ideas of dissidents in the former Soviet bloc through *Samizdat* and the toppling of the Shah of Iran through secret tape recordings and religious sermons. In each instance, the idea that journalism could do a more effective job of representing unarticulated interests has appealed to many who have been dissatisfied with the performance, demeanour and perspective of mainstream news organizations at a particular time and place.

Aligning itself with particular interests and/or interest groups, alternative journalism tends to use volunteer, non-profit, non-corporate and otherwise independent efforts on the part of individuals or collectives to articulate some notion of social responsibility (*see* **Four theories of the press**). Its devices are multiple but can be unusual in news settings, and they include tape recorders, mimeograph machines, microphones, carbon paper, photocopiers, pirate radio and, increasingly, laptop computers, remote hosting sites, digital cameras, camcorders and telephones. Its reporters use techniques like **eyewitness** accounts, first person **narratives** and non-hierarchical forms of organization so as to be more inclusive and egalitarian than other kinds of journalism. Alternative journalism tends to arise in response to a perception of neglect of issues by mainstream news organizations and is often formed along platforms – such as progressive politics, women's rights and anti-globalization groups – that offset it. Such platforms have extended in multiple directions – to the **underground press** (*The Village Voice*, the *Free Press*, *International Times*), to celebrations of the counterculture (*Oz*, *Rolling Stone*, *New Musical Express*), to the reinvigorated **muckraking** of the 1960s (*Private*

Eye, Ramparts, The Progressive), to the advancement of certain ethnic or gender groups (*Spare Rib, Mother Jones, El Macriado, The Advocate*).

Though many alternative news organizations tend to be short-lived, lacking the infrastructure to keep themselves afloat for long periods of time, certain news organs have drawn long-standing support, such as *The Nation, In These Times, UTNE Reader* and *Spare Rib*. Independent documentary filmakers use online DVD sales and house showings to distribute their films. In the US, projects like the Association of Alternative Newsweeklies (a trade association of alternative newspapers, many rooted in the underground press); Pacific News Service (PNS, or more recently New America Media); and the now-defunct Independent Press Association have all offered ways of co-ordinating alternative journalism that nonetheless kept it distinct from the mainstream. The alternative viewpoints they espouse are documented on a yearly basis by Project Censored. Elsewhere, Venezuela's *El Libertario* or the German *Die Tageszeitung* are examples of vibrant hubs through which to engage alterna-tively with the news. Public access television has emerged too as a viable platform for alternative journalism, and in locations as wide-ranging as Brazil, Belgium and Finland members of the public are regularly given voice.

Alternative journalism has advanced further with the rise of online media. Examples abound: Independent Media Centers (**IndyMedia**), which estab-lished itself in 1999 to cover the World Trade Organization summit in Seattle and has since grown to over 150 centres in nearly 50 countries; Alternet; news **blogging** and **citizen journalism**; and individual postings to YouTube, Flickr, Twitter and other social networking sites.

Anchorperson: the newscaster who fronts a **television news** programme. Used in the US to refer to the lead announcer or host of a newscast who remains on camera as an organizing presence, the term 'anchor' was initially coined by CBS producer Don Hewitt in the early 1950s to describe coverage of the Republican National Convention in Chicago. Likening the coverage to a track relay team, presided over by the team's final person – its 'anchor', then embodied by an up-and-coming Walter Cronkite – Hewitt established the parameters of a live in-studio performance that kept the news programme running smoothly. This was achieved via improvisation, reading from a **tel-eprompter**, introducing **breaking news**, chatting with in-studio guests and co-ordinating the presentation of coverage from journalists on the scene. Anchorpersons – sometimes called 'anchors' or 'news-anchors' – are often involved in writing copy, in going on **assignment** to cover special events and in providing live **eyewitness** reports from the scene. Some of the most well-known US journalists established themselves as anchorpersons, includ-ing Cronkite, David Brinkley and Peter Jennings, and contemporary US anchors are often celebrity personalities as well as information hosts. News organizations elsewhere in the world may not use the term 'anchors', but do have individuals who perform the same or similar tasks, such as the **newsreaders** or newscasters of European television programming. Critics argue that anchors exacerbate an emphasis on surface appearance in broadcast news, turning them into celebrities which can in turn trivialize the traditional role of journalists.

Angle: the chosen perspective, emphasis, **bias** or focus from which a news item is told. News angles draw from multiple aspects of newsgathering circumstances, such as the medium through which an item is being relayed or the **news values** and selection criteria by which it is drawn in as news. Largely understood as the aspect of a news item that gives it worth for the public, the news angle is evident in multiple aspects of news presentation: in the **lead** of the item, in the **headline**, in the quotes that elaborate the lead's main point, even in the **captions** that might adjoin accompanying pictures. **Objectivity** demands that the angle be seen to arise from the apparent facts of the situation, rather than being consciously imposed by a journalist pursuing a specific agenda, though more **partisan** models of journalistic practice display news angles as proof of their perspective.

Anonymity: the state of being unnamed or unidentified. Anonymous writing became particularly prevalent once the printing press made available the circulation of texts separate from the physicality of their authors. Anonymity in journalism is associated with both unauthored news output and anonymous **sources**, and in both cases it undercuts journalism's broader gravitation towards clear disclosure. Often journalists agree to anonymous sourcing so as to gain access to the information the source can provide, but historically accepting anonymity as a stipulation for information sharing has created multiple highs and lows. **Watergate**, for example, would not have been uncovered without the intervention of an anonymous source. In the years since, conventions of anonymous sourcing have often been established because of threats to the source's livelihood or well-being. Problems sometimes ensue, however, including blows to credibility as sources end up not existing, are not able to verify claims or have grudges to bear. Certain journalists have abused anonymity to create fabricated or erroneous stories, with such (relatively rare) instances of misconduct attracting news coverage in their own right.

Art: any visual material – such as illustrations, photographs, maps and graphics – accompanying the news reports in a **newspaper** or **magazine**. Though most attention to the art of journalism tends to focus on the news **picture**, in fact the graphic elements of the journalistic record are far-reaching.

Asian values journalism: a type of journalism practised in Asia that is perceived to foreground harmony, consensus and the collective over freedom of information and the individual's right to know. Though the degree to which Asian news organizations practise it exclusively is variable, it emerged when it became clear that western models of journalistic practice did not fit well within the Asian context. The premise that Asians share a set of core beliefs – favouring the collective over the individual, harmony and consensus over conflict and divisiveness, freedom with responsibility over robust independence, respect for order and authority over criticism – was seen as an alternative way of thinking about journalistic practice. Journalism's performance, it was felt, could be wedded to the goal of national development by following these core beliefs.

In departing from the western model, Asian values journalism's articulated support for extended parameters of social responsibility (*see* **Four theories of the press**) and respect for the government has attracted criticism by some commentators. First, they point out, Asian values journalism is applied variably, and in nation-states with low levels of literacy and high dependence on foreign **news agencies**, the tendency towards more strident government control over the media complicates the operation of a free journalism. Second, Asian values journalism exerts subtle but strategic control. Here critics argue that it persuades Asians to eschew western-style journalism and its concomitant values of democracy and civil society in favour of yielding to the authoritarian bent of local governments. Journalists are encouraged not to be **adversarial**, to avoid **investigative** reporting, to widely cover government speeches and **press releases**, and to ignore signs of opposition to the government. Third, subtle punitive measures exist, such as expensive licensing fees of newspapers (which can be revoked if a news organization becomes too adversarial), expensive security deposits, government control of newsprint, and laws concerning security, public order, sedition and **libel** that are applied to both journalists and publishers.

Assertion journalism: a type of journalism in which information is presented with little time or effort given to establish its veracity independently. Largely an outgrowth of **talk shows**, punditry, **infotainment**, **blogs** and opinion-driven broadcast programming, the journalism of assertion unfolds so quickly that journalists cannot substantiate facts as they were presumed to have done with traditional journalism. Coined by Kovach and Rosenstiel (2001) to assess the impact of 24/7 news programming characterized by corporatization, the rise of cable news and the internet, and the deregulation of the US broadcasting industry, assertion journalism remains more focused on getting topics and events into public discussion than on verifying the **accuracy** of their details. Critics argue that a constant foregrounding of speed for its own sake comes at the expense of responsibility and accountability.

Assignment: a specific story or reportorial task, sometimes associated with a **beat** or **patch**, which a news editor has given to a particular journalist to pursue. On occasion, a journalist makes the case for an assignment of his or her choosing, but the suggestion requires an editor's approval from the outset. In some news organizations, an 'assignment editor' is a specific role for an individual overseeing the breadth of coverage – either generated on a given day or anticipated in future – so as to facilitate an efficient allocation of resources.

Attribution: a formal acknowledgement of the **source** for material appearing in a news report. Proper attribution enhances the credibility of the news organization, whereby acknowledging statements credited to an individual or copyrighted images supports the transparency of the newsgathering process. Conventions of attribution continue to change, however, as the journalistic environment changes. For instance, news **pictures** in their early evolution were often, though not always, attributed to the photographer, while more recently credits make note of the archival or picture agency that owns the picture. Sometimes attribution is a problem for those offering information, and in those cases **unattributed sourcing** practices may prevail.

Autocue/Teleprompter: a technical device that projects the slowly scrolling words of a news script in front of a television news **anchor** or **newsreader**. The device allows the presenter to look directly into the camera, saving them from memorizing large amounts of text or from reading a hard copy of the script.

Automated news aggregator: software designed to gather and present news reports from across the internet on to a single website without relying upon the news judgement of a human **editor**. The term emerged shortly after the beta (or test) version of Google News, the first automated news aggregator, went live in September 2002. Though it glosses over the reliance of the news site on the efforts of thousands of editors and journalists to generate its content in the first place, the site enables users to conduct searches on any subject, and then links them to news stories from more than 10,000 news sources (some 4,500 in the English language) around the globe. Its main page arranges the leading news stories without human intervention, presenting the most relevant news first, and it is updated every 15 minutes. Clusters of related links for each story make the reading of multiple reports straightforward. Each 'top story' is clearly time-stamped and sourced, and sorted by robotic 'spiders' into genre categories, such as World, Business, Sci/Tech, Sport, Entertainment and Health. Pages can be filtered – 'customized' for UK users or 'personalized' for US users, for example – on the basis of news from different regions and languages, as well as by the individual user's own interests and preferences. Google refuses to divulge its precise ranking criteria, beyond a general indication that relevance to search words, timeliness and the reputation of the news source figure into its calculations when collating stories. For the news organizations included in its sweep, it provides a much greater audience of users – 'eyeballs' in advertising parlance – than they might otherwise attract on their own, and a portion of any generated advertising revenue is shared among them.

B

B-Roll: video footage or images prepared for illustrative purposes in a news item that are usually intended to supplement a newscast's more central material. While the term originated in the days of film, when a distinction was made between A (primary) and B (secondary) rolls, B-Rolls are now used to cover a reporter's **voiceover** or to help link together otherwise disparate visual elements when unwanted footage has been removed.

Back-pack journalism: a type of journalism whose reporters use multiple tools of relay in crafting their news stories. Also called **multimedia journalism**, back-pack journalism typically combines the use of self-provided video and audio clips, graphics, animated graphics, still photographs and texts into one non-linear news story. One of the first groups of back-pack journalism was developed by Video News International, the *New York Times*'s television platform, in the mid-1990s. Associated with **VJs** (video journalists), it has taken on creative forms among **MoJos** (mobile journalists) and **SoJos** (solo journalists) in numerous places around the globe.

Backtime: a time calculation made by counting backwards in broadcast news. In television news, for example, one minute into a three minute news segment means that two minutes of backtime remain. News directors and producers must be necessarily adept at monitoring backtime in order to ensure smooth narrative flow throughout the newscast or **bulletin**.

Bagger: a **soft news** television report prepared earlier and left 'in the bag' for later use. Also called leaving a story 'in the can' or 'on the shelf', news organizations value baggers because they can be retrieved for use when there is a gap in the **news hole** that needs to be filled. The **zinger** is one kind of bagger that can be retrieved generally without concern for the elapsed time since it was made.

Balance: the maintenance of a state of equilibrium between two or more sides, opinions or perspectives. One of the long-standing aspirations of **neutral journalism**, balance refers to a journalist's or news organization's ability to remain even-handed in news coverage. Closely allied with **impartiality** and fairness, balance suggests that journalists try to recognize different sides of a topic or issue and give equivalent voice to the most prominent or relevant among them. Though balance does not mean giving equal time or space to every side, it does suggest a reasoned, dispassionate approach to the simultaneous existence of more than one perspective and the various aspects of a topic or issue that they raise. Balance tends to be invoked most often in **public service broadcasting**, where it features frequently in discussions about news quality. Critics of balance maintain that in searching for a state of equilibrium journalists often miss the crux of the stories they report and, in driving for balance, they reduce complicated stories to only two sides.

Banner/Streamer: a **headline** that stretches across the entire width of the newspaper page or webpage. Banner headlines tend to be reserved for unusual, critically important or **breaking news** stories. They are used with reserve by mainstream news organizations, while tabloids rely on their use more frequently.

Beat: a regularly covered geographic or specialized area. Also called 'specialities', 'specialisms' or **patches**, beats offset a news organization's reliance on **breaking news** and help journalists plan for stories to fill the varying and often unpredictable size of the **news hole**. Both geographic beats (the White House, the Middle East, the suburbs) and speciality beats (the courts, the police, health, local government) are useful for gauging and controlling for the instability of news. Beat reporters are expected to track events and issues in their beat area and report on them regularly. They remain the first point of contact when news unfolds in their area and are often engaged to help organize wide-ranging coverage that involves **breaking news** or more than one reporter. Though beats are valuable in organizing workload, they have been criticized for overly narrowing a reporter's focus and rendering him or her too close to the beat area to retain a truly independent perspective. Part of the folklore associated with the successful US coverage of the **Watergate** scandal was its involvement of journalists across beats, by which crime reporters were engaged in an account of governmental misdemeanour. The assumption was that the story may not have broken if only White House reporters had been involved.

Bias: a slanted **angle** or partial perspective on a news event or issue. In journalism, to detect bias is to suggest that journalists are failing to present the world as it is or emphasizing one area of coverage over another. Long aligned with **partisan journalism**, **participant journalism**, **advocacy journalism** and **alternative journalism**, bias constitutes a problem in those parts of the world where models of **neutral journalism** and norms of **objectivity**, **impartiality** and **balance** have ascended with the professionalization of journalists. Though scholarship on social perception has underscored the inevitability of bias in basic cognitive and perceptual mechanisms (leading to a recognition that non-biased reporting is an impossibility), the notion of bias still remains a trump card in the **public sphere**, where pleas for and against certain views regularly feature in news coverage. Bias is said to be most often found in the selection of topics for news presentation and in the **framing** strategies of news organizations and journalists. It may be similarly perceived to be embodied in word choice, **source** choice, the selection and presentation of quotations, **headlines**, presentation on a page or lineup, and **captions**, suggesting that bias rests in some form in nearly every aspect of news presentation and selection (Zelizer *et al.* 2002). Having multiple origins, it can be personal, organizational or structural, conscious or subconscious, official or unofficial, formal or informal. At the heart of each of these attributes is a presumption that in presenting a news event or issue in one way and not another, bias works to shape coverage and, by extension, the response of the public to the news story. For that reason, partisan bias – or bias that follows some kind of ideological line, usually liberal or conservative – is seen as the real culprit undermining quality journalism, unless reporting follows partisan lines as a matter of course.

Big Media: a disparaging label given to the mainstream news media by critical voices in the **blogosphere**. In the case of **citizen journalism**, for example, the virtues of 'amateur' reporters have been championed for the role they play in offsetting Big Media, and their perceived capacity to escape complicity in 'professional' (predominantly corporate) **gatekeeping** machinations.

Blogosphere: the totality of **blogs** available on the internet, envisaged as a distinct realm or sphere in its own right. Implying a degree of connectivity across blogs, the term is thought to have been coined in the late 1990s as a humorous play on the term 'logosphere', the Greek combination of 'logos' (word) and 'sphere' (world). Today the blogosphere is often referenced as a gauge of public opinion, though with varying reliability, and multiple tracking sites, such as Technorati and BlogScope, regularly follow a topic as it travels from blog to blog.

Blogs/Weblogs: blogs, short for weblogs, are diaries or journals written by individuals seeking to establish an online presence. The typical format revolves around a shared practice whereby each new entry is placed at the top of the page, its posting instantly time- and date-stamped. Not only is this reverse-chronological ordering expedient for the 'web enthusiast' turned weblogger (called a 'public diarist' or 'journaller' in the early days), but it also allows users to see at a glance whether or not the weblog has been updated since their last visit. This format quickly caught on because of its ease of use, enabling regular and even daily postings to appear in a logical sequence. When the number of posts became too large for convenient scrolling, they could then be archived for future reference. The majority of early weblogs were 'personal' weblogs, that is, authored by a single person (as is the case today), although some 'portal-like' or 'content aggregator' weblogs involved the collective efforts of a group of like-minded individuals making fresh contributions.

Debates regarding which weblog should be heralded as the first to appear continue to attract attention. Much depends, of course, on how 'weblog' is defined. For some, the first website may be considered the first weblog, in which case the site built by Tim Berners-Lee at CERN (http://info.cern.ch/) deserves proper recognition. Other contenders include the ubiquitous 'What's New' pages, such as the one hosted by the National Center for Supercomputing Applications (NCSA). Still others nominate the 'microportals' or 'web musings' – rumoured to have been written by Netscape creator Marc Andreeson – that began to appear on a regular basis in 1993.

There appears to be something of a consensus – to the extent it is possible to discern one in the **blogosphere** – that credit for the invention of the term 'weblog' itself belongs to Jorn Barger of Chicago. His 'Robot Wisdom' introduced the term in December 1997 as a means to describe a format that was slowly being formalized into a daily net journal (thereby displacing an earlier rendering of 'weblog' as a term for the traffic record of a web server). The 'log' in 'weblog' was generally interpreted as referring to the way such sites provided a log or record of their owner's surfing in the form of a collection of links to other locations online. While alternative histories about the origins of weblogs continue to spark debate, there is little doubt that weblogs emerged in form and practice – however unevenly – prior to the arrival of the term itself (Allan 2006).

Body-bag journalism: reporting based upon a sensationalist conception of **news values** – encapsulated in the dictum 'if it bleeds, it leads' – associated with the worst excesses of **tabloid** or **local news** coverage of **crime**. Studies suggest that in placing a disproportionate emphasis on violent crime for its ostensibly entertaining shock value, audiences are encouraged to believe that their communities are more violent than crime statistics would suggest. Moreover, body-bag journalism may elicit strong feelings of fear, cynicism and resignation among some audience members, especially children and the elderly. At times bordering on **moral panic**, this type of journalism has been shown to benefit conservative 'law-and-order' rhetoric.

Breaking news: a type of news that is unfolding at the moment of – or very near to – its presentation. Though breaking news constitutes only a portion of journalistic outlay over a given period of time, many journalistic practices and much of journalistic folklore are geared towards the potentiality of breaking news and its centrality in the evolving **news hole**. Because breaking news tends to involve fast and pressured decision-making, high stakes, unpredictable circumstances, near-instant reallocations of resources, and changing decisions about what to feature most prominently in a relay, newscast or newspaper, it requires standardized practices and routinization that facilitate instantaneous and widespread attention from the members of a news organization. Missing a breaking news story is tantamount to eschewing the obligation to cover the news, and journalists thus associate breaking news with an implicit set of craft expectations – about agility, organization, clarity and speed – for which journalists must always be prepared.

Broadsheet: a term used to describe the (relatively large) format of a newspaper, usually in comparison with the smaller **tabloid** alternative. Broadsheet newspapers are typically situated at the 'serious' end of the quality continuum, where they are contrasted with the 'popular', 'sensational' tabloid press. Originating in the 1600s and early 1700s, when wooden presses required large pages to be singly pressed for typesetting, the gradual evolution of different print features – such as greater use of graphics or the possibility of fewer columns – increased the appeal of the smaller pages made available by tabloids. Broadsheets continue to flourish in some parts of the world, the larger size still aligned with perceptions of prestige and credibility, but the difference between broadsheets and tabloids began to disappear in many locations by the mid-1990s when finances made broadsheets a less tenable choice of presentational format. In the UK, for instance, most national broadsheet titles moved to a tabloid format in recent years, with the *Daily Telegraph* the main exception and the *Guardian* moving instead to the mid-size 'Berliner format' – similar to France's *Le Monde* – in 2005. In the US, by contrast, certain newspapers moved from broadsheet to tabloid style only on certain days of the week, such as the *St Louis Post-Dispatch*, while others, such as the *New York Times*, shrank the size of their broadsheet page.

Bulks: copies of newspapers given away to members of the public for free or at a discounted price in order to promote sales. Examples include distributing copies in hotels, airports or university campuses in order to encourage prospective readers to discover a paper's merits. For accuracy's sake, bulks are typically not included in circulation figures.

Bulldog: an early edition of a newspaper, such as one intended for distribution in the suburbs or a rural region, prepared before the main edition is **put to bed**. A bulldog also refers to a news story put together prior to a specific date or time for release, such as a business item about a new company written before its stock is floated later that day.

Bulletin: a British term for the delivery format of broadcast news. Often called a newscast in the US, bulletins comprise the core of the network's assembled news reports and related types of content, such as weather information, positioning them at a specified time in the schedule.

Bureau: an office established by a **news organization** to extend its operation by gathering news reports from distant locations. While most news bureaux are defined by their geographical location (e.g. a **news agency**'s Beijing Bureau), some offer specialized reportage associated with a certain topic and are called a **beat** or **patch** (e.g. a sports bureau for the Olympic Games).

Business journalism: reporting about the economy, business, finance, commercialism and consumerism. Business journalism aims to inform the public about major events and issues related to the economic side of life, and most contemporary news organizations employ individuals with business acumen who can address business news as it unfolds.

Early forms of mercantile journalism were among the first justifications for distributing news beyond a specific location, and shipping information, exchange rates and commodity prices were regularly shared among members of the merchant class in Venice and Antwerp as early as the mid-1500s. As mercantile activity shifted geographically, so did the publications, and its spread to Amsterdam in the seventeenth century and to London, Boston, Philadelphia and New York City in the eighteenth and nineteenth centuries spawned business-related publications in multiple places. For instance, the *New York Herald* was among the first newspapers to regularly report on business news in 1835, while the *Wall Street Journal* was founded in 1889. Joined by periodic journals in the early nineteenth century under titles like *Commercial Advertiser* or *Merchants' Magazine*, business journalism became increasingly part of mainstream news as newspapers became more diverse in scope. That development required a shift from what had been until then a mostly uncritical filing of issues of interest to the companies that were being covered towards a more critical approach to business affairs that did not necessarily coincide with the interests of business leaders and their firms. Central in this regard was the appearance of a number of weekly and monthly business magazines, such as *Business Week*, *Fortune* and *Forbes*, begun in the US in the 1920s and 1930s. The first consumer periodical – *Consumer Reports* – also appeared at this time.

Following the Second World War, business journalism rose in stock as financial affairs were seen as having direct relevance to everyday life, and multiple business newspapers – among them the *Wall Street Journal* in the US and the *Financial Times* in the UK – began reporting on general economic trends and forecasts and their relevance to the public at large. This in turn led to more comprehensive coverage of business by mainstream journalism, which today provides a large swathe of connected topics and events – including wide-ranging news about the economy, specific companies, stock market quotes, economic regulation and policy, and consumerism. Business journalism began to appear on television by the late 1960s, when special business shows – such as *Wall Street Week* – anticipated the development of cable stations devoted to business journalism, such as CNBC or Fox Business News. Business journalism rose further in centrality in the 1990s with large-scale investments in the stock market and continued to grow in importance with the financial crisis of 2008 and beyond (despite widespread criticism of business journalists for failing to predict the scale and severity of the crisis). Today business journalism's often sceptical mode of engagement remains generally at odds with the companies at the core of its coverage.

Byline: a line of type that designates the author of a newspaper article. Bylines were encouraged by the **trade press** during the end of the nineteenth century, because using a byline was linked to receiving a salary. Until writers added names to their articles, the argument went, they would not be able to claim higher status and better wages. Bylines were widely instituted in the US during the 1920s and 1930s, when, according to Schudson (1978), they became an instrumental tool for separating personal values from objective reportage. Bylines also were related to the rise of **professionalism** and to the recognizable expertise of journalists in conveying the news in an authored fashion. Not only did they confer status on certain reporters, but readers began to look for articles written by named journalists whom they believed they could trust.

Bystanders' journalism: a title for **war journalism** that tries to be objective. The term was first used by former BBC journalist Martin Bell (1998: 15–16) who argued against war reporting that was concerned 'more with the circumstances of wars – military formations, tactics, strategies and weapons systems – than with the people who provoke them, the people who fight them and the people who suffer from them' (*see* **Journalism of attachment**).

C

Caption: the title adjoining an illustration in the news. Often one of the more underdeveloped aspects of the intersection between words and images, captions have long been expected to tell the public what it sees in the adjoining image. Standards for caption writing did not develop at the same time as the use of captions proliferated, such that today's caption use remains one of the loosest, most variable practices of news presentation. Captions are often written without a one-on-one correspondence with the depictions they are presumed to describe, though they serve to anchor the image within some meaningful frame (Hall 1973). They easily gravitate towards broad description, favour symbolic over concrete information and generally identify the most formulaic parameters of what is represented (Zelizer 1998), thereby generating often erroneous and incomplete descriptions of the adjacent news **picture**.

Cartoon: a drawing or illustration that opines on a news event or issue, often with humorous intent, and is typically displayed on a newspaper's **editorial** page. Though the cartoon is often interchangeably called a caricature, the difference between them is primarily one of tone: the cartoon can offer either positive or negative views on its subject, while the caricature generally portrays negative views by exaggerating the most characteristic feature of an issue or person in order to satirize or ridicule it.

Cartoons and caricatures are long-standing features of journalism, in which they have served pictorial, editorial, entertainment and commercial purposes. They appeared as early as the 1650s as a way of visually addressing the English civil war, and they emerged in the US during the 1750s as it contemplated independence. Arguably the first of such representations of the colonial union, credited to Benjamin Franklin, depicted a snake cut into eight parts (signifying the eight colonies) under the caption 'Join, Or Die' in 1754, though some believe it actually represented support for England during the French and Indian War. Cartoons and caricatures rose in stock during the 1800s, when their appearance in the British *Punch* magazine highlighted what came to be known as the 'Golden age of British caricature'. French caricaturists widely disseminated their drawings at the same time by taking photographic pictures and making hundreds of inexpensive prints of them, exemplified by Honoré Daumier, who in the 1830s produced over 4000 lithographs that satirized social and political conditions in France and Europe. Thomas Nast began distributing his cartoons during the US Civil War, though they generated wide-ranging acclaim when he used them to tackle the corruption of New York City's Tweed Ring in the late 1860s. Early cartoons in both Britain and France tended to lampoon politicians, specifically the government and monarchy, while US drawings were more inclined to poke fun at newspaper editors and only over time at politicians and other public figures.

Routinely appearing in the printed page from the late nineteenth century on, usually on the same page in each issue of a journal or newspaper, cartoons and caricatures offer an ironic, sardonic, humorous or satirical perspective on current events and issues, achieved through visual form. Called by Seymour-Ure (2008: 75) 'editorials in pictures', cartoons and caricatures emerged as particularly powerful when they combined a receptive audience with a negative perception of a powerful subject worthy of scorn and a cartoonist who was able to mobilize that scorn creatively into visual form (Lordan 2006). Cartoons have regularly generated outrage when the targets of their critical depiction disagree with their portrayal. From Boss Tweed's demand to stop Nast's pictures of Tammany Hall during the 1860s and 1870s to the murders that followed the portrayal of the prophet Mohammed in the Danish press in 2005, the illustrations generate intense emotion surrounding the legitimacy of whatever is being depicted. When cartoons are assembled into single or multiple panels which recount a continuous sequence of action over days, they are called comic strips. Although some comic strips are simply instruments of humour, many also use comic drawings to engage with political or social concerns of the day. Among the most famous was a US cartoon entitled 'Hogan's Alley' which depicted tenement life of the late 1890s. One of its key characters was a boy in a long yellow nightshirt, known as 'The Yellow Kid', who later came to emblematize the Hearst–Pulitzer newspaper rivalry and the so-called **yellow journalism** that ensued. Other venues for the display of cartoons and caricatures proliferated too, including *Private Eye* in the UK, *Mad* and *National Lampoon* in the US and *Le Canard Enchaine* in France.

Censorship: the suppression of expression, ideas or information considered dangerous, harmful, threatening, objectionable or otherwise undesirable by those in power. Coming from the Latin word *censere* – 'to give as one's opinion' – and originally associated with the reputable actions of an individual of high prestige in ancient Rome, contemporary censorship has undergone multiple degrees of redefinition, both in function, nature, scope, demeanour and effect.

Censorship has experienced various manifestations during different time periods. It ranges from the pervasive, explicit censorship that characterized the control of printed materials in seventeenth-century Europe, for example, to the inferential modes of **self-censorship** (such as where matters of **professionalism**, or even 'good taste', are concerned) taken for granted today in multiple democracies. Censorship derives from various impulses, of a religious, political, military, corporate or moral nature, or any combination thereof. It has also been differently shaped when journalism operates under different kinds of political regime. A key attribute of so-called authoritarian states, censorship is thought to be one of the most powerful instruments of repressive state control. In democracies too, however, the yielding to censorship increases in times of perceived threat. For instance, in 1798 the passage of the Alien and Sedition Acts in the US provided the opportunity to imprison and fine persons convicted of writing, printing or publishing anti-Federalist sentiments. And though today freedom of speech and freedom of the press are protected in the US by the **First Amendment**, the tendency towards self-censorship, **libel** suits, wartime censorship, secrecy, official acts of withholding, government or corporate pressure, and even language choice all make it easier to censor than might be imagined.

Not surprisingly, over time censorship has fomented various creative practices of evasion: international newspapers were published widely in the seventeenth century in the Netherlands so as to circumvent domestic censorship, while caricatures during the Restoration of Louis-Philippe – drawn both in newspapers and public spaces – offered an opportunity to critique the French monarch more easily than was available in words.

Chequebook journalism: the payment of money or monetary benefits to individuals for the exclusive right to publish their account or testimony concerning a news event. Often called 'pay for play', the practice is widely condemned by politicians and lawyers for being unethical, particularly when it is feared that it will pervert the course of justice, as in court trials. Chequebook journalism has a long history – some sources note its first appearance in 1912 when a journalist paid a survivor of the *Titanic* $1000 for the story of the ship's sinking – and it has been practised by otherwise upstanding news

organizations, including payments by the Hearst newspapers of Bruno Hauptmann's legal bills in 1935 as he stood trial for kidnapping the Lindbergh baby, by *Esquire* to Lt. William Calley for his version of the Mei Lai Massacre in 1968, and by CBS News for interviews related to the **Watergate** scandal in 1975. Some news organizations, however, prohibit chequebook journalism in their codes of ethics. In the UK, the **Press Complaints Commission** has proposed safeguards but not yet a ban on such payments. Defenders of chequebook journalism insist that it can be used safely and effectively in the course of **investigative reporting**, not least to secure statements from **sources** otherwise disinclined to co-operate.

Churnalism: the outcome of the increasingly intense pressures placed on journalists to churn out copy. Coined by Nick Davies (2008) in his book *Flat Earth News*, the term presumes that life in 'a news factory' is grim, with reporters busily recycling second-hand material provided by **news agencies** and **public relations** companies, usually without sufficient time or resources to independently verify the claims being made – let alone pursue their own stories using the tried and tested methods of independent report-ing. Davies argues that quantity supersedes quality, reducing journalists 'to passive processors of whatever material comes their way, churning out stories, whether real event or PR artifice, important or trivial, true or false' (2008: 59). Usually designed to serve the political interests of those who provide the news, churnalism may be exacerbated with news websites, where there is even less time to check facts because of the relentless drive to be first with **break-ing news**.

Citizen journalism: a type of journalism in which ordinary citizens adopt the role of a journalist in order to participate in newsmaking, often spontane-ously during a time of crisis or tragedy when they happen to be present on the scene. Citizen journalism includes the provision of first-person **eyewitness** accounts, audio recordings or video footage and mobile and digital camera snapshots, and it is typically shared online through blogs, wikis, personal webpages, social networking sites and web-based communities. It is seen by some as an outgrowth of earlier forms of **public or civic journalism** and is associated with the rise of online communication and new forms of citizen media from the late 1990s onward. The name 'citizen journalism' was coined in the immediate aftermath of the South Asian tsunami of December 2004, when individuals' accounts and imagery were widely heralded for uniquely contributing to mainstream journalism's coverage. Multiple newspapers declared citizen journalism a startling upheaval, if not outright revolution, ushered in by internet technology. News organizations were in the awkward position of being dependent on amateur material to tell the story of what transpired on the ground.

Despite its ambiguities, the term 'citizen journalism' appeared to capture something of the countervailing ethos of the ordinary person's capacity to bear witness, thereby providing commentators with a useful label to characterize an ostensibly new genre of reporting. In the years since the tsunami, it has secured its place in journalism's vocabulary (for better or otherwise in the view of many news organizations), more often than not associated with a particular crisis event. It is described variously as 'grassroots journalism', **'open source** journalism', 'participatory journalism', **'hyperlocal journalism'**, 'distributed journalism' or 'networked journalism' (as well as **'user-generated content'**), but there is little doubt that it has recast crisis reporting's priorities and protocols in profound ways (see also Allan and Thorsen 2009).

In tracing the emergent ecology of citizen journalism, it is apparent that its diverse modes of reportorial form, practice and epistemology – typically defined narrowly around 'revolutions' in technology – have been crafted through the exigencies of crisis reporting. In the months following the tsunami, two such crises consolidated its imperatives, effectively neutralizing claims that it was a passing 'fad' or 'gimmick' among all but its fiercest critics. Citizen reporting of the aftermath of the bombs that exploded in London on 7 July 2005, like the devastation wreaked by Hurricane Katrina the following month, necessarily figure in any evaluative assessment of how citizen journalism rewrote certain long-standing reportorial principles.

In the years since, there has been no shortage of crisis events that have similarly figured in appraisals of the changing nature of the relationship between 'professional' journalism and its 'amateur' alternatives. Examples are numerous, including the citizen reporting of the Buncefield oil depot explosion in the UK, the Mumbai train bombings, the protesting monks of Myanmar, the execution of Saddam Hussein, the shootings at Virginia Tech University, the Wenchuan earthquake and the protests over the Iranian election.

Classified ads: a form of advertising typically appearing in a specific section of a newspaper or magazine, where readers pay to briefly list an item or service they wish to sell to another reader. The fee for running the ad is usually charged on a per word basis or by line of text, while the length of the ad's run reduces its per diem rate. Subsections typically include help wanted, property for sale, lost and found, pets available, automotive, romantic companions, and so forth. Also called 'small ads', classifieds remained a mainstay of newspapers' business model from the time they emerged in the nineteenth century until 2000, when newspapers began to incorporate online platforms that included classified ads. Today, this form of advertising has increasingly gravitated towards the internet, where the incorporation of search and find features, vertical sites which show a single category such as 'pets', and aggregation make online classifieds easier to search than their print counterparts.

Coffee houses: an early venue for sharing and distributing news. The importance of coffee houses for the emergence of what may be described as an embryonic **public sphere** in various European countries was first discussed by Habermas (1989), and the coffee house he envisioned – with its idealized projection of 'a kind of social intercourse that, far from presupposing equality of status, disregarded status altogether' (1989: 36) – evolved into the central institution of the English public sphere. Its ascendant popularity corresponded to the celebrated ambience it enjoyed as an establishment open, in principle at least, to any ordinary citizen inclined to 'learn the news and discuss it'. Individual premises served as meeting places, usually for a specific type of clientele sharing an interest in a particular kind of news or information. **Newspapers**, along with broadsides, pamphlets, journals and similar tracts, were distributed via coffee houses, where they were passed about from one patron to the next.

Apparent from the outset was the formative role coffee house sociability played in the creation of public opinion, the collective force of private individuals' deliberations wielding considerable influence. The remarkable appetite of participants for news – as well as for political discussion of its significance – recurrently attracted the attention of authorities concerned with controlling the flow of information. Habermas observed that coffee houses were sometimes castigated as seedbeds of political unrest. On these grounds, Charles II's government responded to the 'great complaints' that were 'daily made' of the 'license that was taken in coffee houses to utter most indecent, scandalous and seditious discourses' by seeking to suppress them by proclamation on 29 December 1675. This attempt was abandoned shortly thereafter, however, when it became apparent that the order was being ignored. In addition to government proclamations, other efforts mobilized against coffee houses over the years included those of Christian authorities convinced that free speech was helping to cultivate atheism, purveyors of rival beverages (including critics fearful that the demand for English grain used in ale would be undercut) and women alarmed by the amount of time their idle spouses spent newsmongering.

Although egalitarian in theory, actual participation in the typically boisterous, uninhibited discussions of the coffee house was largely confined to middle and upper class men able to afford the price – and conspicuous leisure time – to indulge their coffee-drinking habit on a regular (frequently daily) basis. In contrast with the salons of France, women were seldom welcomed to partake in conversation in this milieu, their custom tending to be discouraged for entirely sexist reasons characteristic of the period. Records indicate that some were present in the role of proprietor (a 'coffee woman', who was often a widow), or more typically in a service capacity, but in any case were ordinarily excluded from taking part in 'rational-critical debate' (Habermas 1989) due to the gendered culture of what was a predominantly masculinized domain.

Collaborative journalism: news coverage of an issue or event which draws upon the contributions of both professional and amateur ('pro-am') **citizen journalists** to craft a report superior in quality to what could be produced by either group working alone. This process is typically made possible through internet sharing (such as via email, blogs or instant messaging), often arising spontaneously with little or no organizational contact beforehand. The emphasis on collaboration helps to distinguish this mode from other forms of participatory journalism.

Collective memory: the practices by which the past is reconfigured for present aims. Journalism's capacity to act as a vehicle for collective memory rests on overturning a long-held assumption that the news provides the first draft of history which it then turns over to historians for deeper engagement. When seen through the prism of collective memory, journalism in fact reveals a wealth of practices associated with the past. As Lang and Lang (1989) noted twenty years ago:

> even cursory perusal reveals many references to events no longer new and hence not news in the journalistic sense. Thus past and future together frame the reporting of current events. Just what part of the past and what kind of future are brought into play depends on what editors and journalists believe legitimately belongs within the public domain, in journalistic conventions, and of course in personal ideologies. (1989: 126)

References to the past help journalists build connections, suggest inferences and create story **pegs**, act as yardsticks for gauging an event's magnitude and impact, offer analogies and provide shorthand explanations. News practices like rewrites, revisits to old events, commemorative or anniversary journalism and even investigations of seemingly 'historical' events and happenings make the past so central to journalism that it has emerged as an unspoken backdrop against which the contemporary record-keeping of the news takes place (Zelizer 2008). Journalism acts in the service of collective memory via all of its tools of information relay – words, **headlines**, **pictures**, among others. Zelizer (1998), for instance, showed how images of the Nazi concentration camps were systematically recycled as a mnemonic template for western journalism's coverage of atrocity in other times and places.

Column: a personal, authored and often recurring opinion article which typically addresses public events or issues. Developed from the essay of the 1800s and at first limited to humour, gossip and politics, columns are usually written by the same person or persons, appear in the same length (between 300 and 800 words), are published on a consistent and predictable cycle in a fixed place in the newspaper or journal (such as the front of a local news section or on the opinion page) and tend to address different topics over time.

Often called the human face of journalism, columns in broadcast news programmes take the shape of 'essays', 'opinions' or 'viewpoints'. Always signed or otherwise authored, columns differ from the unsigned **editorial** that reflects a news organization's official voice. They offer a chance to opine personally on events or issues, to offer advice or commentary and to review public events, books, movies or the arts. Columns began appearing by the 1800s in numerous places around the globe; the first column in the US – 'Journal of Occurrences' – was distributed in Boston in 1768. Additionally, the pre-Civil War decade included luminaries Karl Marx and Friedrich Engels (writing on European affairs for the *New York Tribune*) among its columnists. But the golden age of columnists is thought to have been between the two world wars. Widely read and thereby often **syndicated**, they adopted multiple tones – serious, analytical, moralistic, satirical and humorous.

Columns have ranged across the political divide, with some newspapers of a strong conservative orientation, including several titles in **business journalism**, employing liberal or left columnists with alternative political perspectives (and *vice versa*). Some columns are intended to inject levity into the paper, thereby offering temporary relief from the seriousness of **hard news**, or to address everyday concerns, as with **confessional journalism**. Examples range from the gossip items of Louella Parsons or Walter Winchell in the US from the late 1920s onward, to Fleet Street diary writers such as Nigel Dempster, who once famously wrote: 'If the trade of the gossip columnist is trivial, then all of life is trivia.' **Agony aunt** (or, less typically, agony uncle) advice columns, such as Dear Abby or Ann Landers in the US, or Marjorie Proops's campaigning 'Dear Marje' in the *Daily Mirror* in the UK, became a mainstay of the twentieth-century press. Today popular contemporary columnists rank among the most well-known journalists – most countries having their top tier of voices – but they do not escape criticism by many others within journalism, sceptical about the value of their contribution. Harold Ickes was rumoured to have called them 'calumnists', because he was bothered by what he saw as undeserved power to shape agendas and public sentiments. Contemporary **blogs** constitute a new form of journalistic column, using the internet to set forth personalized views on current events and issues.

Column-inch: the amount of text per spatial area within a newspaper. Often called 'legs', columns vary in size and width, and their placement across spatial inches varies the amount of information they can provide. Though column-inches were historically the means by which article size was determined in the press, today's information environment and its dependence on digital platforms makes predetermined notions of length less relevant. Nonetheless, column-inches still remain a loosely referenced measure in journalistic circles, as reporters strive to produce copy in conjunction with **editorial** notions of a story's size, prominence and centrality.

Commodification of news: the transformation of news into a commodity, where financial profitability is prioritized over and above the public interest. Though early forms of commodified **news** date back to its first mass distribution, with the development of the printing press and emergence of capitalism, the often subtle, seemingly 'commonsensical' ways in which corporate interests influence news content have generated numerous questions regarding the impact on news of owners intent on maximizing their profits for the benefit of shareholders. This bottom-line mentality encourages journalists to internalize the values of media owners as consistent with **professionalism**, as problematic as that might be. In the case of the media proprietor Rupert Murdoch, for instance, **news values** are narrowly defined within the corporate culture of his empire.

Compassion fatigue: the concern that extensive news coverage of the human suffering engendered by crisis and **war journalism** leads to audiences becoming tired of learning more about it. Elaborated as a concept by Moeller (1998), compassion fatigue suggests that due to repeated coverage audiences become less sympathetic to those caught up in the events, however tragic.

Computer-assisted reporting (CAR): news reporting of stories made possible through the use of computer technologies, including the gathering and interpretation of complex datasets (sometimes called 'database journalism' in the 1950s, prior to the rise of the personal computer). CAR enables journalists to bring to bear a methodologically rigorous approach to their work, including activities like testing hypotheses, calculating probabilities, analysing public records, conducting surveys and so forth. Often associated with analytic or **precision journalism**, use of the term itself is fading as computers become increasingly central to **newsgathering** of all types.

Confessional journalism: highly personal **columns** revealing private details of a columnist's life. Often sharing emotional responses to the trials and tribulations of everyday, usually middle-class, life, confessional journalism is thought to help draw attention to under-reported topics, such as issues concerning self-esteem, raising children, eating disorders, sexual relationships and financial problems. Critics, however, question its status as 'proper' journalism and express concern about the impact on the columnists themselves, some of whom may be under pressure to disclose ever more intimate revelations in order to sustain reader interest.

Confidentiality: the promise made by a journalist to his or her **source** to keep their identity confidential, even in the face of intense pressure to reveal it. A long-standing tenet of **professionalism**, this commitment to source **anonymity** has been recurrently tested in the courts, where it is typically regarded as distinct from the codes of 'professional–client confidentiality' associated with medical doctors, lawyers and religious leaders. Promises of confidentiality emerge as particularly important in types of journalism that call to the foreground a journalist's involvement in the issue or event being covered (such as **participant journalism**, **partisan journalism** or **advocacy journalism**), because they highlight the journalist's motives in keeping his or her source anonymous.

Conflict of interest: a breach of **ethics** said to occur when a journalist with a personal interest in a story's outcome lets it interfere with the story's shaping. The implication of personal interests – such as family considerations, a financial investment or religious beliefs – in the news is always a danger, reflecting the basic fact that journalists are also family members, residents of neighbourhoods, voters and the like. But when journalists fail to ensure that those interests do not unduly influence or interfere with the reporting process, the perceived conflict calls into question their capacity to be fair and **balanced** in their reporting. The same principle applies to news organizations, when a decision to cover a story in a certain way or even to ignore it altogether is traced to a concern that proper procedures would upset the owner or an important advertiser. News is presumed tainted by a conflict of interest that in turn undermines editorial integrity, and thereby the reputation of all those involved. Because conflicts of interest are natural occurrences, they should be openly acknowledged so as to minimize the damage they potentially cause.

Contact: an individual of interest to a journalist for purposes of gathering the information she or he may be able to provide. Often sought out due to their specialized knowledge (e.g. a contact in the police force during a crime investigation or in a trade union during a strike), contacts are cultivated into potential **sources** by journalists with care. Journalists often rely on them to help secure access, to alert them to **breaking news** or to keep them appraised about developments unfolding behind the scenes.

Contempt of court: a court judgment that an individual or group should face punishment – possibly a formal rebuke, a fine or even imprisonment – for having committed an act which the court considers detrimental to the interests of the legal process. While interpretations vary in different countries, contempt of court provisions are generally intended to ensure a fair trial for the defendant, and as such place restrictions on what can be reported, how and when. Journalists and editors must therefore take considerable care when covering court cases to ensure that the outcome of the trial will not be affected. In the view of some, these restrictions can represent an undue constraint on a free press, such as when a journalist is jailed for refusing to divulge the name of a source or for reporting details they consider relevant and newsworthy. Consequently, intense debates have addressed the need to strike an appropriate **balance** between the defendant's right to a fair trial, on the one hand, and the journalist's right to act pursuant to a perceived public interest, on the other. The long-standing principles at stake in these debates are currently being recast anew by 24-hour news coverage, **bloggers** and social networking sites, namely because efforts to police the breaching of reporting restrictions are proving increasingly difficult to enforce.

Convergence: the bringing together of two or more otherwise disparate elements in what is ostensibly a technology-driven form of consolidation. Though a wide array of definitions of 'convergence' (or 'digital convergence') are in circulation, many highlight the ways in which digitized information is shared across different media contexts, such as when a website combines audio, text and video material, or when a cell or mobile telephone allows its user to take a photograph or watch the full streaming of a live newscast. In some newsrooms, what counts as news is recast as a 'multi-platform product' in light of these changes, inviting fresh thinking about how news can be produced and delivered in ways to engage elusive audiences, especially young people disinclined to follow 'old' media. Multi-skilled journalists are increasingly expected to multi-task in converged multimedia environments; that is, in addition to preparing news copy, they are asked to repackage their stories (up to and including the post-production stage) for diverse audiences. Convergence thus emerges as a dynamic, highly interactive process rather than an achieved or fixed outcome. Convergence also refers to the transference across component platforms of storytelling strategies and techniques which, in previous times, were regarded as medium-specific. More broadly, convergence is sometimes described as a form of media consolidation, especially when news organizations find themselves competing in different markets or are controlled by owners intent on exploiting 'synergies' in their 'convergence investments', such as between news output and entertainment products. A celebratory rhetoric of convergence (with an emphasis on collaboration and co-operation afforded by technological innovation) is thus sometimes used to justify 'cost efficiencies' for companies primarily concerned with 'bottom-line' profitability.

Copy: the written material in a **newspaper, magazine,** broadcast or online news site.

Copy approval: a request from **sources** to see the **copy** for a news item in which they have been interviewed, prior to its publication or broadcast. Seen as a way for sources to confirm personally how their words have been used, some may insist upon the right to copy approval before agreeing to co-operate, although journalists generally avoid agreeing to such terms, if possible, for fear that it will place an undue constraint upon their ability to report the facts as they see them.

Copy taster: a subeditor who assesses the quality of **copy** forwarded by journalists (or **news agencies**), making a preliminary judgement about what looks promising for purposes of inclusion. He or she either forwards the copy to the editors or returns it to the reporter for additional information.

Correspondent: a journalist responsible for covering a specific topic and/or geographical area, such as a war. Often used in conjunction with a **foreign correspondent** reporting from the **field** or a **news bureau**, correspondents can also operate closer to home, where they may be associated with a particular **beat** or **patch** where news is generated on a regular basis.

Craft: the art of journalism, with reference to its special skills, strategies and knowledge. The craft of journalism demands intuition, a flair for language, an interest in exploration and discovery, initiative, resourcefulness, drive and a certain determination. Notions of journalism as a craft are often contrasted with journalism as a **profession**, with critics maintaining that professionalized trajectories in **journalism education** have all but eliminated the craft dimension of journalism (Bromley 2006). More recently, some critics blame the internet for further undermining its specialized status, not least with regard to a diminished recognition of the special skills-set necessary to be socially and ethically responsible (see, for example, the current debate about **citizen journalism**).

Crawl: a stream of words moving (effectively *crawling* at a slow enough pace to be read) along the bottom of the television screen during a newscast. Sometimes called a 'news ticker', a crawl or crawler usually consists of **headlines** of 'top stories', financial information (stock market data) or **breaking news**, and is most likely to appear on 24-hour cable or satellite newscasts. Web users can often download a crawl or news ticker from their preferred news site to run on their desktop.

Crime journalism: a type of journalism devoted to crime. Often associated with the rise of **popular journalism** and its focus on sensational news topics that easily draw the public, the coverage of crime in the news in fact goes back to the earliest newspapers around the globe. European papers reported on witchcraft trials during the sixteenth century, while in the US the colonial press regularly reported on crimes like counterfeiting, robbery and piracy. It was during the mid-nineteenth century, though, that a growing recognition of the value of crime reporting helped develop the press in various locations. In Britain, Sunday papers such as *News of the World* offered a popular forum for reporting the proceedings of the police courts. At the same time, the US **penny press** focused what had been diffuse crime reporting into a predictable news section drawing from the nearby registries of police precincts. The appearance of crime journalism underscored its popular appeal with the public, and the penny press reached new heights of **sensationalism** when it relayed coverage of the first murder case of a prostitute – the Helen Jewett case – in 1836.

Though crime coverage became closer to what we recognize today during the late nineteenth century, relying on **eyewitness** accounts of details from the crime scene, differences in style prevailed in different countries. The early US coverage was moralistic and sensational, British coverage of crime was terse and filled with decorum. Differences also were sustained across the various types of newspapers that covered crime. **Tabloids**, for example, gave crime lurid coverage that was replete with graphic **news pictures**, while **broadsheets** reported violent crime in a more dignified fashion. Finally, crime journalism differed across time period. So-called jazz-age journalism in the US, for instance, marked the 1920s as a period replete with graphic crime reportage as it impacted upon known celebrities, such as the murder trial of actor 'Fatty' Arbuckle.

As the commercial draw of crime journalism became increasingly evident, news organizations assigned reporters to crime **beats** while police precincts developed their own **media relations** departments to deal with ongoing investigations. Crime coverage became particularly associated in the 1970s with **local news** in the US and elsewhere, as city TV stations sought ways of differentiating themselves from national networks. The excessive gravitation towards crime journalism also earned numerous local TV stations accusations of engaging in **body-bag journalism**. Contemporary crime journalism tends to focus less on the proceedings of police precincts and more on large profile cases due, in part, to news organizations' reductions of the human and technical resources required for sustaining a crime's investigation. The rise of 24-hour news and the internet have also had an impact on crime journalism.

Nonetheless, even thirty years ago studies suggested that as much as one quarter of all news coverage focused on crime (Graber 1980). Much crime reportage is also associated with **moral panics** (Cohen 1972), by which disproportionate amounts of crime coverage intensify public fear towards the type of crime being covered. Critics of crime journalism lament its focus on violent rather than non-violent crimes, on working-class crime among marginalized communities rather than white collar crime, on individual over structural causation, and on the victim rather than the perpetrator or context for the crime.

Crop: the act of excising parts of a **picture** or photograph. Cropping has multiple effects, good and bad. Though it can reduce the size of an image or improve its composition, it can also distort what is being depicted. Given long-standing debates about **photojournalism** and **objectivity**, where questions regarding verisimilitude come to the fore, cropping can also raise questions about the wilful manipulation of news pictures. In cases where the same photograph might be used by different news organizations, the decision by one to crop while the other leaves it as it is highlights the extent to which strategic decision-making undercuts the presentation of images in the news.

Crowdsourcing: grassroots or citizen-led initiatives whereby individuals are encouraged to share information that can be gathered for purposes of producing a rigorous, comprehensive piece of reporting. Crowdsourcing draws upon news organizations' long reliance on audiences to act as **sources** and help share the task of gathering information, and extends it onward, such as a **breaking news** event, the environmental record of a specific company, or the campaign of a local politician. Initially outlined by Jeff Howe in an article in *Wired* magazine (2006), the term crowdsourcing referenced the **open source** software movement (where volunteers contribute programming code to a collaborative project), Wikipedia (an online encyclopedia composed of entries written by users) and websites such as eBay and MySpace. Some news organizations rely upon crowdsourcing to process large datasets, because when extensive official records are released to the public, the challenge for journalists to sift through them alone is formidable. By eliciting the involvement of a news site's users, the dataset can be read by literally thousands of volunteers to help identify potentially newsworthy details.

Cub reporter: a reporter at the start of his or her career, just beginning to learn the **craft**. Inexperienced and often young, cub reporters are thought to learn the craft of journalism by osmosis, watching others in the **newsroom** more than being told explicitly what to do (Breed 1955).

Current affairs: a genre of news broadcasting. News reporting that is more issue-centred, and thereby less event-driven, in its approach to covering public life than **hard news** journalism. Typically it offers a more in-depth treatment of an issue in the news, conducted over an extended period of time, than would be possible under the constraint of a 24-hour **news cycle**. Examples include *Panorama* (BBC) in the UK and some of the **television news magazines** in the US, such as *60 Minutes* (CBS).

Cut-aways/Noddies: video shots taken of a journalist for interspersing into the final broadcast footage. Taken during a one-camera shoot, cut-aways help smooth over visual transitions or cuts, where they might show an interviewing journalist nodding, shaking his or her head, frowning or listening attentively. They are usually shot after the **interview** has been conducted for possible use at the editing stage.

Cuttings/Clips: a collection of previously prepared news reports. In journalistic parlance, news items are literally 'cut' or 'clipped' from the pages of a **newspaper** and filed together as a resource for further stories to follow. A 'cuttings job' is a story put together by drawing upon this collection. In news broadcasting, a short taped excerpt of audio or video (e.g. a **soundbite**, **interview** footage or **actuality** sound) is sometimes called a 'cut' or 'clip' when inserted into a news report.

D

DA-Notice: a notice distributed by UK government officials requesting that journalists avoid publishing or broadcasting a news item because it is perceived to be sensitive to national security. Formerly called D-Notices, Defence Advisory Notices aim 'to prevent inadvertent public disclosure of information that would compromise UK military and intelligence operations and methods, or put at risk the safety of those involved in such operations, or lead to attacks that would damage the critical national infrastructure and/or endanger lives' (as stated on its website). Although they reflect a voluntary code without legal force, pressures can be brought upon journalists to encourage co-operation. Overseen by the Defence Press and Broadcasting Advisory Committee, members of which are drawn from both government and the media, the DA-Notice Secretary negotiates disputes over what can and cannot be published, the effect of which is usually to remove 'genuinely secret details' from a news story that might be otherwise blocked in its entirety through litigation. The five standing DA-Notices presently include:

1   Military operations, plans and capabilities;
2   Nuclear and non-nuclear weapons and equipment;
3   Ciphers and secure communications;
4   Sensitive installations and home addresses; and
5   UK security and intelligence services and special services.

Dateline: a line of type in print journalism that describes where and when a news story was crafted. Though the dateline emerged during the mid-1800s, over time it has changed in function as evolving news technologies have created different ways of sharing information across news organizations. Usually appearing at the top of a news story, the dateline lent credibility and stature to the newsgathering apparatus at a time when the establishment of **journalistic authority** relied, in part, on organizing a standardized, professional set of reportorial practices and conventions. Signalling news that had been gathered from distant locations, the dateline appeared with increasing regularity through much of the twentieth century. Today, however, as news organizations have cut back on the distant geographic **assignments** of reporters, datelines are more likely to highlight the distribution of news by intermediary institutions, such as **news agencies**, rather than via the exclusive placement of a news organization's own reporter. Critics maintain that the assignment of datelines can be misleading. A **stringer** positioned in a distant location, for example, provides sufficient justification for a news organization to employ a dateline, even if the stringer plays little role in the article's actual crafting. Though datelines do not exist *per se* in broadcast news, a reporter's location is often formally stated by news announcers, suggesting their modification to fit broadcast parameters.

Dead air: the unexpected interruption of a news broadcast occurring when the signal is temporarily lost. Dead air produces on-air silence in the case of radio news and a blank screen or frozen image in television news.

Deadline: the latest time or date by which a news story must be in hand if it is to run in the next edition of the **newspaper, magazine** or broadcast bulletin. Because process drives content in newsmaking, the deadline is the point of no return. Once a deadline passes, editors can no longer process a given account as news within the continual **news cycle** of newsgathering, presentation and distribution.

Death-knock: a type of **interviewing** in which journalists seek contact with members of bereaved families or their associative circles. Critiqued as an invasive journalistic practice that violates **privacy** and intrudes unnecessarily on a grieving individual, the death-knock is often instrumental for news organizations attempting to retrieve information, quotes or pictures following someone's demise, including a known figure or celebrity or a victim of a crime or natural disaster. Death-knocks may involve telephoning family members, schools or places of employment and knocking on the doors of private residences (hence the name of the practice). Journalists are often advised by news organizations to make single attempts at contact and, if rebuffed, to abandon the task.

Defamation: an instance in which the information presented in a news report is false, and as such harms the reputation of an individual or group. With defamatory statements resulting from malice or simple negligence in fact-checking, instances of defamation are evaluated as either **libel** or **slander**, depending upon the medium of representation. **Truth** is a fundamental defence to a defamation claim, although it may be difficult to prove in a court of law (and possibly expensive in light of the costs associated with litigation). Here the distinction between what a journalist may sincerely believe to be true and what he or she can actually demonstrate to be true becomes important. Fears that the burden of proof may be too onerous for a given news story may lead to it being temporarily **spiked** or even abandoned altogether. In this way, the prospect of a defamation claim may have a 'chilling effect' on the news organization, effectively undermining the viability of **investigative reporting**.

Development journalism: journalism that focuses on developmental processes in its coverage, usually in developing nations of the global South. Seen as a response to a one-way flow of news that privileged the priorities of the global North, the study of development journalism was an outgrowth of scholarly work by Daniel Lerner and W.W. Rostow on modernization. Their research proffered a one-directional model for modernizing traditional nations, positioning the news media as part of the modernization process. In the 1960s, Filipino journalists Alan Chalkley and Juan Mercado at the Press Foundation of Asia (PFA), reconceived development journalism with the intention of finding a kind of newsmaking that could better fit the agendas of countries in the region, directly reflecting an interest in socio-economic development.

Focusing on the poor, marginalized and disempowered, proponents of development journalism see the needs of disenfranchised populations as an instrumental gateway to adapting journalism in the service of resolving the problems it seeks to uncover. They argue for a mode of journalistic practice that draws less from imported models of colonialism and more from the immediate needs of proximate nations. Doing so means that development journalism goes to great lengths to evaluate existing development programmes, processes and policies and to explain their impact to affected populations.

Co-ordinating across the mass media, folk media and other modes of small group communication, development journalism regards the incorporation of disenfranchised individuals as central to effective developmental planning and nation-building. Critics of development journalism argue that it creates extensive paths for government intervention and restricts freedom of information in the nations in which it is practised. Moreover, they cite instances of **censorship**, government suppression, and the restriction and punishment of journalists as reasons for a greater distance between national interests and journalistic agendas. Proponents maintain that development journalism remains at heart **adversarial** to government, although they recognize that its aim of constructive criticism can be achieved even alongside government involvement.

Direct quote: a statement made by a **source** that is directly quoted – verbatim – in a news item. Quotation marks are used to signal that the words in question are recorded speech and that they were actually stated as presented, in contrast to paraphrased remarks.

Dish: short for satellite dish, the parabolic (dish-shaped) microwave antenna used in the **field** by journalists to relay electromagnetic signals with communications satellites passing overhead.

Disinformation: false or inaccurate information intentionally relayed to a journalist by a **source** for purposes of deception. Contrasted with **misinformation** that derives from an error or mistake, disinformation commonly occurs in cases of **propaganda**, fakery or malicious **spin**.

Dispatch: a news item relayed to a **news organization** by a **news agency** or **correspondent** in the **field**.

Docudrama: an audio or visual re-enactment of current (or historical) events. Offering a hybrid of fictional storytelling about factual events, docudrama emerged in US journalism in the 1930s, when *The March of Time*, affiliated with CBS, re-enacted historical events first as an audio relay and later as a **newsreel**. Though docudrama comes in many forms, today it is most prevalent in **television news magazines**, where often **crime news** stories are told through docudramatic re-enactments.

Documentary: the use of visual material to create a fact-driven account of actual events or issues, as in a non-fiction movie or broadcast programme. Documentaries typically marshal evidence to sustain a specific argument or point of view, in contrast with the ostensibly dispassionate stance of journalism. Though documentary is regarded as placing an emphasis upon interpretation and analysis while journalism is primarily concerned with reporting, the centrality of documentary efforts within journalism nonetheless provides an important venue for applying visuals in the service of reportage. Efforts to clarify conceptual boundaries between the two terms are fraught with difficulties, not least with regard to their respective treatment of the **ethics** surrounding **truth** claims, factuality and **objectivity**. Documentary pioneer John Grierson's definition of documentary as 'the creative treatment of **actuality**' contravenes journalistic convictions that actuality must be rendered dispassionately at all costs.

Doorstepping: a journalistic practice whereby journalists surprise a potential **source** by an encounter at the door, with the hope of securing a newsworthy statement from them. Widely considered to be an essential strategy for gathering information and often used to lend a news account a greater sense of drama, doorstepping is used regularly by journalists worldwide. At the same time, some news organizations, such as the BBC, explicitly forbid the practice if it risks being overly-intrusive, except as a last resort, due to concerns about people's right to **privacy**. Fewer qualms are expressed when the individual in question is a public figure.

Double-ender: a broadcast **interview** between two people situated in different places who can hear but not see one another. Double-enders often connect a news **anchor** or **newsreader** with a news **source**, whose words are relayed via microphones and earpieces.

Double-spread: two **newspaper** or **magazine** pages facing one another that are devoted to a single story. Double-spreads also may involve a cluster of related stories.

E

Eavesdropping: the practice of surreptitiously listening in on a private conversation. Though variously used in journalism, eavesdropping raises questions of **ethics** primarily because the listening journalist tends not to have self-identified to the speaker. Ethical issues draw from a more general discomfort with subterfuge in journalism, unless it can be justified as being in the public interest and the material in question cannot be gathered through more straightforward means. Eavesdropping may offer information of limited value in any case, because the journalist probably cannot corroborate its veracity if the person quoted denies making the statement. When a clandestine listening device or hidden camera is used or a telephone call or email intercepted, legal charges may ensue. Further complications can arise for news organizations drawing upon **user-generated content**, where it is sometimes impossible to determine the circumstances under which the information was acquired.

Editor: an individual who oversees a news organization's various **editorial** decisions and is in charge of its news content. First used to denote a book publisher in the 1600s, today the 'editor' references a hierarchy of individuals who manage the various tasks necessary to keep a **news organization** running smoothly. These include the executive editor or editor, who reports only to the publisher or broadcast executive; the news director, who oversees decision-making in broadcast operations; the managing editor, who oversees process and reports to the editor; multiple producers, news editors, **copy** editors, **picture** editors, **assignment** editors and page editors. The number of editors depends on the size of the news organization, though tighter financial constraints have reduced their presence within most news organizations. Moreover, editors increasingly find themselves assuming responsibility for more than the editorial side of a news organization, taking on new duties associated with advertising/sponsorship and circulation/viewership. Technology has also changed an editor's responsibilities over time: the move, for instance, from typesetting and printing presses to computers eradicated the 'cut and paste' orientation towards editing that was originally accomplished with scissors and glue, while computers have made the graphics editor significantly more central than was previously the case. Most importantly, the gravitation to online journalism has further reordered the long-standing responsibilities of editors, as much of the **user-generated content** used by traditional news organizations bypasses editing altogether.

Editorial: both a statement of opinion written under the collective responsibility of a news organization's **editor** or publisher and a descriptive term for news-related activities within the organization which are distinct from advertising/sponsorship, technical production and circulation/viewership. The editorial in form has appeared for over two centuries. Originally attributed to an editorial account in the US press that appeared in response to events during the American Revolution, by 1800 the editorial had become **anonymous**, was regularly appearing on page 2, used the editorial 'we' to frame its commentary and was often italicized. Since then the editorial has endured waves of enhanced and waning centrality. Seen as the way in which news organizations explicitly articulate their **partisan** or ideological slant and draw in like-minded segments of the public, the editorial is also important to those who read it because it helps policy-makers, politicians and activists gauge public opinion (and members of the public to do likewise).

In the US, the editorial became particularly important with the rise of the **penny press**, where expressions of opinion were mostly confined to the editorial page, as is the case with **neutral journalism**. In Europe, Latin America and countries where **partisan journalism** is prevalent, the editorial reflects ideological lines that are already present, to varying degrees, in a news organization's **hard news** reporting. In this regard, the function of the editorial tends to increase in centrality when journalism strives for **objectivity** over partisanship and decreases as media consolidation and **convergence** render editorial opinion larger than any one newspaper or journal. In some places, opinions have become the habitat of **columnists** and signed **op-ed** pages, rendering individual editorials marginal. Also called 'the leader', the editorial always tends to appear in the same place (such as the top left hand corner of a newspaper's second page or at the end of a newscast) and has particular impact during electoral campaigns, when the support of a news organization can critically impact the race. Most newspapers tend to feature multiple editorials on a given day which engage with pressing issues. Some use an editorial board or group of editors to decide the perspective to be taken.

Because editorial activities are so central for news organizations, the second use of the term – as an umbrella reference for all activities within the news organization that are related to the journalistic tasks proper – has become widespread. References to the editorial side of a newspaper, for instance, position newsmaking at its core and differentiate these practices from the technical or business dimensions of journalism.

Editorialize: the act of engaging in **editorial** activity. Editorializing refers to the articulation of **partisan** statements which detract from **balance** and **impartiality**. In news organizations which strive for **objective** modes of information gathering and presentation or models of **neutral journalism**, editorializing is kept separate from news relays. Consequently, it is funnelled to areas of the news organization which admit a blending of fact and opinion, such as **editorials**, **op-eds** and the like.

Effects of news: the impact of news on individuals and collectives. Though the effects of news are many, among those most cited are comprehension, **agenda setting**, **framing**, priming, learning, opinion formation, attitude change, generating fear, **stereotyping**, recall, consensus building, facilitating public engagement, inducing **moral panics**, constructing reality, and acting as vehicles of **collective memory**. The widespread nature of the list of journalism's possible influences on its audiences underscores how many expectations are attached to journalism, particularly in democratic systems of governance in which the news media are assumed capable of keeping the government in line and on target in informing a healthy body politic. The rise in scholarly attention to news effects took place primarily in the United States during the post-Second World War period, when observers were attempting to understand the role that the news media had played in the rise of the Nazi party in Germany. Hoping to prevent a recurrence of its **propagandistic** function, scholars in different disciplinary fields set about identifying different effects of the news as being of primary importance; political science researchers, for example, viewed the effects of journalism on the public as instrumental to understanding a functioning democratic polity (Zelizer 2004). At the same time, the implicit focus on audience impact offered a prism for understanding the news that has since been contrasted with ongoing work on news production, in which emphases on news practices, **rituals** and **routines** were seen as alternative focal points to news effects but nonetheless necessary for understanding journalism.

Embargo: an agreement between journalists and **sources** to delay publication of a news story until a specified later date and hour. Often accompanying **press releases** about stories with material that can be circulated ahead of time, such as speeches or lists of award nominees, an embargo is useful for both journalists and **sources**: embargoed material helps journalists fill the **news hole** before the crunch of **deadlines**, while it plays to the **source's** interests by maximizing a story's **circulation** and impact. Embargoes can encourage **news management** and manipulation, however, when sources time a story's publication or broadcast so as to either play down or up its importance in accordance with their interests.

  Science journalists tend to be particularly concerned about the embargo system. Scientific publications, including several of the leading peer-reviewed journals, often rely on embargoes, sending out advance details about scientific research to journalists on condition that they withhold reporting on them until the embargoed time elapses. Kiernan's (2006) analysis of the embargo's impact demonstrates how science journals exercise considerable control over the range and diversity of science stories, with their **editorial** judgements having an especially strong influence on non-specialist journalists struggling to cope with scientific complexity. Nonetheless, this occurs with the full co-operation of those journalists who prefer a level playing field with rival news organizations. The embargo system thus makes **scoops** harder to come by, but reduces the risk that a news organization will miss a major story.

Embedded reporting: a form of **news management** by which journalists are 'embedded' or physically positioned with the military while on the battlefield. Though embedded reporting was introduced in the US as a practice of

war journalism during the second war in Iraq in 2003, in fact it is an updated version of the **pool** reporting set in place during the earlier world wars. Embedding involves assigning a reporter to a military unit for a specified period in an ongoing operation, with the expectation that the reporter will provide a bottom-up **eyewitness** view of combat. By contrast, journalists not embedded with the military – called unilaterals – are free to travel and report, but secure none of the military protection or assistance given their embedded colleagues. Though the former Bush administration saw embedding as a response to media criticism that the US government had given insufficient access during earlier conflicts, particularly the first war in Iraq in 1990–91 and before that the invasion of Grenada in 1983, the questions associated with whether fair and **balanced** reporting was possible given the proximity to military units raised criticism to a new level (Allan and Zelizer 2004; Tumber and Palmer 2004). Critics also argue that embedding reporters minimizes what they can see, limits their coverage to small slices of the action and prevents the provision of context about the factors shaping the waging of war.

Envelope journalism: a form of bribery by which journalists are given an envelope containing a cash payment in exchange for prominent or favourable reporting. Sometimes taking the form of a promised gift or service, envelope journalism can be a chronic problem in countries where journalists are not paid an adequate wage.

Environmental journalism: reporting focused on environmental, ecological and green events and issues, largely revolving around the perceived impact of humans on nature. While non-fiction writing about conserving the natural world is hardly new, it was not until the 1960s that environmental journalism emerged in its own right in Europe and North America. That decade witnessed the formation of the environmental movement, which mobilized public concern about issues such as pollution (helped by publications such as Rachel Carson's *Silent Spring* in 1963), together with a shift in orientation as **science journalism** embraced more critical forms of **investigative reporting**. News events came to be increasingly framed in environmental terms, including the break-up of a super-tanker off the coast of Cornwall, England, in 1967, the 1969 Santa Barbara Channel-Union Oil leak in the US, and the 1969 Apollo II moon landing. Engendering sustained discussion among interested stakeholders, these events opened a range of debates over 'the environment' that featured prominently as news and required new strategies to interpret its complex issues. As environmental stories spread across domains otherwise concerned with business, politics, science, technology and medicine, 'environment **beats**' were developed to generate more appropriate types of reporting: *Time* magazine, for example, introduced an 'Environment' section in its 1 August 1969 edition. Further, news organizations increasingly recognized the need to hire specialist journalists on **beats** better able to critically appraise the scientific and technical claims being made by special interest groups associated with the environment. An ensuing 'information explosion' underpinned the environment's transformation into a major news story. At the same time, the steady rise in environmental awareness during the 1970s in North America and Europe sparked a corresponding intensification of efforts amongst corporate **public relations** agencies, such as Earth Day.

By the start of the 1980s an 'ecological conscience' had begun to penetrate multiple news organizations in Britain and the US. However, many of the deficiencies inherent in environmental reporting are attributable to a mismatch between journalistic modes of telling and the complexity of environmental issues. For instance, the journalistic search for the novel and unusual and for dramatically compelling news **pegs** confinable within episodic **narratives** creates a tendency to represent environmental crisis as a specific event-oriented catastrophe rather than an outcome of administrative calculations and decisions about risk. Consequently, an array of environmental concerns have not received sustained high-level news coverage despite being long-term threats, in part due to their non-event-oriented characteristics. Moreover, **sources** able to address long-term environmental consequences or speak to issues of mitigation and prevention are routinely displaced from journalistic **hierarchies of credibility** or else made to adapt their message to the rules of exclusion and inclusion that are in operation.

Ethics: principles of good practice as applied to journalism. Seen as a safeguard against potentially errant or problematic journalistic practice for the good of a scrutinizing public, journalistic ethics are associated with the shaping of journalism into a **profession** and have evolved as journalism itself has changed. While journalistic ethics are articulated in shared codes of action that are thought to apply to members of a news organization, a journalistic sub-field (such as RTNDA – Radio-Television News Directors Association) or employees of a specific medium, the first ethical code for journalists emerged in the US in 1910 by a group of elite editors trying to discern standards of action for members of the burgeoning profession. Today, most journalists in democratic countries subscribe to some notion of social responsibility (*see* **Four theories of the press**), by which they are expected to work for the public good. Loosely associated with norms of **accuracy**, truthfulness, **impartiality**, diversity, fairness and public accountability, codes of ethics have been seen as organized responses to changes in news practice, transformations in technology and altered aspirations concerning the role of journalism and its relationship with the public. Ethical violations have ranged across style, content and form. They involve relationships with **sources**, invasion of **privacy**, **conflicts of interest**, the misuse of news **pictures**, questions of fairness and diversity, fabrication, deception, misrepresentation and **plagiarism**, among others. There have been multiple attempts to co-ordinate common principles across various codes of ethics: the most well-known examples are *EthicNet* (which collects ethical codes from countries associated with the Council of Europe) and *MAS* (Media Account-ability Systems, developed by Jean-Claude Bertrand in 2000). Moreover, certain practices – such as **ombudspersons**, organs for media criticism or the journalism review – have developed as programmatic ways of enforcing optimum ethical practice. Nonetheless, ethics remains a disparate set of expectations and principles.

Ethnographies of news: sociological studies of journalism which explore how journalists approach and accomplish **newswork**. Also called participant observation and borrowing largely from the concepts and techniques of ethnomethodology, news ethnographies were a prominent mode of scholarly address towards journalism during the 1970s in the UK and US, when their examination of the workings of primarily large urban news organizations offered a detailed and grounded picture of newsmaking that proved consistent across the various studies. Providing a personal and particularistic glimpse of the settings in which news is crafted, news ethnographies were driven by grounded questions that tried to see the world through the newsworker's point of view, generating detailed accounts of the news **routines**, **rituals**, conventions, practices and rules by which work took shape. From Tuchman (1978), Gans (1979) and Fishman (1980) in the US to Tunstall (1971) and Schlesinger (1977) in the UK, they remained for over thirty years the standard of ethnographic work about journalism. Critics lamented the lack of updating to their findings, with scholars only recently addressing the degree to which the earlier studies held up against new turns in the contemporary journalistic work environment. Such developments – including a stronger corporate pres-ence, the centrality of **convergent** and online technologies, **multi-tasking** journalists, multi-platform journalism, among others – suggest a more limited shelf-life for the original news ethnographies than they have enjoyed until now.

Exposé: an **investigative** news report that exposes otherwise concealed wrongdoing – such as a scandal, **crime** or form of corruption – to public attention.

Eyewitness: the title given to reporters or news organizations which are on the spot as news unfolds. Lending news organizations on-the-site **journalis-tic authority** for reporting events and establishing a physical presence that makes it possible for reporters to accomplish newswork, claims of eyewitness presence are so central to journalism that they are often incorporated into the **mastheads**, titles and logos of news organizations around the world. News organizations most often use eyewitnesses to report events that cannot easily be confirmed, challenged or tested but are made more credible by virtue of a correspondent's on-site presence. Eyewitness presence demonstrates how central is the authenticity that tends to accrue around 'being there' in establishing the authority of a news report, particularly so in **war journalism**, and it has been variously claimed over time in conjunction with changing notions of the eyewitness report itself, the role it puts into play, and the technology it uses (Zelizer 2007).

Early eyewitness reports were written by Xenophon, who wrote of wars during the time of Christ, but they are wide-ranging: Edward R. Murrow, with his Second World War radio broadcasts and early documentary programming *See It Now*; various news programmes during the early days of television – NBC's *Eye Witness* or CBS's *Eyewitness to History*, both broadcast during the 1960s; **Pulitzer Prize** winning **photojournalists** who captured news **pictures** of people falling to their deaths from house fires; Peter Arnett's famous eyewitness coverage of the Vietnam conflict and the first Persian Gulf War; and the amateurs who videotaped Rodney King's beating in 1991 or Saddam Hussein's hanging in 2006.

During the early 1960s a number of **local** TV **news** stations gave the eyewitness another meaning, incorporating eyewitness journalism as a proprietary trade name that signified a more folksy and informal delivery, so as to humanize the newsgathering process on the local broadcast level. Offering an emphasis on visuals and live reports, **weather** and **sports** segments, and the use of telegenic co-anchors, local eyewitness news strove to be different from the more straight-laced delivery of the national news. Though it was decried by national news organizations as **sensationalist**, by the 1990s eyewitness news programming on the local level was adopted as the signatory style of all local news programming in the US and was exported as well to Germany, the UK, Latin America and some East and Central European countries.

Critics of the eyewitness claim that the subjectivity and interpretation associated with its reportage undercut journalism's reliance on straight facts. Proponents nonetheless support its centrality as a particular form of grounded engagement with the world. Given these tensions, Zelizer (2007) argued that claims of eyewitness presence have been used strategically by news organizations over time, and that today the eyewitness is associated less with an identifiable reporter being on the spot than with either **citizen journalists** using mobile instruments of information gathering or technological devices like seemingly unmanned live cameras. In both cases, they allow the news media to claim that they 'have been there' as witnesses of events that they did not witness.

E-zine: an electronic (hence 'E') news magazine (hence '-zine'), typically produced by an individual or small group motivated for personal reasons to cover a topic, issue, event or concern they believe is being ignored or underreported by the mainstream media. News-related e-zines are usually distributed via the internet free of charge and without advertising, and they are produced in a stylistic manner akin to the **underground** or **alternative** press. Other genres include fanzines.

F

Facticity: the condition or quality of being a fact. First used by the German philosopher Johann Gottlieb Fichte, the term originally emerged in debates about facts and factuality in nineteenth-century positivism. Over time, facticity took on multiple intellectual meanings, particularly in the areas of phenomenology and hermeneutics, and variant meanings were drawn out by thinkers as wide-ranging as Dilthey, Sartre, Heidegger, Merleau-Ponty and Habermas. In journalism, Tuchman (1978) delineated what she called the 'web of facticity', by which saying that 'A said B' is useful as part of journalistic coverage, even if 'B' is false.

Factoid: a factual point of information presented in a manner akin to a **soundbite**, simply to engage the attention or curiosity of the reader, listener or viewer in an entertaining manner. In a newspaper, factoids may appear in a **sidebar**, while a radio programme otherwise devoted to music may offer a factoid as an interesting form of trivia.

Facts sheet: in **public relations**, a sheet or two of paper (or email equivalent) listing key facts, claims or points of information considered relevant to a news item. The facts sheet is distributed to journalists in hopes that they will incorporate these details into their news report, thereby facilitating a publicity strategy.

Fairness Doctrine: a principle originally upheld by the **Federal Communications Commission** (**FCC**) that a US-based radio or television station must provide equal time for different points of view to be advanced with regard to a controversial public issue. From the mid-1950s onwards, news and current affairs programming on the main US TV networks – ABC, CBS and NBC – became increasingly ratings-driven, due to the high sponsorship revenues they could demand. In general, network newscasts did their best to avoid controversy for fear of offending either advertisers or government officials. Such apprehensions routinely led to **self-censorship**, thereby calling into question the networks' provision of **impartial** journalism consistent with the public interest. Meanwhile the FCC sought to ensure that the networks observed the tenets of what would eventually evolve into a fully fledged 'Fairness Doctrine' as part of their licence obligations. Attempts had been made by the FCC even before a statutory basis for the doctrine was established in 1959 to enforce a principle whereby the right of stations to **editorialize** on the air would be strictly limited.

These attempts at regulating fairness, promoted under the FCC's report *In the Matter of Editorializing by Broadcast Licensees*, revolved around a declaration that:

> Only insofar as it is exercised in conformity with the paramount right of the public to hear a reasonably balanced presentation of all responsible viewpoints on particular issues can such editorialization be considered to be consistent with the licensee's duty to operate in the public interest.

In general, the FCC's efforts met with little success throughout the 1950s, partly due to its inability to adequately police agreed requirements. A further contributory factor was the Commission's internal confusion over how best to delimit a **balance** between **advocacy** on the part of the broadcaster, on the one hand, and the rights of those expressing opposing views, on the other (these issues were clarified to some extent in the Communications Act (1960), although not to the satisfaction of any of the parties involved). The net effect of the fairness requirements was to encourage the makers of news and current affairs programmes to avoid items likely to attract the attention of the FCC even if, as was probably the case, its strictures would lack sufficient bite to be meaningful. When the Fairness Doctrine was abolished by the Supreme Court in 1987, following the Meredith Corp. v FCC case, Congress voted to put it into law on a statutory basis. President Ronald Reagan vetoed the legislation, a move repeated in 1991 by President George H.W. Bush. Currently some hope is being expressed by advocates that the Obama administration will decide to reinstitute a Fairness Doctrine, in part to curb the ideological excesses of strongly **partisan journalism** such as Fox News.

Fake news: popular culture's **fictional representations of journalism** intended to blur fact/fiction distinctions for purposes of **satire** or comedic effect. In parodying the forms and conventions of news – including its **news values**, **routines**, priorities, and **framing** strategies – this type of fakery throws into sharp relief the normative assumptions underpinning 'proper' news in a manner that is intended to be both entertaining and revealing. Examples include deliberately falsified stories (e.g. the Great Moon Hoax of 1835), pranksters handing out spoof newspapers as a hoax (e.g. free copies of the *New York Times* headlined 'Iraq War Ends' edition in November 2008), the 'news' website *The Onion*, or Comedy Central's *The Daily Show* and *The Colbert Report* on television.

Fashion journalism: a diversity of styles of reportage concerned with all aspects of fashion consumerism. A key component of **lifestyle journalism**, the history of fashion journalism is intertwined with the fashion industry it effectively services, with journalists typically assuming the role of advocates in their coverage. A mainstay of women's **magazines** from the eighteenth century onwards, and often a distinct section in the daily press of today, fashion journalism has been slow to gain credibility as a form of reporting in its own right – in part due to sexist attitudes towards its predominantly female practitioners. In most western countries the majority of fashion journalists work on a **freelance** or contract basis, with little job security. They rely on extensive networks of **contacts** for **breaking news**, information (e.g. about the latest fads and trends) and **tips**, and crucial access to backstage events and social gatherings. While few have formal training, considerable expertise is necessary in fashion design, labels, brands, purchasing patterns, and the history of designers and their fashion houses. Much of the ensuing coverage is image-led, revolving around pre-scheduled events such as fashion shows, with one effect being that certain models become household names. **Advertorials** are common at the glossier end of the journalistic continuum, while **investigative reporting** into the multi-billion pound/dollar industry is rare. Pressures engendered by the symbiotic relationship between the relatively closed industry and those covering it decisively shape what is reported and how, with the result that much coverage is timid, superficial and conservative. Some critics go further, arguing that fashion journalism perpetuates body images that are unhealthy, is patriarchal in its representation of femininity, and elitist in its celebration of excessive wealth in the name of style, taste and beauty. On the web, fashion news **blogging** is proving increasingly popular, even credited in some countries – such as Sweden – for playing a key role in attracting public attention to blogs in the first place.

Feature: a distinctive or prominent **newspaper** article or broadcast story that is usually longer and more extensive than those surrounding it. Contrasted most often to the straight or **hard news** story, the feature tends to be a pre-eminent example of **soft news**, which caters to the **angles** of an event or issue likely to be of greatest interest to the target audience though not necessarily about those of most importance. The feature can differ by emphasis, catering to the ironic or bizarre; by impact, evoking strong emotion or entertaining rather than primarily informing; and by genre, tending to align with people and **human interest** rather than just facts. Because the feature integrates a greater mix of writing styles and lengths, it is presumed better able to address complicated stories than can hard news. Features are not driven by the same notions of **newsworthiness** that characterize hard news, but they deal with topical issues in greater depth than can a simple news report. They do so by accommodating the presence of the reporter, his or her opinions, multiple quotes from multiple personalities that come to life in the feature, anecdotes and extensive description. Sometimes the feature refers to **editorial** content writ broadly – as in reviews, advice **columns**, **interviews** and think-pieces – but its distinctive attributes become most prominent when defined as that which is not 'hard news'.

Federal Communications Commission (**FCC**): an independent agency established in the US by the Communications Act of 1934 to licence and regulate communication by radio, wire and cable. Today the FCC regulates interstate and international communications by radio, television, wire, satellite and cable, but does not possess the authority to censor news content or challenge a broadcaster's selection or presentation of news items. The FCC's own documentation, available on its website, states that 'rigging or slanting the news is a most heinous act against the public interest', and that it will act to protect this public interest where sufficient documented evidence is received. This type of evidence includes 'testimony, in writing or otherwise, from "insiders" or persons who have direct personal knowledge of an intentional falsification of the news. Of particular concern is evidence about orders from station management to falsify the news.' Here it cautions that in the absence of such evidence, it is unable to intervene. Exceptions to its authority include instances in which it is guided by decisions made by the courts to prohibit obscene, indecent or profane language.

Fictional representations of journalism: the fictional representations of journalism in popular culture, including novels, comic books, theatre, cinema and television. Though such representations are as old as journalism itself, they have tended to follow formulaic parameters, positioning journalists as either heroic public servants who defend the truth from modern day evils or as immoral social misfits lurking in the shadows as they relentlessly dredge up scandals. Movies such as *The Front Page* and *All the President's Men*, novels like *Scoop* or the Swedish *Millennium* trilogy, theatrical productions like *Night and Day* or *Frost/Nixon*, and television series like *Lou Grant, Drop the Dead Donkey* or *The Wire* oscillate between some notion of journalism in the real world and the collective vision of creators and producers working in a given medium under generic, economic, technological and narrative constraints. Many existing representations of journalism have been classified by the University of Southern California's Image of the Journalist in Popular Culture Project, which counts over 71,000 films, TV shots, novels, radio shows, **cartoons**, comics, commercials and songs among its inventory.

Field: the world beyond the newsroom. Journalists in the field pursue news that demands that they be able to offer a firsthand account of what is transpiring on the ground. Field experience tends to be valued more highly than desk experience, namely because of the challenges associated with reporting under difficult or dangerous circumstances, such as when the field refers to the battle zones of **war journalism**.

Fifth Estate: an undecided term that refers to the establishment of governance beyond the executive, legislative and judicial branches of government, bolstered by the **Fourth Estate** of the news media. Some employing the term use it to refer to 'the public', while others suggest that political commentators constitute a Fifth Estate of sustained, informed criticism and debate. This latter definition has been extended by some to include **bloggers**, who suggest that their voices combine to form a Fifth Estate in the **blogosphere**. Still others believe that a Fifth Estate is only now beginning to emerge via the networked spaces afforded by the internet and related digital technologies, optimistically arguing that new forms of citizen-led, **investigative** reporting will emerge in these spaces, thereby playing a positive role in helping to hold other institutions socially accountable.

Filler: news stories of secondary importance. Filler is deployed as needed to help fill time (broadcast) or space (print publications) and, given the unpredictable unfolding of news events, is critical for filling the **news hole**.

First Amendment: the section of the US Bill of Rights that prohibits the infringement of either freedom of speech or freedom of the press. Submitted to the states for ratification in 1789 and adopted in 1791, the First Amendment declares:

> Congress shall make no law respecting an establishment of religion, or prohibiting the free exercise thereof; or abridging the freedom of speech, or of the press; or the right of the people peaceably to assemble, and to petition the Government for a redress of grievances.

Current debates over these rights resonate at a number of levels within journalism, especially when a news organization is determined – in the face of government opposition – to exercise its First Amendment right to publish information that it believes bears on a matter of public interest. The relative degree of privileged protection afforded by the First Amendment to individual journalists continues to be tested in the courts (*see* **Shield law**). Moreover, precisely who qualifies as a 'journalist' is proving to be a vexing issue in this regard, not least when questions are raised about whether **bloggers** or **citizen journalists** claiming 'First Amendment' rights are in fact protected under the First Amendment.

Five Ws and H: the long-held necessary elements of a newspaper **lead**, specifically employed in **hard news** format. The five Ws and H refer to the critical questions that need to be answered in the lead or first paragraph or two of a news story: Who, what, when, where, why and how? As a convention, these commandment questions are linked to the rise of **objectivity** and **professionalism**, the ascendance of the **telegraph** and the associated emergence of the **inverted pyramid**, by which the most important information of a news story is presented first. The five Ws and H were memorialized by Rudyard Kipling in his 1902 *Just So Stories*, and were already being taught in US high school journalism classes by 1917. Though some observers contend that they dated back to early forms of biblical study, the five Ws and H today constitute a somewhat contested form of journalistic relay that is nonetheless referenced as a useful guide for targeting the relevant core points of a news story. They are also unevenly realized, as Carey (1986) famously argued in his discussion of the ways in which 'how' and 'why' eluded journalistic and public attention in much of US news.

Flack: derisory term for a **public relations** practitioner, press agent, publicity agent or information officer. Chiefly in use in the US and Canada (where it is a play on the word **hack** for journalists), flack and its related term of flackery are invoked primarily to connote slickness on the part of those who turn information to a client's advantage, despite evidence to the contrary.

Flag: a display which a newspaper positions at the top of the page to designate the newspaper's **layout**. Typically flags can be used either to mark the tops of section pages and/or special pages, such as **sports** or entertainment sections, or, in a fashion similar to nameplates, display vital information about the newspaper on its front page.

Flak: a measure by which news organizations and/or individual reporters escape criticism that is targeted at them by those alert to perceived shortcomings. Referenced as 'dodging flak', the term traces its origins to anti-aircraft artillery during the First World War, when pilots were forced to take evasive action to avoid having their aeroplane hit by shells fired from the ground. Flak, in journalistic terms, implies a similar sort of manoeuvre. Most would agree, however, that 'catching flak' is part of the job. While those firing flak often have strong **partisan** or ideological motives, sometimes primarily concerned about issues of **bias** or slant rather than factual inaccuracies *per se*, a steady barrage of flak can engender a powerful chilling effect in news organizations. It may encourage subtle forms of **self-censorship** when preparing news reports that risk contravening the declared interests of those behind the flak attacks.

Fleet Street: a reference to the national press in the UK. Known alternately as the 'street of adventure' and the 'street of shame' and servicing London's press corps for over 500 years, Fleet Street was home to the British national press from 1500 onward. Taking its name from the old Fleet River, Fleet Street connected the City of London and the City of Westminster, rendering it an active intersection in which **sources** from governmental, financial and commercial circles all interacted. Filled with taverns, pubs, clubs and **coffee houses**, at its height it housed the offices and printing presses of nearly every national news organization and many regional journals. In the mid-1980s, the widespread move of the British newspaper industry to Wapping replaced the social networks of Fleet Street with a starkly different fortress-like environment at the same time as the printing presses were replaced with computer technology (*see* **Wapping dispute**). Although the titles are now dispersed to other parts of the city, most notably London Docklands, Battersea and Kensington, the term is still commonly used to describe the British national press.

Folio line: a **newspaper's** identification heading. Usually found in the top corner of a paper's inside pages, the folio line typically details the publication date, name of the newspaper and page number.

Follow-up: the practice of returning to a previously published or broadcast news story in order to pursue an updated **angle** on it. Called by Tuchman (1978) 'continuing news', follow-ups can update a story in multiple ways, by providing a fresh angle to familiar information, reviewing earlier separate developments in new relationship with each other or covering further developments to actions reported earlier.

Footage: material captured on tape, whether shot via a video camera for television news, filmed for a documentary, or recorded in audio for radio news. 'Raw' footage is unedited.

Foreign correspondent: a journalist who works in a distant country of **assignment** and reports to the home news organization about the events and issues of that country. Emerging as an occupational speciality during the second half of the nineteenth century as a way for primarily US and European newspapers to cover distant events, foreign correspondents remain an elite and desirable posting within news organizations which combines an outsider's independence with an insider's knowledge. Unusual in that they are generalists in every sense of the term, foreign correspondents occupy a **beat** or **patch** in which they are responsible for explaining the history, politics, economics, culture and all other aspects of the location to which they are assigned. In an era of shrinking news budgets, however, this often becomes a regional rather than national **assignment**.

While foreign correspondents date to the earliest evolutions of news, they have risen and fallen with the economic and political tides of journalism. An integral part of the earliest newspapers which distributed chronicles written from already distantly placed political or business correspondents, from the middle of the nineteenth century onward correspondents were sent from the home base to distant locations, prevailing in record breaking numbers for nearly a century of journalistic practice. Through the middle of the twentieth century, as global communication and transportation infrastructures made it possible and valuable to know more about the world beyond one's immediate grasp, foreign correspondents reigned as one of the prized postings in a news organization. They need to have a flair for **multi-tasking**, for improvising and for adapting quickly to unfamiliar environments. Usually sent for a predetermined 'tour of duty' of three to five years in a given place, they struggle with the already hectic pace of **newswork** together with the additional pressures of language barriers, cultural sensitivities, suspicion from local authorities and publics, safety concerns and often restrictions on access. Many of the problems associated with the reporting of foreign correspondents

– involving **pack journalism** or 'groupthink', superficial reporting and **stereotyping** – draw from unsuccessful ways of dealing with these multiple pressures.

By the end of the twentieth century, the foreign correspondent began to dwindle as a viable posting for news organizations. As the fortunes of news organizations began to decline, foreign bureaux decreased in number, news budgets for distant events shrank and alternative sources of foreign news became ever more prevalent and available, the role of foreign correspondent started to die out. Adjacent and somewhat reconfigured adaptations of the traditional foreign correspondent include **parachute journalists** who arrive temporarily to cover distant events as they happen, **stringers** who are residents of the distant location but work on adjunct contracts for the news organization, and local **citizen journalists** who have no contractual obligation to news organizations but work on a case by case basis. The relays of **news agencies** are also used to compensate for the on-site reporting that is no longer provided by the traditional foreign correspondent.

Four theories of the press: a normative schematic introduced by Siebert *et al.* (1956) to elucidate varied conceptions of journalism's role in different political systems. Offering idealized and prescriptive representations of how the news media should function in each circumstance, they coined four theories to encompass the possible variations in journalistic performance: authoritarian theory positioned the press as supportive of and subordinate to government; in libertarian theory the press acted as an autonomous check on government; Soviet (communist) theory saw the press as a propagandistic arm of government that was subordinate to the interests of the working class; and social responsibility theory envisioned the press as responsibly raising conflict to the plane of discussion. In each case, the four theories underscored an assumption that the news media always reflect larger systems of political control. Since they were first coined, the four theories have undergone repeated revision, with multiple attempts to tweak their Cold War era assumptions and make them more workable for different mostly non-western contexts. Seen as part of an approach to news that is more descriptive than analytical, today most critics question the value of the approach's assumptions for understanding contemporary journalism (Nerone 1995). At the same time, various international watchdog associations, such as the Paris-based Reporters Without Borders, regularly assess press freedom using some of the parameters it suggested.

Fourth Estate: a term historically used in classical liberal theory to denote the press, now broadened to refer to the news media – in particular, their role in ensuring a functioning democracy. Originally attributed in England by Thomas Carlyle to Edmund Burke in his late eighteenth-century response to the French Revolution, the Fourth Estate stood for the independent emergence of the British press as a defender of public interests in opposition to the first three estates of the French *ancien regime* – the church, the nobility and the commoners – and now it similarly stands alongside the executive, legislative and judicial branches of government. In its optimum form, the Fourth Estate implies that the press, now the news media, can only act as a **watchdog** to other strong social and political institutions, bringing the errors of the powerful to light, if it remains independent of them. Relying on **investigative** and independent journalism, the idea of the Fourth Estate allowed the British press to position itself respectfully as part of the British institutional landscape. Critics of invocations of the Fourth Estate note that the increasing proximity between the news media and government has meant less of an independent role than the notion originally implied.

Frame/Framing: the way in which the news media organize reality for presentation to the public. News frames are employed by journalists, via tools of language – such as metaphors, exemplars (or historical lessons), catchphrases, depictions and visual images – to impose order on the social world so as to render its happenings into a series of meaningful events.

Framing draws from the writings of sociologist Erving Goffman to elucidate its characteristics. Gitlin (1980) argued that frames constitute a way in which journalism naturalizes the social world in accordance with certain discursive conventions. News frames, he argues, make the world beyond direct experience look natural; they are 'principles of selection, emphasis, and presentation composed of little tacit theories about what exists, what happens, and what matters' (Gitlin 1980: 6). The subject of often intense negotiation between journalists and their editors, as well as their sources, frames help render 'an infinity of noticeable details' into practicable repertoires. Frames thereby facilitate the ordering of the world in conjunction with hierarchical rules of inclusion and exclusion. Once a particular frame is adopted for a news story, its principles of selection and rejection ensure that only information material seen as legitimate within the conventions of **newsworthiness** appears in the account. Frames focus attention, privileging certain areas of emphasis over and above alternative possibilities in a manner held to be appropriate within its own terms of reference.

Arguing that frames define problems, diagnose causes, make moral judgements and suggest remedies, Entman (1993) contended that the framing of certain facets of events or issues facilitates making connections among them; the deeper the cultural resonance, the greater the potential for influence. As such, framing is frequently a contested process – not least between journalists and their **sources** (as well as between journalists and their **editors** within a news organization, where decisions about placement, **headlines**, **pictures**, **captions** and the like become important). Frames also have far-reaching implications for how claims made by sources are selected (or not) as newsworthy, the **narrative** conventions guiding the ways in which they are reported, and the possible consequences for generating **effects** on public perceptions. Critics express scepticism about their heuristic value, arguing that framing constitutes primarily a second-level instance of **agenda setting**, renames narrative analysis in conjunction with effects-oriented research, and blurs the distinction between theory and method.

Freebie: an item that is offered to journalists ostensibly for 'free' but which suggests an implied payment in exchange for positive news coverage. Such items, which might include a pen or T-shirt, concert tickets or a laptop computer, are seen as compromising the autonomy of the reporter's judgement. Bearing this in mind, some journalists refuse all freebies as a matter of principle, unwilling to risk their integrity being called into question. Others accept them, drawing a line only where a perceived **conflict of interest** arises in their judgement. Still others regard them simply as a perk of the job, as in **travel journalism**, when airlines offer 'free' tickets to exotic destinations.

Freedom of information: the citizen's basic right to request and receive access to information held by public institutions. In the absence of a valid reason to deny a request (the obligation to make information available being placed on the institution in question), the applicant can reasonably expect to receive it promptly and at minimal cost. Legislative efforts to ensure 'freedom of information' vary markedly from one country to the next, where they exist at all. The Freedom of Information Act (2000) is a relatively recent innovation in the UK; citizens – and journalists among them – in the US have been afforded the advantages of their Freedom of Information Act since 1966. The latter has made possible an array of major news stories over recent decades which would have been virtually impossible to investigate without this provision.

Freelance: a journalist who is usually self-employed with a short-term commitment – at best – to one news organization at any particular time. Some work to an agreed contract to deliver specific types of news stories (or audio, video or photographs), while others sell their news items on a piece-by-piece basis. Usually a flat rate or fee is agreed, although others prefer to negotiate terms on an *ad hoc* basis. Perceived advantages include improved remuneration, as well as a wider, more diverse array of stories to pursue; drawbacks include a lack of steady income and the absence of company benefits (legal protection as well as paid holidays, health insurance, pension, etc.). At a time when many news organizations are rapidly 'downsizing', with severe consequences for the number of posts available, it is not surprising that salaried staff members are often compelled to consider a change of status. The relative proportion of UK and US journalists working as freelancers has increased dramatically over recent years. Many find work on the internet, which makes available an array of journalistic opportunities outside mainstream news organizations.

Freesheet: a newspaper given to members of the public for free, whose associated costs are usually covered by advertisers intent on reaching the readership with their messages. Examples range from the efforts of individuals producing their own freesheet to distribute within the local neighbourhood or community (e.g. news items presented on photocopied sheets of paper folded to make a newsletter of sorts), on one end of the continuum, to major initiatives – backed by national news organizations – on the other end. On rare occasions, funding is provided by a corporate sponsor or via government support. Critics argue that the availability of freesheets undermines the market for newspaper sales, and that the content is typically lacking in quality.

G

Gag order: a court-ordered ban on journalistic coverage. Typically invoked in association with public proceedings and acting as a form of **prior restraint** because it suppresses information before harm can occur, the gag order can be requested from the courts by governmental, commercial or private entities which seek to suppress information and prevent it from being shared through the news media. Though the frequency with which gag orders are invoked depends on the degree of authoritarianism in the associated political system, gag orders are common even in environments that favour free speech generally. Typical circumstances that encourage the invocation of gag orders are those in which news coverage might prevent due process, such as the identification of jurors mid-trial, or the interference of the news media in police activity, such as during a hostage taking situation. At times gag orders are invoked when the need for them is questionable and governments are seen to act strategically to prevent the distribution of national security information, official secrets or details of ongoing military activity, as occurred in the US government's suppression of coverage of the activities in Guantanamo Bay during the so-called 'war on terror'.

Gatekeeper/Gatekeeping: the filters for either inclusion or exclusion of information from a given system. Drawn from the work of US social psychologist Kurt Lewin on consumer choice, the idea of gatekeeping was applied to journalism by White (1950) as one of the first areas of post-war academic inquiry into journalism. The gatekeeper was seen as controlling the gates of information flow, which acted as codes by which people admitted or refused the entry of certain information into a system. Studying a single newswire editor's selection of incoming news items, White observed that eight news items were rejected for every one that was deemed newsworthy and allowed to move past the gate of the wire-editor, a finding which underscored the systematic subjectivity of news selection. The metaphor of the gatekeeper became a widely applied notion in understanding information flow, and numerous studies tweaked and refined its approach. Gatekeeping was found to be impacted by **social control**, to be stable across gender, had repetitive attributes at later points in time, was more pronounced in **local news organizations**, and was influenced by notions of **professionalism**. Applied to individuals, organizations, sets of practices, norms, judgements, newsgathering **routines** and external constraints of a social, political, economic, legal or technological nature, gatekeeping eventually came to include more broadly the idea of 'knowledge control' or 'information control'. Capable of blocking, adding and changing information, gatekeeping invited consideration of what happened to a news story once it entered the channels of newsmaking. The gatekeeper and gatekeeping studies have not gone uncritiqued, however. Critics argue that they are too simplistic and psychological; they favour individual selection over organizational or institutional constraints; they underplay the work of construction; and they isolate one stage of a complicated process and tend to overplay its significance.

Get: the accomplishment of an exclusive story or **scoop**. Securing a get in the face of competition from rival journalists is a marked journalistic achievement that bolsters **journalistic authority**. In most cases a get is accomplished via a **tip** provided by a **source**.

Gonzo journalism: reporting that draws upon fictional techniques to describe non-fictional situations. Coined by US writer Hunter Thompson who was assigned to cover the 1972 US presidential campaign for *Rolling Stone* magazine but who instead developed his own narrative about drugs and alcohol (*Fear and Loathing on the Campaign Trail*), gonzo journalism has been associated more broadly with **new journalism** proponents like Norman Mailer and Tom Wolfe. Gonzo journalism sees a journalist's subjective, hands-on experiences in events and issues as central to the coverage that results. It engages the public in a prose **style** that tries to replicate the feeling of that direct experience. Often taken to mean a privileging of participation over observation and of style over substance, various literary features – such as hyperbole, exaggeration, profanity, extended first-person **narrative** and **satire** – characterize its output to varying degrees. Gonzo journalism also often incorporates texts in process – snatches of dialogue, transcripts, unfinished notes – as part of its reportage.

Gotcha journalism: a type of **interviewing** designed to entrap the interviewee into revealing more information than he or she initially intended to share. Typically, the information revealed is damaging to the interviewee's character, self-esteem or repute, and the journalist uses it to craft a story that portrays the interviewee in an unfavourable, even detrimental, light. Said to have evolved from a 1982 headline in the *Sun*, the British paper that proclaimed 'Gotcha' after an incident during the Falklands/Malvinas conflict, gotcha journalism today embraces a range of questionable practices – such as falsely framing the goal and topic of the interview (and/or switching them midstream), baiting the interviewee on sensitive topics with leading questions, or confronting the interviewee with problematic material mid-way through the interview. Gotcha journalism has arisen in multiple political contexts in which politicians and celebrities claim that the media have engaged in unethical newsgathering practices. During the US national election in 2008, Republican vice-presidential candidate Sarah Palin complained that she had been victimized by gotcha journalism on several occasions.

Graveyard shift: a term for the late night shift in a newspaper office, when it is relatively quiet because there is little news to report. Sometimes called the 'lobster trick' (its origins possibly deriving from New York slang for 'a fool or dupe'), the graveyard shift usually stretches from midnight to 8.00 a.m. and builds on the assumption that a wiser journalist works during the day. By contrast, a 'swing' (evening) shift overlaps the regular daytime and late night shift.

Gutter journalism: sensationalist, irresponsible reporting in pursuit of a story with little regard to the veracity of the claims made or the **ethics** involved in their being made public. Gutter journalists typically do not heed the possible implications for innocent parties vulnerable to the ensuing repercussions.

GV: a term used to denote general views in visual footage. GVs generally provide static background scenes that feature buildings or landscape but no humans and are often used in broadcast footage.

H

Hack: slang for a journalist. In some quarters, the term 'hack' has come to connote journalists who fail to uphold an appropriate standard of conduct in their reporting.

Hammer head: a large **headline** that is intended to achieve maximum impact. Typically consisting of one or two words – 'ALIVE!', 'GOTCHA', or 'IT'S WAR' – the hammer head is usually followed by a **kicker**.

Happy news: a style of broadcast news **talk** and presentation that foregrounds a positive approach to the events and issues comprising the coverage. Largely associated with a certain period of **local news** programming in US television, happy news was suggested by consultants during the

1970s as a strategy to win over viewers who were repeatedly voicing discontent with the sombre news received from the networks. Though an earlier move towards happy news was evident on US radio during the Second World War period, when commentators like Paul Harvey or Gabriel Heatter signed on or off with a positive news titbit or slogan, the move towards happy news on television reflected a more strategic marketing decision to follow the advice of consultants who were trying to create local news as a distinctive brand of TV journalism. The implementation of happy news had several attributes: single **anchorpersons** were replaced by co-anchoring teams, usually male/female, who used part of their on-air time to engage in 'happy talk' (on-air banter in which they personally reacted off-script to the events and issues of the day). Though 'happy talk' sometimes gave way to comedic routines on air, the informal banter later became one of the characteristic traits of the **eyewitness** news format that took over local television news.

Hard news: a type of news associated with importance, significance, **immediacy** and relevance which reflects the news that the public 'needs to know'. The hard news account is defined in opposition to other types of accounts, such as **soft** or **human interest** news (as well as **editorials** or leaders, which foreground matters of opinion). Initially characterized as a genre of newspaper narrative, it organizes facts within a distinctively hierarchical structure – typically described as an **inverted pyramid** – based on notions of newsworthiness and timeliness, as determined via a 24-hour **news cycle**. The **lead** – or opening paragraph – usually provides a summary or abstract of the hard account's essential **peg** or hook which projects, in turn, the story in a particular direction or **news angle**. The **five Ws and H** (the who, what, where, when, why and how most pertinent to the news item) are likely to be identified here, although the 'why' invites interpretation, which risks upsetting the codified strictures of **objectivity**. Most journalists claim that they know hard news when they see it, but many admit difficulty in defining it. It can turn out to be more a choice of presentation than an intrinsic set of qualities characterizing the news itself. As Tuchman (1978) showed over thirty years ago, the distinction between hard and soft news is so untenable that the same news event can take on the attributes of both types of news depending on the strategies of the journalists crafting the story. Such blending is increasingly the case today as multiple modes of news presentation across media platforms have brought the two in increasingly close quarters.

Headline: a one-line sentence or phrase at the top of a news article or broadcast news bulletin that signifies its contents, typically in an attention-grabbing manner. Headlines not only distinguish one news story from another, they indicate the relative importance of the stories. In print, the headline is typically written by the subeditor (i.e. not by the journalist), who draws it from the **lead** of the news story in order to forefront its main point.

Usually headlines employ active tense, together with clear language evoking vivid imagery. Headlines are in competition with one another with respect to play and prominence. **Banner** headlines, which stretch across the entire news page, denote very important and/or **breaking news**. In broadcast news, headlines function as **teasers**, coming at the top of a newscast and reflecting the most significant or interesting stories to follow. When headlines are used on television, they tend to be supported with accompanying news **pictures**.

Helicopter journalism: a type of journalism that literally offers a view of a news event as it unfolds from the vantage point of a helicopter hovering above it. Though opinions differ regarding the origins of this term, many trace its emergence to the time when local television news stations in the US began using helicopters (otherwise deployed to generate rush-hour traffic reports) to gain exclusive video footage of **breaking news**. Controversial examples abound, with one of the most notorious being the 'OJ Simpson Bronco chase' in June 1994. Millions of viewers watched the former football star Simpson – who would eventually stand trial for the murders of his ex-wife and her friend – attempt to flee police in a white Ford Bronco in a slow-speed chase along Interstate 405 through Los Angeles. Advocates point to the virtues of bird's-eye reports for the unique perspective they offer, while critics, alarmed by the prospect of more 'hacks in choppers', decry what they perceive to be the superficial, **sensationalist** reporting that typically ensues. The latter often point to examples where this genre of journalism has relayed graphic news **pictures**, which would not have found their way into a newscast otherwise.

Hierarchy of credibility: the hierarchical placement of individuals as prospective news **sources**, with those at the top regarded as most credible and those at the bottom least so. Becker (1967) employed this notion to specify how, in a system of ranked groups, participants take as given that the members of the highest group are best placed to define 'the way things really are' due to their 'knowledge of truth'. Implicit in this assumption is the view that 'those at the top' have access to a more complete picture of the bureaucratic organization's workings than members of lower groups, whose definition of reality, because of this subordinate status, can be only partial and distorted. As Becker (1967: 241) noted, 'any tale told by those at the top intrinsically deserves to be regarded as the most credible account obtainable ... Thus, credibility and the right to be heard are differentially distributed through the ranks of the system.' By this rationale, then, the higher up in this hierarchy the news source is situated, the more authoritative his or her words will be for the journalist processing the information.

Horse race journalism: a type of election campaign coverage that implicitly likens the competing political candidates and/or parties to horses racing toward the finishing line. In **framing** elections as a spectator sport, horse race journalism focuses on who is edging ahead and who is falling behind while distracting attention from the campaign as a forum for airing policy ideas and debate, context, positions on issues or qualifications of candidates. Called by Patterson (1977) the 'quiet revolution' of US political reporting, horse race journalism has existed in some form since the colonial period but has become particularly prevalent over the past forty years as journalists around the world struggle to make election news interesting to sceptical publics. Using opinion polling data, details about campaign strategy and gossip about political personalities, horse race journalism seeks to give the race a defined shape – an organizing **narrative** – that generates excitement. Its proponents defend it on the grounds that it increases voter interest in politics, putting a human face on policy abstractions.

Human interest: news that incorporates a human **angle** to straightforward information relay. Human interest stories have long been a mainstay of **popular journalism,** namely because they address the lives of individuals and the community in accessible, often emotionally resonant, ways. In an early study, Hughes (1940) marked them as an important and necessarily democratic development in news, which helped turn the masses into a reading public. Emotive and skilled at drawing public interest in an empathetic way, human interest stories put a human face on straight facts. Associated with **soft news,** proponents argue that human interest stories fulfil multiple social functions, including facilitating social cohesion, creating a shared knowledge base and group identification, and helping to maintain a functional **public sphere.** Critics maintain that they trivialize the news and detract from what people need to know, simplifying deep-seated structural issues by positioning them as the result of serendipity and luck. Curran *et al.* (1980) argued that human interest stories service elite interests by disempowering their readers.

Hyperlocal journalism: the **local news** taken to an extreme. Hyperlocal journalism is 'hyper' to the extent that it focuses on local events in such a specialized way that it effectively precludes the interest or attention of those situated outside the targeted community. While hyperlocal journalism is arguably a long-standing feature of good community newspapers, the internet enables the 'community' in question to be defined in far narrower terms. The absence of a viable business model to support hyperlocal journalism is often a serious problem. As a result, reporters working in the hyperlocal patch may be ordinary citizens acting as **citizen journalists** rather than paid journalists.

Hype/space dilemma: the hyping of a news story in order to secure it the necessary space for inclusion. Debates in the newsroom over how best to fill the available **news hole** may lead a journalist to 'hype' her or his story in order to secure it the necessary 'space' for inclusion. Wilcox (2003: 243) called this tension the 'hype/space dilemma', which unfolds in **science journalism** as follows: '[T]he media require scientific studies to provide dramatic new findings and dramatic conflicts, while the conventions of scientific journalism require that the results of single studies be de-emphasized in favour of the scientific context of the research.' Condit's (2004) assessment of the tensions between hype and space suggested that the journalist's struggle to make a story interesting, even **sensational**, in relation to other stories competing for the same space, conflicts with the reaffirmation of professional ideals of truth-telling and **balance**. Precisely how this conflict is negotiated has consequences for what gets covered, but also for the standards of **accuracy** applied to the news.

I

Immediacy: the timeliness of an event or occurrence which is unfolding or happening now, and as such a defining characteristic of its perceived **newsworthiness**. What counts as immediacy varies from one news medium to the next, but all treat it as a virtue of **breaking news** (especially where **scoops** or **exclusives** are concerned). The less time that has elapsed between an event and its reporting as news, the better – immediacy serving as a key criterion when judging performance and as such a marker of prestige, efficiency and reputation. Moreover, it is perceived to be a **news value** highly desired by journalists and news audiences alike for its apparent directness, in part due to its ostensibly unmediated quality (allowing viewers to 'see for themselves' in the case of television news or with respect to **actuality** in radio news). Critics argue that all too often immediacy is prized for its own sake, with the near-obsession to be first frequently engendering inaccurate, superficial or **spectacle**-led reporting.

Immersive journalism: the use of specific strategies or techniques, especially those made possible by digital technologies, to create a heightened sense of lived experience for audiences following a news story. At one end of the continuum, the term refers to mundane factors such as dust, dirt or water on the camera lens, blurred focus or shaky camerawork and the sound of the journalist's personal reaction to what is being recorded (such as discomfort, surprise or alarm). At the other end, it includes devices intended to encourage audiences to interact with story elements or information in a manner that engenders a personalized perspective. The latter includes the use of digital gaming features within virtual environments, as when visitors to an online news site are presented with the opportunity to negotiate the virtual experience of being on an aeroplane that has crashed earlier that day. Advocates regard immersive journalism as a way to supplement traditional, **objective** reporting with a more subjective sense of connection, one that invites empathy and understanding. Critics, by contrast, liken it to **infotainment**, suggesting that it offers an egocentric form of reporting that confuses dazzling visuals with substantive insight.

Impartiality: a commitment to scrupulously **accurate, neutral** and dispassionate reporting in the interest of **professionalism**, usually associated with broadcast news. Even for those journalists who believe impartiality is an ideal impossible to realize in practice, many nonetheless strive to achieve it. In the UK, impartiality is a long-standing feature of **public service broadcasting**. Since the BBC was transformed from a private company to a public body under a royal charter in 1927, its news programmes have been required to be politically impartial over a period of time. By contrast, the Television Act of 1954 which authorized the launch of ITN contained a clause demanding that 'due impartiality' be demonstrated within each individual news programme via a 'proper **balance**' of views. In the US, although the word 'impartiality' appears in the first canons of journalism adopted by the American Society of Newspaper Editors in 1923, its more typical association with news broadcasting tends to revolve around the issues of **balance** and fairness (*see also* **Fairness Doctrine**). The late Walter Cronkite, anchor of the CBS Evening News from 1962 to 1981, was often credited for being the embodiment of impartiality. His daily sign-off line – 'And that's the way it is' (followed by the date) – gave expression to this implicit claim, thereby ostensibly aligning his personal integrity with that of the newscast's journalism.

IndyMedia: a network of independent and **alternative** individuals and organizations offering grassroots, non-commercial and non-corporate coverage of the news. The origins of IndyMedia can be traced to what became known as the 'battle of Seattle' in November 1999, when thousands of people took to the streets of the city to protest against the impact of global free trade relations, as embodied in the meetings of the World Trade Organization. News of the events unfolding on the streets of Seattle made headlines around the world. Playing a vital role in this regard was the Independent Media Centre (IMC) with its all-volunteer team of journalists and alternative media activists – including independent video makers, radio producers and web techies – dispersed across Seattle. The type of democratized journalism being performed by these individuals – described as 'part-activist, part-journalist' – represented **open source reporting** in the eyes of advocates. 'Don't hate the media; be the media' quickly proved to be an effective rallying cry for the rapidly fashioned Seattle IMC.

Today over 150 independent media centres are situated in about 50 countries across six continents. While each local IMC admitted into the network shares the aspirations of the collective, each is also relatively autonomous, defining the details of its mission statement, finances and logistical approach on its own terms. Accordingly, although there is a degree of co-ordination from the centre with respect to technical decisions and editorial policy, each IMC enjoys sufficient freedom to pursue its own agendas. In refusing to be 'a conscious mouthpiece of any particular point of view', IndyMedia itself avoids any direct association with a **partisan** position or stance while enabling those who seek to post non-corporate news, information or analysis to be heard. Its aim in encouraging people to 'present their own account of what is happening in the world' on its newswires revolves around a desire to empower individuals to effectively 'become the media' themselves. As such, it is intended to be a 'safe place' for dissent to be articulated, given that no formal prohibition is placed on the points of view expressed, other than that they are respectful of the editorial policy. On those occasions when offensive outbursts of hate occur (sexist, racist, homophobic, and so forth), the discussion can be temporarily blighted until the item in question is 'hidden' from sight – even then, in the case of most centres, it remains viewable behind the main pages. Ever sensitive to questions of **censorship**, activists seek to ensure as open a dialogue as possible.

IndyMedia does not seek to set an overall news agenda, choosing to depend instead on its reporters – and readers – to determine what should be covered, how and why. Each of these users, it goes without saying, exhibits their own **biases**, so the site advises everyone to read its contents with a critical eye. Those objecting to the content of what is posted can express their alternative view by using the 'add your own comments' link situated beneath each post. This strategy, while sound in principle, can be ineffectual at times, as reasoned critique is sometimes lost in a flurry of heated rants and diatribes. The thorny question of whether or not an individual contributor posting a news item qualifies as a 'journalist' is left by IndyMedia for each person involved to decide for themselves. In the early days, much of the news coverage focused on up-to-the-minute reporting of various demonstrations following in the wake of Seattle around the world. What the activists turned DIY reporters lacked in journalistic experience, they typically made up for with enthusiasm and commitment. Gradually, as the network grew and its resources improved, the range of news items expanded to encompass a much wider array of stories and reporting styles. Informing the efforts of many contributors is a keen desire to make available news that can be used to effect social justice and generate an alternative, non-commercial resource for citizen power (Allan 2006).

Infotainment: a term used to describe a genre of text where information and entertainment values converge in an effort to attract as wide an audience as possible. Infotainment is often perceived to be a derogatory term in the eyes of journalists committed to relaying factual information for its own sake.

Injunction: a court order prohibiting a journalist or news organization from releasing specific details concerning a particular news story. Usually the result of a request made by an aggrieved **source** to the courts, injunctions are imposed to protect the aggrieved from some form of harm (i.e. to their reputation, employment status, need for confidentiality) that may ensue should such details be made public. In the event that the judge agrees to an injunction, it may entail the pulping of newspapers carrying the story or the suspension of a planned broadcast. Critics point out that injunctions can be used by the wealthy and privileged to undermine press freedom.

Interpretive community: a term for the commonality that emerges among journalists through shared discourse and collective interpretations of key public events and issues. Drawn from literary studies, anthropology and folklore, the term 'interpretive community' was applied to journalism by Zelizer (1992, 1993), who argued that journalists create community through a continuous discourse that proliferates in informal talks, professional meetings and trade reviews, memoirs, interviews on talk shows and media retrospectives. When that discourse creates shared interpretations of events, journalists invoke them to make their professional lives meaningful and address dilemmas that arise while engaging in newswork, thereby solidifying their **journalistic authority**. Offered as an antidote to notions of journalism as a **profession**, the boundaries of the interpretive community offer a marker of how journalists see themselves as journalists.

Interpretive journalism: a type of journalism that provides perspective, context, explanation and analysis of the facts central to covering an unfolding event or issue. Contrasted with **neutral journalism** and norms of **objective** or straight reporting, interpretive (or interpretative) journalism involves accounting for the larger unstated motives, agendas, patterns or complications that inflect upon an issue or event because it sees them as critical to ensuring public understanding of its coverage. Rather than report only on facts that can be attributed to **sources**, as is the case with **neutral journalism**, interpretive journalism gives journalists the leeway to evaluate the unarticulated reasoning behind an issue or event.

Though interpretive impulses have long been present in the news, interpretive journalism was thought to emerge in the US in the 1920s, in response to criticism that journalists had not ensured that the public understood the news as then conveyed. It has alternately grown and diminished over time, its popularity associated with multiple developments. First, it is aligned with the degree of literariness in a given news environment – the more literary the journalistic tradition, the more interpretation will appear – and it remains strong in southern Europe, Latin America and Africa. Second, it is associated with time periods characterized by a questioning of government and key public issues: it was particularly strong in the US during the 1930s as the debate over the Great Depression and the economic role of government ensued; it reappeared decades later in the late 1960s and early 1970s with ascendant questions over political assassinations, the Vietnam War and the **Watergate** scandal. Third, it tends to emerge with journalistic formats that encourage interpretation, such as opinion **columns** or the 'week-in-review' sections of newspapers and magazines. For critics wedded to **objectivity**, however, worries are expressed about **bias**, and the concern that interpretive journalism is more akin to **editorializing** than to news reporting.

Interview: an interchange between a journalist and **source**, in which the journalist secures information from the source, usually in a Question and Answer (Q & A) format. Both a tool for gathering information and a particular sort of presentational news format, interviews have been the mainstay of reporting for the last century or so but primarily gained public prominence with the ascent of broadcasting and **current affairs** programming that was based on taped or live interviews. Journalists gather multiple kinds of information in interviews, including fact checks, elaborate details and confirmatory quotes. In the US, interviews were first given for the record in the 1830s with the rise of the **penny press**, but they were not published or quoted verbatim until the end of the nineteenth century. Interviews were adapted to radio already in the 1920s, and by the beginning of the twentieth century were increasingly seen across Europe as levels of **professionalization** intensified and **public relations** firms were introduced, both developments which saw value in the act of interviewing. By the early 1970s, interviews appeared on television, where over time they generated half-hour and hour long interview programmes that facilitated Q&A formats with public figures as well as appearing on **television news magazines**. Today interviews may take place face to face, on the telephone or on the internet, involving spontaneous exchanges around a formal or informal list of prepared questions.

Interviews range from prearranged lengthy conversations to on the spot **doorstepping**, in which the reporter waits for the source at the entrance to buildings. Clayman and Heritage (2002) addressed a set of discursive rules by which televised interviews unfold: interviewees need to show a willingness to respond in a straightforward fashion while sharing only the information they want known; they must not appear evasive or non-compliant and must tread a thin line between seeming genuine and self-promoting. By contrast, interviewers strike a blend of **neutrality** and **adversarial journalism**. That is, they typically maintain a neutral stance towards their interviewees by restricting themselves to asking questions, avoiding overt forms of agreement and disagreement, and avoiding flat assertions; they pursue adversarial journalism by the content of their questions, raising alternative viewpoints and challenging responses. Sometimes interviews are organized with panels of interviewers or interviewees, which helps offset the divergent expectations placed on both roles. The ascent of televised interviews has brought with it a tendency towards more aggressive questions on the part of journalists, less deference towards the interviewees and a more blunt and direct style of questioning. These and related factors have made the interview a powerful instrument of public accountability.

Inverted pyramid: a style of newswriting in which relevant information is presented in a descending order of importance. The summary **lead**, an initial paragraph which summarizes the **five Ws and H** – who, what, when, where, why and how – of the news story, generally tops off the inverted pyramid, while the remainder of the news story provides supporting information for the points made in the summary lead. The least essential information is left to the end of the story.

Associated with **objectivity** and factuality, the inverted pyramid is assumed to have come into widespread use by the end of the nineteenth century with the Progressive Era, though some observers claim evidence of its sporadic use by the Secretary of War during the US Civil War. Its evolution was spearheaded by technical, social and cultural developments, including the ascent of the telegraph and the consequent development of the **news agencies**, the rise of science and consequent privileging of facts as a mode of understanding reality, and a rising public demand for information and its presentation in a so-called **neutral** or un**biased** manner. The inverted pyramid had practical effect on journalistic form and practice, in that it helped introduce a brief, concrete newswriting style into journalism, facilitated the smooth processing of raw information into a story format, allowed news editors to cut the news story from the bottom up when faced with fitting stories to constrained space under **deadline**, and aligned itself easily with aspirations towards **objectivity**. It also assumedly made news copy easier for the public to read, once accustomed to the convention. Contrasted with the journalistic essay, the first person narrative and the flamboyant, detailed, chronological account, the inverted pyramid emerged as particularly useful for **breaking news**, and today it tends to appear on the front pages of newspapers and taglines of internet relays. Proponents see the inverted pyramid as a basic building block of newswriting that forces journalists to summarize the story through its key facts. Critics of the inverted pyramid decry its artlessness and unnatural mode of information relay, seeing it as an 'anti-story' form that tells the news story backwards and loses its audience. They also claim that the inverted pyramid stifles critical thinking.

Investigative journalism: journalism which excavates hidden or obscure aspects of public events and issues to the surface, usually involving the exposure of wrongful conduct, malfeasance or corruption of the public good. Investigative journalism, whose reporters Ettema and Glasser (1998) call 'custodians of conscience' because they expose the violations of valued public norms, has had various forms since journalism's earliest days.

Recognizable, at least in retrospect, from the earliest conceptions of journalistic form and practice (not least with respect to related movements over time, such as the **muckraking** era of the early 1900s), investigative journalism reached new heights with the mistrust of government and social upheaval that arose during the 1960s and onward. In comparison with other modes of reportage, investigative journalism tends, in reporter Martha Gelhorn's view, to report 'from the ground up' and to involve longer and more protracted efforts by its reporters, who use public records, buried or hidden documents, multiple **interviews**, and often undercover observation to piece together their stories. Investigative reports usually offer a more in-depth, comprehensive treatment than other kinds of news stories. Certain news organizations have been long associated with investigative reporting, including in the US exemplars such as CBS's *60 Minutes*, or journals such as *Mother Jones* and *The Nation*, and, in the UK, newspapers like the *Sunday Times* in the 1960s or, more recently, the non-profit Bureau of Investigative Journalism initiative or the BBC's flagship *Panorama* programme.

Connected in large part to long-standing aspirations about journalism's ability to uncover and expose official wrongdoing, investigative journalism has always had its supporters in the non-profit and commercial worlds. For instance, in the US it has been supported since 1975 by the IRE (Investigative Reporters and Editors), a national organization that trains journalists in the methods of investigative reporting, while the Fund for Investigative Journalism (FIJ) came to acclaim when its grant of $250 enabled reporter Seymour Hersh to begin his investigation of the My Lai massacre in Vietnam during the late 1960s. By the late 2000s, multiple organizations modelled on IRE were set up in Europe, Latin America and Asia, and Global Investigative Journalism, an international network of over 30 countries, was established in 2003 to share resources. More recently, as multiple newspapers folded in 2009, the news and opinion website *The Huffington Post* began bankrolling its own investigative journalism unit as a means of supporting unemployed investigative reporters. Critics maintain that investigative journalism can be harmful in that it undermines public confidence and leads to cynicism, and, if not done well, focuses public attention on insignificant aspects of public life.

J

Journalese: specialized vocabulary among journalists. Often referring simply to jargon, journalese is employed by journalists (and editors) in the course of communicating with one another in their everyday work.

Journalism: the broad range of activities associated with newsmaking. Referenced in the 1700s in France by Denis Diderot as the 'work of a society of scholars', the word 'journalism' was later applied to the printed reportage of current events. In contemporary usage, it refers to the organized and public collection, processing and distribution of news and **current affairs** mate-rial. Implied has been a sense of the evolving **crafts**, **routines**, skills and conventions employed in **newswork**, spanning the occupational roles of **editors**, reporters, correspondents and photographers, among others. These have varied over time, but, as Adam (1993) noted, they fundamentally involve judgement, reporting, language, narration and analysis. Alongside these impulses, references to journalism are associated with a slew of secondary notions, none of which can be applied across the board of all that constitutes journalism but which nonetheless are regularly invoked as both actual description ('what journalism is') and subjunctive aspiration ('what journal-ism could be'). These include an intersection with modernity, by which journalism is seen as a decidedly modern day phenomenon that aligns itself with post-Enlightenment notions that one can observe and know the world; with an association to politics, shaped either as an **impartial** and **objective** arbiter that acts for the public good or in **advocacy** for a narrow slice of politics as in **partisan** practice; and with notions of **truth**telling, by which journalism is expected to be a reliable and honest broker of information about the world.

Journalism education: the teaching of journalism as a vocation. Though journalism education can take place at multiple points in the process of becoming or already working as a journalist, it almost always involves some combination of practical training and broader understanding of journalism's place in the world. From practical skills like writing or editing to grasping how journalism intersects with government or the law, journalism education takes shape through apprenticeship on the job, journalism training institutions and university degrees. It has had different evolutionary trajectories around the world. In the US, journalism education began first in the humanities around 1900, focusing on journalistic 'skills' like news writing or the history of journalism, and in the social sciences a quarter of a century later, when early attempts expanded into schools of journalism. Curricular developments reflected the concerns of the time, as when multiple US universities, worried over whether vocational training was sufficiently academic, instituted the 25/75 rule by which only 25 per cent of available courses could focus on journalistic skills. In the UK, journalism education developed much later, against a long-standing tradition of learning through apprenticeship, and it was only when a burgeoning interest in journalism came from the social sciences during the late 1960s that journalism began to occupy a core position in the new field of media studies. Even today, much course division undergirding journalism education is driven by whichever media are taught, and technologies of production often remain separated from each other; with TV, magazines, radio, the press and online journalism taught in separate sequences. The resulting curriculum, in Carey's (2000:13) view, continues to lack 'historical understanding, criticism or self-consciousness' and despite multiple calls for change (e.g. Dennis 1984) remains on the whole conformist, unevenly addressing the academic projects typical of journalism studies in its curricular mix. Journalism education is supported by multiple professional associations in different countries, where an emphasis tends to be placed on improving standards and quality in teaching and learning contexts.

Journalism of attachment: an approach to journalism which sees journalists attending first to the emotional and human costs of the wars they cover rather than serving as conduits for political or military interests. A term coined by veteran BBC foreign correspondent Martin Bell (1995) as part of a controversial argument against what he called **bystanders' journalism** during the 1990s war in the former Yugoslavia. Bell argued that the war journalist should not attempt to stand neutrally between 'good and evil, right and wrong, aggressor and victim'. A journalism of attachment, he maintained, is a 'journalism which cares as well as knows', and 'engaged' journalism takes sides by assuming an empathetic role. Not surprisingly, the term sparked fierce debate, especially by those angered by what they perceive to be a dangerous blurring of **objective** reporting into the realm of **advocacy journalism**. Moreover, critics argue that it creates unrealistic expectations of journalists' roles in wartime, suggesting simplistic distinctions between 'good' and 'evil' (as well as 'us' and 'them') and positioning journalists as moral arbiters even if they are not qualified to act so.

Journalist: a broad label for the range of people who engage in activities associated with newsmaking. Broadly a reference to those who 'write in a journal', the term 'journalist' now connotes those who systematically keep records of certain happenings within a specified time frame and make that record public. Traced at least as far back as the French *Journal des Sauvants* during the seventeenth century, today the term refers to individuals who engage in a slew of related activities – in Adam's (1993) view, 'reporting, criticism, editorializing and the conferral of judgment on the shape of things'. But tensions over the boundaries of who is a journalist persist. Is a teenage girl who produces daily entries in her diary and shares them with her friends a journalist? She could be, especially if her diary is a **blog**. The same could be said of the freelance writer sitting in a jail for contempt of court and claiming protection while refusing to reveal her sources. Various institutions, ranging from **IndyMedia** to major news organizations, from the courts to the United Nations, have sought to offer a definitive definition. Who is a journalist promises to be increasingly difficult to specify as journalism's functions continue to proliferate across multimedia platforms.

Journalistic authority: a term for the ability of journalists to promote themselves as authoritative and credible spokespersons of events transpiring in the real world. First applied by Eason (1986) in his discussion of the Janet Cooke affair, a scandal involving the revoking of a **Pulitzer Prize** from a

Washington Post reporter following evidence that her front-page story had been fabricated, the term journalistic authority refers to the multiplicity of ways in which journalists informally and subtly credential themselves while working as journalists, gaining and securing prestige, stature, salience, power and career advancement through their **newswork**. Building upon what Park (1940) called 'synthetic knowledge' – the kind of tacit knowledge that is 'embodied in habit and custom' rather than that which forms the core of formalized knowledge systems – journalistic authority forces attention to the cues by which journalists think about journalism and the world and how they incorporate such cues into newsmaking. Driven often by critical incidents, that is, hot moments which give journalists an opportunity to air questions and challenge assumptions about how best to act as journalists, journalistic authority constitutes a way for journalists to mark their placement as journalists. Zelizer (1992), for instance, showed how the US television coverage of the John F. Kennedy assassination and its retellings over time were as much about the TV journalists who gave the story voice as they were about a slain US President.

Journalistic field: a concept referring to a journalistic microcosm with its own laws, perspective, structure and interests. Introduced by Bourdieu (1998), the journalistic field – which possesses a relative degree of autonomy from other fields of cultural production, such as the juridical, literary, artistic or scientific fields – reveals the social conditions underpinning journalism as a collective activity which 'smoothes over things, brings them into line, and depoliticizes them' to the 'level of anecdote and scandal'. Despite the fierce relations of competition which exist between different news organizations, the quest for exclusivity (or **scoops**) recurrently yields coverage which is as uniform as it is banal. Consequently, Bourdieu argued, once the decisive impact of the journalistic field upon other fields is taken into consideration, the current extent of public disenchantment with politics is hardly surprising.

Journo: slang for journalist.

Jump-line/Spill-line: the line at which a **newspaper** or **magazine** news story 'jumps' or 'spills' from one page to another. When jump-lines occur, the reader is instructed where to find the remaining portion (e.g. 'Story continues on Page 5') so as to carry on reading to the end.

Junk journalism: a term referring to journalism with little or no integrity. Constituting a play on 'junk food', junk journalism refers to reporting with little nutritious value – tasty perhaps, but harmful to the health of the body politic.

K

Kicker: a journalistic presentational feature that draws public attention to the adjacent item. Several different definitions of kickers are in circulation within journalistic discourse. The kicker can refer to:

1   a short, lead-in headline (usually in a small font), situated just above or below the main headline, intended to catch the reader's eye;
2   the final paragraph or two of a news report, which should work to invoke **narrative** closure in a satisfying way (*see also* **Zinger**); or
3   a word or short phrase that introduces the **caption** for a news photograph.

Kiss and tell journalism: a form of reporting highly valued by the **tabloids** or **popular journalism**, whereby a source provides intimate (kiss and tell) revelations about a sexual relationship with a public figure (politician, celebrity, sports star, etc.) in exchange for financial payment from a news organization. This type of **chequebook journalism** can generate sales, but it is becoming increasingly risky (and expensive) to pursue in countries where the courts can be used to protect the **privacy** of the rich and famous.

Kite-flying: the leakage of information by individuals so as to test public, official or journalistic response. Also called trial balloons, kite-flying can be initiated by a range of individuals: they include **anonymous sources**, such as individuals within a political party, who selectively **leak** potentially controversial information to journalists with the purpose of ascertaining journalists' reaction and/or gauging public response. They can also include journalists, who outline a scenario to a source (**off the record**) with a view to seeing whether or not it prompts a formal (**on the record**) response. In both cases, kite-flying facilitates decision-making on the individual's part as to how best to proceed with the information, safe in the knowledge that should it prove problematic any association with it can always be denied.

L

Labour journalism: a type of journalism associated with labour issues, labour movements, working conditions and workers' rights. Labour journalism emerged during the nineteenth and early twentieth centuries when multiple localized publications created a platform for concerns related to labour, and in the US context these focused on the possibility of reform in working conditions and the improvement of workers' rights, high on the progressive agenda of the time. Associated often with the **muckrakers**, most labour publications depended on subscriptions and donations and were thereby short-lived. Others, though developed ties with political parties and survived by generalizing their concern for working conditions and workers' rights beyond specific locations. Labour journalism made slight headway into broadcasting, where in the US organized labour helped address labour issues in a handful of broadcasting markets, such as Chicago. But when only a few national publications survived into the twenty-first century, mostly as monthlies or bimonthlies with updated websites, the task of covering labour issues fell to the mainstream news media. Much mainstream coverage of labour and management conflicts (Glasgow University Media Group 1976, 1980) tends to reflect labour negatively and management positively.

Layout: the arrangement and design of articles, **pictures** and advertisements on a **newspaper** or **magazine** page. Layout refers to how the house-style is implemented for a particular page's design and format, with the aim of making transitions between features clear and easy to follow. Decisions are made about the amount of space to devote to a news item, its placement, prominence (with regard to advertising copy, photographs, graphics, sidebars, and the like) and typographic style (including column width, type sizes and type faces). Layout usually varies from page to page so as to draw reader interest. Barnhurst and Nerone (2001) traced various styles of graphic design that have come into play in newspapers over time, all of them addressing the visual priorities of readability. Worked upon by page designers and/or subeditors, the layout of a page often proceeds from a template that pre-designates where pictures, articles and advertisements might be placed. An early version of the layout plan, which may be subjected to considerable reworking before completed, is sometimes called a 'blueprint' or 'dummy'.

Lead/Lede: a news story's initial sentence or paragraph that summarizes its main point. Often spelled 'lede' from Old English and sometimes called 'the intro', the lead is expected to convey the story's essential facts. Usually between 25 and 30 words long, the lead typically follows the rule of the **inverted pyramid**, by which the most important information is presented first, and attempts to address the **five Ws and H** (who, what, where, when, why and how). Journalists craft leads with considerable care, given that they are widely assumed to either catch or lose the news story's audience. The lead story on television refers to the most important news story of the day. Burying a lead refers to positioning the lead too deeply in a news story and/or erroneously forwarding the wrong **angle** as its most important information.

Leak: a seemingly unauthorized release of **confidential** information by a **source** to a journalist or news organization. Once called oil in the machinery of government, two types of leaks regularly occur in journalism: one refers to material disclosed despite attempts to keep it secret; the other to material disclosed with strategic intent. Although 'leak' was coined in the early twentieth century as a specific term for an inadvertent slip of information picked up by reporters, today it refers broadly to an array of practices involving the sharing of information, including authorized leaking, **whistleblowing**, settling grudges, culling favours, drawing attention to policy initiatives, signalling foreign governments, **kite-flying** and releasing trial balloons so as to discern early public response. In some national contexts, leaks occur on a routine, even daily, basis as a **public relations** strategy for **agenda setting**. Additionally, there is similar variation in the effects of leaked information, which only sometimes benefits the public good. Though much journalistic lore associated with leaks plays up their dramatic nature and influential impact – such as the leaks involving Daniel Ellsberg and the **Pentagon Papers**, **Watergate** and 'Deep Throat', the Iraqi armaments and suicide of British weapons expert David Kelly, or the Weapons of Mass Destruction fiasco – in fact most instances of leaking information are mundane and have little effect. In the best of cases, leaks encourage the journalists who receive them to cross-check and corroborate the information they offer.

Letters to the editor: letters written by members of the public to a news organization, expressing opinion or other kinds of response to some aspect of its news or editorial coverage. From the earliest newspapers, letters to the editor offer ordinary individuals a chance to opine on events and issues in the news. Presumed to be generally older, more educated and wealthier than the general population, writers of readers' letters are not necessarily expected to reflect general public opinion, with studies finding results on both sides of the question of their representativeness. Because news organizations do not publish or air all readers' letters, the ones that do appear signify the boundaries of what the news organization considers fair or legitimate public response (Wahl-Jorgensen 2007). Letters are often processed by a specialist subeditor, grouped together in presentation so as to provide meaningful clusters of opinion, and used as signals for larger debates about ongoing topics in the news. Sometimes editors select letters that advance an opinion contrary to that appearing in the news and editorial content of the news organization. Should an objectionable letter (e.g. sexist, racist or homophobic in content) appear, it does so with the tacit approval of the news organization that facilitates its appearance.

Libel: an instance of **defamation**, where a false but damaging statement or image has been made in a published or otherwise fixed medium. Appearing in newspapers, magazines or websites, libel is shown to have damaged the good reputation an individual or group is otherwise entitled to possess.

Lifestyle journalism: a genre of reporting that is primarily concerned with the minutiae of everyday life. Lifestyle journalism encompasses a diverse range of consumer-oriented subjects. Perceived to be an increasingly popular type of **feature**, both with readers and advertisers, lifestyle journalism emerged in the 1970s (in part as an updated form of both women's pages and society pages that had existed in many **newspapers** and **magazines** since the late 1880s). Often associated in its US form with the *Washington Post*'s 'Style' section begun in 1969, contemporary examples of lifestyle journalism address **fashion**, home, cuisine, nightlife and **travel**. Typically upbeat in tone, the coverage is sometimes described as 'news you can use'. It prioritizes practical information as well as assessments of current ('what's hot') trends in consumption, frequently appearing in specialized sections and/or supplements in newspapers and magazines. Critics argue that news organizations have become dependent upon lifestyle journalism because of its close synergies with advertising, which means that the reader is addressed as a consumer rather than as a citizen in the interests of boosting revenue. It is seldom the case, they point out, that companies benefiting from such coverage find themselves subjected to 'real', investigative reporting (making it a form of **infotainment** in some views). At the same time, many news publications still produce the women's and society pages that lifestyle pages were expected to supplant.

Lift-out quote/Pull-out quote: a quotation drawn from a news item and presentationally highlighted so as to draw interest to the news item. Appearing in print publications, a lift-out quote typically uses a different or enlarged font and may be positioned in a box or **sidebar** so as to give the reader a flavour of the adjoining news item.

Literary journalism: a type of journalism that uses techniques associated with literary writing to convey a larger truth about the world. Also called **'new journalism'**, 'creative non-fiction' and the 'non-fiction novel' and often associated with **gonzo journalism**, literary journalism is largely thought to have emerged in seventeenth-century England, when Daniel Defoe – and following him Jonathan Swift, Samuel Johnson and Charles Dickens – used literary techniques to craft stories about real life problems and concerns. Literary journalism spread to the US in the nineteenth century, when writers like Samuel Clemens/Mark Twain, Walt Whitman, Dorothy Day and Lincoln Steffens used literary techniques in their journalistic accounts, offering what Stephen Crane called a 'feel of the facts.' In the twentieth century, Truman Capote, Tom Wolfe and Norman Mailer took the category one step further in trying to develop a different kind of journalistic storytelling that put **narrative** and style on an equal footing with or sometimes before substance. Situating themselves against conventional journalism and its norms of **objectivity**, **accuracy** and fact verification, literary journalists used techniques like composite characters, scene setting, irony and satire to drive a different kind of engagement with their material (Sims 2007), though some observers claim that it went beyond mere writing to suggest a movement about political style and engagement, writ broadly (Pauly 1990). Much literary journalism has been published in book form, but as newspapers moved increasingly towards objectivity and its related presentational forms, it often moved to magazines. Who constitutes a literary journalist continues to be debated, however, as some novelists only dabbled in journalism – such as George Orwell – while many journalists employed literary attributes in their writing – such as Daniel Defoe. Others – Albert Camus, John Steinbeck, Ernest Hemingway and Emile Zola, for example – inhabited both worlds in an equally committed fashion. Contemporary trends towards narrativization in news and its crafting into a movement towards 'creative non-fiction' since the 1990s offered yet another experiment with new forms of journalistic storytelling akin to the literary journalism of the 1960s.

Lobby briefing: a type of UK **press briefing** during Parliamentary session for journalists that affords privileged access to official sources of information and comment by government spokespersons, typically on a non-attributable basis ('inside sources say …'). The system dates to the 1870s – when certain reporters were allowed to meet MPs in the lobby or hallways of the Houses of Parliament before or after debates – and has often been used to considerable advantage by politicians and civil servants seeking to shape the news agenda. In November 1997, however, the Labour government moved to formally place such briefings **on the record** (along similar lines to the US custom) for accredited lobby correspondents. Since 2002, the briefings have been open to specialist and foreign journalists as well, although the 'lobby rules' – e.g. sources are not named, nor can opposition MPs be approached for a reaction – remain in place. The number of passes in issue to lobby correspondents varies from one year to the next, but is typically about 250 at any one time.

Local news: information relay that is geographically proximate to its audience. Primarily of interest to residents of a specific locale, local news tends to perform a networking function for community members and is organized in three interrelated ways: **beats** associated with local institutions, like the police, schools, courts or municipality; **breaking news** that generally focuses on local accidents, criminal activity and natural hazards; and the softer and more timeless local **lifestyle** and **feature** sections, which track the area's major ongoing social, cultural and political activities. In form local news ranges from simple lists of transactions – real estate transfers, marriages, obituaries, weather updates – to full length articles about community hearings, trends and problems.

While early examples of local news date to the 1690 organ *Publick Occurrences, Both Forreign and Domestick*, which reported briefly on local crimes and agriculture, local news has long been charted with facilitating community integration and local civic involvement by observers as wide-ranging as Alexis de Tocqueville, John Dewey and Robert Park. At the same time, local news runs the risk of sliding into economic boosterism, by which its interdependence with the local power structure increases the possibility that it becomes a cheerleader for local business interests. Though local news is used as an umbrella term for many types of news content produced locally, in fact the different media that provide local news produce content that varies considerably from each other. Local news in print has moved from being aligned with cities to embracing multiple types of communities. While during the mid-nineteenth century rise of **popular journalism**, local print news was largely tied to urbanization, over time it broadened to reflect the concerns of many kinds of communities, and there arose multiple daily and weekly newspapers, city and regional magazines, a suburban press and free neighbourhood papers. Local television arrived on the scene along with television's more general popularity but struggled to find a way to differentiate itself effectively from the more national programming. It experimented with a variety of innovations, including '**happy news**', '**eyewitness** news' and 'action news', and wrestled with critics who saw it as focused on **crime**, accidents and disaster to the near exclusion of all else.

Currently local news has gravitated to '**hyperlocal**' spaces, where it is found in city-based websites that extend far beyond the boundaries of traditional journalism. Typically produced online by **citizen journalists** using camera phones, email, newsgroups and **blogs** to share information, this 'amateur' reporting helps to cover events and issues missed by the other local news media.

Lock-up: the consignment of rival journalists to a room with severed communication ties to the outside world, so as to allow privileged access to exclusive information. Lock-ups are often implemented prior to events providing major or large-scale official announcements, such as a government's notification of the year's financial budget. Advocates maintain that lock-ups provide journalists with sufficient time to sift through documentation in detail, thereby allowing them to make a more informed assessment than would be otherwise possible under **deadline** pressure. Critics contend that journalists sequestered under such circumstances open themselves up to possible manipulation by officials seeking to **spin** the data or, at the very least, risk engendering the perception that they have compromised their independence.

Look-live: footage on **television news** that looks as though it is being recorded live. Though look-live ostensibly relays events occurring at that moment in front of the camera lens, it does not reveal that the footage was taped beforehand.

M

Magazine: printed publications appearing on a regular basis which are devoted to reportage and/or commentary about news events transpiring since the previous edition. Ranging across various modes of periodicity – weekly in the case of *Time*, *Maclean's*, *Der Spiegel*, *L'Express*, *Kalakaumudi* or *Veja* – the word 'magazine' was derived from the Arabic term for 'storehouse'. Histories of the news magazine as a genre of periodical observe that its origins can be traced back to the earliest classifications that emerged as distinctive from specialized journals. The first self-described magazine was the *Gentleman's Magazine: or, Trader's Monthly Intelligencer* founded in 1731, which offered a news digest of events in London. Definitions continue to vary – *The Economist* prefers to call itself a newspaper, for example – but most revolve around a commitment to furnishing the reader with an informed (often politically **partisan**) treatment of topical news that exhibits greater scope and depth than can be typically found in the daily press. Given that most news magazines tend to attract a relatively elite readership in terms of social and economic capital, they are often perceived to wield a greater influence on opinion formation than their **circulation** figures might otherwise suggest. In some countries, the Sunday newspaper performs a similar function to the news magazine.

Market-driven journalism: a type of journalism in which editorial judgements about news content are made primarily through considerations about news as a saleable commodity. Contrasted with news that gives priority to **professional** judgements about quality, the integrity of reporting or the public interest, market-driven journalism emerged during the 1970s, when newspapers turned to consultants and marketing research (opinion surveys, focus groups, interviews, etc.) to identify and satisfy the needs and interests of their readers. Newspapers were re-envisaged by accentuating their most marketable elements, which led to specialized sections devoted to single topics or themes (closely aligned with relevant advertising), as well as a new emphasis on **human interest**, entertainment, **lifestyle** and **local** news. This trend, which has continued to gain momentum over the years across the news industry more widely, is sometimes described as **tabloidization**.

Masthead: the title or motto of a newspaper or journal; alternatively, a newspaper or journal's list of publishers, senior staff and contact details. Derived from a nautical term for the tallest part of a ship, the masthead is usually printed in a conspicuous place on a newspaper's front page or journal's cover, in the first instance, and on the **editorial** page, in the second instance, where it might also present a statement of the news organization's editorial vision, statement of purpose, or subscription and advertising rates. In standard usage, the masthead often refers metonymically to the publication itself.

McJournalism: a term which refers to the standardization of journalism as a packaged commodity. Coined by Franklin (2005), who drew upon George Ritzer's conception of McDonaldization as a process of rationalization and bureaucratization within the fast food industry, it refers to the local press in Britain, where the sustained decline in the number of published titles (and corresponding concentration of ownership) is associated with marked increases in advertising revenue and profit. Franklin argued that the local press is aligned with the key principles of McDonaldization – namely efficiency, calculability, predictability and control – in a manner detrimental to journalistic quality. Two consequences are engendered by this process of McJournalism:

1 news is increasingly 'spoon fed' to readers in ever more accessible ways;
2 readers are 'force fed' a 'relentlessly *uniform* and *predictable* diet of news presented in ever more *uniform* formats'.

Media relations: a specialized function of **news management** that focuses on shaping news media interest by encouraging, sustaining or combating interest in a specific event, topic or issue. Broadly synonymous with **public relations**, media relations involves a number of strategies, including the preparation of '**press kits**' (promotional materials) by 'media officers' which aim to ensure that journalists remain 'on message' with the desired publicity aims and objectives.

Microblogging: a kind of **blogging** that shares text messages via social networking sites, such as **Twitter**. Sharing entries smaller in size than the typical blog, microblogging offers short posts that are distributed by email, mobile phones, the internet and instant message relays. Even social networking sites like Facebook and MySpace accommodate microblogging through their status updates features.

Misinformation: false or inaccurate information relayed to a journalist by a source in error or by mistake. Contrasted with **disinformation**, misinformation is communicated without deliberate intention to deceive.

Moblogging: a shortened term for mobile blogging. Moblogging refers to the use of a mobile or cell telephone (or related handheld device) to post blog entries on the internet. When the device is equipped with a camera, first person accounts can be supplemented with photographs or video. Moblogging by **citizen journalists** attracted considerable attention in the aftermath of the South Asian tsunami (2004), the London subway bombings (2005) and Hurricane Katrina (2005).

MoJo/SoJo: multimedia slang for a mobile journalist (MoJo) or solo journalist (SoJo). Both terms refer to a journalist who works without the benefit of an accompanying crew in the field. Also called **back-pack journalism**, the MoJo or SoJo takes sole responsibility for all aspects of news production, including recording video footage, writing copy, editing, and then transmitting or posting the finished report. Working without a landline telephone, let alone a desk in a **newsroom**, these journalists are almost constantly on the move. 'Anywhere there's wifi, we're there', wrote Patrick E. Tolbert on his blog, *Just a MoJo.* 'We carry all of our equipment, laptops, cameras and recording devices, to provide you with what's happening and what it means to you.'

Moral panic: an academic term for the capacity of the news media to generate a sense of crisis surrounding a particular event, issue or activity. Initially formulated by Cohen (1972) as a means of explaining the media's response to the emergence of 'Mods' and 'Rockers' as subcultural styles in Britain during the 1960s, the term moral panic addressed the media debates over deviancy that arose in response to occasionally violent clashes between the two groups and the disclosure of their attitudes towards sex, vandalism and drug-taking. Hall *et al.* (1978) further elaborated the term, analysing the moral panic generated by the conservative press around 'mugging', which subsequently led to harsher 'law and order' legislation. Today examples of moral panics highlight how certain individuals or groups (pregnant teenagers, asylum seekers, HIV/AIDS patients, 'lager louts') or issues (pornography on the internet, dangerous dogs, knife crimes, violent video games, eating disorders) can be stigmatized in news reporting. Typically they are **framed** as a serious threat to the social fabric, and thereby deserving of strong moral censure and possibly prosecution, depending upon the 'folk devil' in question. The ensuing news coverage often invites a sharp 'us' and 'them' dichotomy, which can prove prejudicial to minority or marginalized groups.

Morgue: the library linked to a newsroom, most commonly associated with newspapers. In addition to the usual reference resources, the morgue is likely to include old newspapers, **clippings** and news **pictures** in storage. Today most newsrooms rely on an electronic archive system.

Muckraking: the investigation of corruption and its exposure as news. The muckrakers are largely thought to have come of age at the beginning of Progressivism in the US, a time when the **professionalization** of journalists was reaching new heights. While the first decade and a half of the twentieth century has generally come to be known as the muckraking era, early instances of muckraking stretched back to the last years of the nineteenth century. Nellie Bly's 1887 exposé of the Blackwell Islands insane asylum, photojournalist Jacob Riis's portrayal of New York City's ghettoes in 1890, and Ida Tarbell's columns in *McClure's* of the 1890s were all forerunners of the impulses that would soon lead US journalism into twentieth-century muckraking.

In its early years, billowing corruption in the political and business worlds of the time drove a group of magazine journalists, critics, novelists and authors to make its exposé their mission. Largely responding to the social upheaval of the Gilded Age and holding a firm belief in journalism's ability to expose wrongdoing through the collection and publication of facts attesting to its existence, muckrakers believed in a better society that could be improved by journalism creating an informed public. Historically, the term 'muckraking' has been understood in two ways, both as the defence of the vulnerable from those in power and as a tasteless digging in the muck for sensationalistic stories. Though US President Teddy Roosevelt originally coined the term in 1906 by drawing from a passage in John Bunyan's *Pilgrim's Progress* – which referenced a man with a muck-rake who never looked up but continued to rake 'the filth of the floor' – muckrakers later came to be seen in multiple and often contradictory ways: as moral crusaders or dirt diggers, as liberal reformists or conservative defenders of the status quo, as responsible advocates for the weak and disenfranchised or as overzealous sensationalists. Most observers agree that the Progressive movement would not have achieved its reforms without the popular appeal generated for social causes by the muckrakers. Noted muckrakers have remained among the most revered of journalism's investigative journalists, and they range from Lincoln Steffens to Upton Sinclair and include journals like *McClure's* and *Collier's* alongside multiple books. Muckraking drew to a close with the advent of the First World War, both due to the decline of Progressivism, the breadth of its assaults on the corruption wrought by the Industrial Revolution, and the turn of attention to battles abroad. Nonetheless, its spirit still resides in other forms of reporting, namely **advocacy**, **alternative**, **citizen**, **participant** and **partisan** journalism.

Multi-skilling/Multi-tasking: the work of journalists as it ranges across delivery platforms. Multi-skilling refers to situations in which a newspaper journalist in addition to writing news reports also takes photographs, shoots video, posts to a **blog**, and prepares **podcasts** – each of which demand competence with various skills. Managers intent on 'efficiency gains' through cost-savings may actively seek to employ journalists with a suitably 'flexible aptitude' and a 'wide skill repertoire'. In addition, they are likely to cite motivational factors such as increased job satisfaction, improved opportunities for employee development, and greater adaptability to technological change and innovation, among other positive benefits. Critics, by contrast, highlight what they perceive to be the dangers associated with multi-skilling, including the reduction in the number of jobs available. Those who remain face a decidedly more pressurized workplace (with a corresponding impact on stress levels). Moreover, critics contend that the quality of journalism suffers, mainly due to the lack of sufficient expertise in each area – a problem compounded by the speed at which complex tasks must be undertaken.

Multimedia journalism: journalism which draws upon more than one delivery format (text, images, audio, video, etc.) in preparing and presenting a news item. Associated with **back-pack journalism**, **VJs**, **MoJos** and **SoJos**, the ongoing drive towards digital **convergence** is making multimedia journalism increasingly prominent (see also Matheson and Allan 2009). Today journalists are expected to work comfortably across a range of platforms using a wide array of skills previously held to be medium-specific.

Murdochization: a reference to the impact and influence of global media magnate Rupert Murdoch on journalism. As the chair and managing director of News Corporation, Murdoch exercises control over vast holdings in newspapers (e.g. the *Sun*, *News of the World*, *The Times* and *Sunday Times* in the UK; the *Wall Street Journal*, *New York Post*, and others, in the US; *The Australian*, *Herald Sun*, *The Daily Telegraph*, amongst many more in Australia), television (e.g. Fox News), satellite television (e.g. BSkyB, Foxtel, STAR TV, etc.), books (e.g. HarperCollins), magazines (e.g. Australian editions of *GQ, Vogue*, etc.), cinema (e.g. Twentieth Century Fox) and the internet (e.g. Fox.com, MySpace), among others.

Murdoch's proponents contend that he deserves credit for his success as an entrepreneur, one who has consistently led the way in ushering in the changes necessary to ensure the continued viability of corporate news organizations. For instance, in 1986 he introduced electronic production processes to his newspapers in Australia, Britain and the US (*see* **Wapping dispute**). By contrast, critics liken Murdoch to the notorious press barons of old, using the term 'Murdochization' to pinpoint his exploitation of economic imperatives – conglomerization, homogenization, bureaucratization, etc. – in the service of profit. The damaging impact on journalism is all too apparent, they argue, as seen in his transformation of *The Times* of London from a paper of record (albeit one which lost money) into a newspaper increasingly driven by **tabloid** news values.

Myth: a mode of understanding which helps explain the originary evolution of a system and establishes models for behaviour within it. Myth positions the aspects of such a system as natural and given, playing a critical social role in reinforcing certain ideas, values and beliefs about how to maintain the system. In journalism, news **narratives** and news **pictures** offer ways of producing and reproducing familiar and already recycled myths, which in turn ratify pre-existing beliefs, ideals and values. Lule (2001) detailed how journalism fills the roles and functions that myth-making institutions filled in earlier cultures, arguing that by offering originary and instructive accounts of central aspects of society, designating heroes and villains, warning of tragedy and instilling collective notions of order and disorder, journalism takes on the role of myth-maker.

Displaying a larger truth about what society accepts and rejects, myth offers a repository of commonsensical notions about how the world works, and these notions – about heroism, morality, diligence and social order, among others – regularly make their way into journalism and render its stories consonant with larger mindsets. Myths always offer some combination of claims to universalism (seen through archetypes, permanent human truths, timeless exemplars) and a recognition of particular contingencies (that are culture-specific and dynamic across time and space). Because they condense complicated realities into transferable form, however, many myths offer distorted, romanticized or otherwise false aspirations or models for behaviour. Much scholarly work on journalism and myth draws from structuralist anthropology and semiotics, where myths are seen as giving concrete form to abstract concepts and thereby assisting the public in making the news meaningful.

N

Narrative: the organizing structure of a news story that describes in patterned ways the unfolding of public events or issues within the parameters made available by a technological medium. Like storytelling, narrative offers a fundamental epistemological way of knowing the world, involving sequence, setting, perspective, characterization, tone, and a relationship with the public.

Narrative is differentiated both by its content – what it says, the story or plot – and its form – how it says, the act of narration. Though news narrative is generally driven by attributes of selection that establish a story's **newsworthiness**, such as topicality or importance, it is also crafted in conjunction with storytelling news codes and with the possibilities and limitations of the news medium in which it is relayed. A radio news narrative is briefer and more repetitive and uses less elaborated prose than does a journal of essays. A news narrative brings together the various items that comprise it, so that an image in a newspaper will be positioned in some relationship – usually a supportive one – with the verbal text at its side.

While all news narrative tends to be formulaic, in that proven narrative formulae – a story of natural disaster that emphasizes the triumph of the human spirit, for instance – tend to reappear in stories about similar events or issues, there is more than one kind of news narrative (Schudson 1978). The so-called 'information model' of news, associated generally with a chronicle-like form, typically appears on the front pages of a newspaper of record and follows a **hard news** format – the **inverted pyramid** which presents the most important information first. Impassive and omniscient in tone, told in the third person, and presuming a public which needs recounting of details already provided at earlier points in time, this kind of news narrative tends to offer simplified accounts of events or issues that recount the highlights of a story for those who will not entertain its entirety. In this view, crafting a news narrative involves presenting information in a way that allows the information to stand before the story.

A second kind of narrative – the so-called 'story model' of news associated with fictional story-like form – seeks to captivate readers and caters to drama and **human interest** even if they compete with the information provided.

Organized in temporal sequence, this kind of narrative tells a story from beginning to end by offering anecdotes and detailed, chronological accounts of events and issues. It persisted in early newsbooks and ballads, particularly in stories of great catastrophes and disasters. By the middle of the nineteenth century and the rise of **popular journalism**, however, it proved to be an inefficient way to recount hard news. Nonetheless it prevails in different forms and stands among the most well-written news stories – as **human interest** pieces, as **soft news**, as articles in **lifestyle** sections that gravitate towards more dramatic storytelling, as the heart of the **literary** or so-called '**new journalism**' that burst across US journalism in the 1960s, as **documentary** film, even as a new current in contemporary print media, where so-called 'narrative news' has been the topic of workshops and training teams since the beginning of the twenty-first century.

Narrowcasting: a type of broadcasting that attends to a narrow rather than mass audience. Although originally associated with niche marketing, the instability of many news organizations rendered narrowcasting a viable way of capturing specific news audiences in broadcast news. As the formerly 'mass audiences' associated with the broadcast networks became more difficult to sustain, niche organizations appeared that catered to either a small number of people or a specific public. Narrowcasting in news follows technological lines as in 24/7 cable television news or subscription-based websites, political lines as in **talk radio**, ethnic lines as in independent television, and presentational lines as in comedy shows (e.g. *The Daily Show* or *The Colbert Report*) and **satire**. User-driven content – such as **blogs**, **vlogs** and **podcasts** – also provides a useful intersection between formerly 'mass' news organizations and evolving niche markets.

Natsot: an abbreviated term for 'natural sound on tape'. Useful in broadcast news for establishing a sense of place in a given story through background noise, a typical example of natsot – also widely called **actuality** – is the incorporation of sound which establishes the urban nature of a location, like sirens, vehicle horns or moving traffic.

Neutral journalism: a type of journalism in which journalists are presumed to report the news in a value-free fashion. Developed during the mid-nineteenth century as a way to defend journalistic autonomy from political **partisanship**, a rise in **professionalism** promoted a sense of journalists as neutral gatekeepers, messengers and conduits. Set forward for academic scrutiny by Janowitz (1975), who contrasted its orientation with that of **participant** or **advocacy** journalism, neutral journalism's favoured techniques allowed reporters to claim **objectivity** and **accuracy**. They included the rise of **eyewitness** journalism, the rise of the **interview**, the **inverted pyramid** mode of storytelling and the separation of fact from opinion. Neutral journalism experienced a rebirth in the US in the late 1960s and early

1970s, when a crisis of credibility in the news, spurred by the Nixon administration, suggested it was necessary to neutralize journalists so as to prevent
them from influencing the public.

Neutral point of view: a term originated by **Wikinews** for a 'neutral point
of view' (NPOV) to be upheld by its **citizen journalists** at all times in their
reporting. Though the term has since found wider usage, it revolves around
the belief that it is possible to ensure that differing views can be represented
fairly and without **bias**. Rather than advancing a single, **objective** point of
view, each news item on the Wikinews site is expected to avoid advocating
(explicitly or implicitly) a particular position at the expense of alternative
ones. In the site's formulation, the NPOV clause states:

> The neutral point of view attempts to present ideas and facts in such
> a fashion that both supporters and opponents can agree. Of course,
> 100 per cent agreement is not possible; there are ideologues in the
> world who will not concede to any presentation other than a forceful
> statement of their own point of view. We can only seek a type of
> writing that is agreeable to essentially rational people who may differ
> on particular points.

Given the site's acknowledgement that 'people are inherently biased', an
emphasis is placed on encouraging 'intellectual independence' by presenting
multiple viewpoints as fairly as possible so that users can make up their own
minds about what to accept as true. 'Neutrality subverts dogmatism' is a key
philosophical tenet, one to be rendered in practice as 'presenting conflicting
views without asserting them'. That is, it is presumed that NPOV is not
actually a point of view at all, but rather the conviction that 'when one writes
neutrally, one is very careful not to state (or imply or insinuate or subtly
massage the reader into believing) that any particular view at all is correct'.
The belief that 'fact' can be separated from 'opinion' – a long-standing principle of unbiased **neutral journalism** – is in this way given a novel
reinflection to the extent that it is made possible by collaborative contributions from across the community of users. The incentive for users to avoid
exhibiting bias in their writing on the news site is thus readily apparent:
failure to do so means that one's words are promptly rewritten by someone
else.

Neutrality: the quality of having no perspective on a news event or issue.
Long connected with aspirations towards a value-free **journalism**, neutrality
is associated with notions of **balance, objectivity** and **impartiality**. The
belief that journalists can engage with public events and issues without slant
or **bias** has generated strong aspirations among journalists, regardless of the
difficulties associated with its implementation. Critics of neutrality argue that
it is more often associated with practices that establish the illusion of its

presence than its existence *per se*. Thus, for instance, establishing what Tuchman (1978) called a web of **facticity** – by which A said B is true, even if B is false – is a means for journalists to make claims about their neutrality regardless of whether or not they are neutral, constituting more of a defensive posture against criticism (including potential **libel** or **slander** accusations) and other formal attacks than an accurate mode of self-reflection.

New journalism: a name appended to journalism that signals a change in style, method, focus, topic or technique from that which is already in use in the dominant journalism of the period.

Most often used to denote the **literary journalism** of the 1960s in the US, new journalism is a name invoking multiple meanings over multiple time periods. First made famous by British cultural critic Matthew Arnold in 1887, in reference to the popularization of the British press, the term 'new journalism' has long been an umbrella reference to a definitive change on the journalistic landscape. In the US, the **penny press** of the 1830s earned the name of 'new journalism', signalling a change towards cheap, popular papers from the more expensive, subscription-based press of the time. 'New journalism' was similarly associated with the ascent of **yellow journalism** in 1886, when aggressive reporting, stunts and sensationalism distinguished the *New York World* and the *New York Herald* from other more serious newspapers. The British press during the mid-1800s was called 'new journalism' when it turned towards popular features, such as shorter stories and pictures, which were expected to draw working-class readers and women, but which also raised a challenge to the seriousness and political import of the mainstream press. **Muckraking** drew the label of 'new journalism' in 1902, when a group of reporters distanced themselves from what they saw as a sedate and complacent mainstream press, thereby dedicating themselves instead to exposing political, social and economic corruption and the abuse of power. 'New journalism' was most prominently associated with the **literary journalism** of the 1960s, when writers such as Tom Wolfe, Norman Mailer and Hunter S. Thompson adopted literary techniques like scene-by-scene construction, multiple points of view and first person **narrative** to engage head-on with events like the Vietnam War, civil rights, and the women's movement. Here again, they contrasted themselves with the ostensibly **objective**, **neutral** stance of the mainstream news media.

News: new information about an event or issue that is shared with others in a systematic and public way. Roughly in use for the past 500 years and originally thought by some to reference the four corners of the globe – north, east, west and south – news in fact derives from the word 'new', spelled during the sixteenth century in Old English as 'newes' or 'niwes'. With the development of the printing press and the emergence of capitalism, need arose for a word that, unlike the then-current Old English 'tydings', could signify the newly commercial aura that sprang up around journalism. The substitution of 'news' for 'tydings' marked a turn in how the public perceived the status of current affairs information and signalled that its provision resembled that of other commodities, like food or clothing, which were used to secure profit within a larger supply and demand framework.

The evolution of the term, however, is easier to trace than its definition, with journalists long admitting that defining news is a formidable task. Most journalistic guidebooks spend more efforts detailing how to write the news or get the news than defining what news actually is. Answers to the question 'what is news?' tend to produce lists of qualities – timeliness, interest or prominence – over definitions. Though the *New York Times* promises 'all the news that's fit to print', more sceptical observers have proffered views that 'news is what the editor says it is', 'news is what the public wants to read', and 'news is what raises eyebrows'. Some approaches to news draw from Robert E. Park's 1940 discussion of **news as a form of knowledge**, a way of knowing situated midway between the informal and experiential 'acquaintance with' aspect of events and the formal, verifiable 'knowledge about' those same events. In that vein, news is regarded as either a mode of constructing reality or a way of facilitating the discussion of that reality.

Broadly speaking, most contemporary news is produced within a systematic and bureaucratic framework that involves journalists of various numbers working through an organizational set-up on a certain schedule. Coming together with individuals who join disparate but often complementary efforts in the common aim of producing the news, journalists draw from sources in the larger institutional environment to produce a record that reports on the environment's central social, political, economic, legal and cultural impulses to an identifiable audience. They do so by playing to notions of **craft**, invoking consensual **news values**, **routines** and **rituals**, upholding agreed-upon standards of performance and employing consensual interpretive strategies, bonding together as an **interpretive community.** At the same time, they repair to multiple models of journalistic practice, ranging across variant notions of journalism – **neutral**, **participant**, **partisan**, **literary**, among others – so as to produce news on a timely schedule.

News, emergence of: though difficulties in defining what counts as a news account date back over 500 years, the concept of news was already in public use. Its ultimate origins rest in the very development of language in oral or preliterate communities thousands of years ago. Spoken news, whether in the form of gossip, sermons, ballads or tales, was an effective form of communication, though at risk of misinterpretation and faulty memory. Already in its earliest forms, news helped sustain a shared sense of social order. Communities often had their own, usually highly ritualized, customs for disseminating news at a distance, typically relying on strategies such as messengers running relays, fires, smoke signals or the banging of drums.

Communicating news over vast expanses of time and space became easier with the advent of writing. Contemporary archaeologists and anthropologists continue to uncover evidence concerning the advent of a range of different writing devices, and examples include the 'pictographs' written on clay tablets by the Sumerians (who would later invent numerals and, along with the Akkadians, develop 'ideographs') for the purposes of record keeping in southern Mesopotamia around 3500 BC. Another crucial advance came with the use of papyrus reeds by the Egyptians in about 2200 BC. While papyrus lacked the durability of clay, stone or wood, it was possible to inscribe symbols on it much more readily and its lighter weight ensured that it could be easily transported. These advantages were not lost on the Greeks, who were quick to exploit papyrus, together with their elaboration of the Phoenician alphabet, in the larger interests of trade and commerce, education, literature and science. A few centuries later in China, writing would be committed to bamboo (about 500 BC), then on to silk, and finally on to paper following its invention, reportedly by a eunuch named Ts'ai Lun, in about AD 105, towards the end of the Han dynasty. Significantly, paper would not begin its slow journey to the world beyond China for another 500 years, when Buddhist priests initially took it to Korea and Japan.

The invention of paper in Europe, which according to many historians was an event that arose independently from developments in China, would not take place until the twelfth century. Even after paper was first used in Britain in 1309, its popularity did not overtake that of parchment until printing was firmly established. Although credit for the invention of movable type also belongs to the Chinese, western accounts typically cite Johannes Gutenberg of Mainz, Germany, as its originator. Whether or not he was influenced by the evolution of typesetting in China, or the use of metal type in Korea, is a matter of dispute among some historians. In any case, Gutenberg succeeded in introducing a typographical system in the 1440s that quickly revolutionized printing throughout Europe. By utilizing a process whereby each letter was moulded individually and then continuously reused, he was able to produce texts – most famously a 42-line Bible of 1282 two-column pages around 1457–8 – with a wine press converted for the task. The first printing press in Europe astonished members of the public, even frightening some who regarded its capacity to make near perfect copies of texts as the 'black art' of the devil. From then it was a race among printers in different European cities to refine this technology further.

News as a form of knowledge: a phrase coined by Park (1940) to refer to the specific way in which journalism engages with the world. Drawing from William James's notion of two kinds of knowledge – 'acquaintance with', or knowledge acquired in the course of experience and intuition, and 'knowledge about', or formal rational knowledge resulting from systematic investigation – Park argued that news provided its own way of knowing the world that combined both kinds of knowledge. Comparing it with other forms of knowledge, Park argued that journalism resembled history in its concern with events; it was like sociology and political science because it appealed to pragmatic interests and gathered people together in potential political participation and conversation; and it was similar to folklore and literature because it gave people common ground. But as a sociologist of knowledge, he insisted that news boasted its own singular conditions from which knowledge arose: the unusual, unexpected but predictable, transient and ephemeral nature of news content; the small, independent relays that could be easily and quickly understood once published and circulated; and the effect of news in making the public feel at home in the world, in orienting the public towards shared topics of conversation, in facilitating political engagement and in creating a public mind. In Park's view, news resided on a continuum as one of multiple ways of knowing the world.

News as purposive behaviour: a concept of **newswork** that defines news events through the practical purposes they serve for those with access to the news media. Coined by Molotch and Lester (1974) and drawing from research on the social construction of reality, news as purposive behaviour rests upon the recognition that the activities of news promoters, assemblers and consumers define news as a continually evolving accounting procedure. Offering a typology of event types – routines, accidents, scandals and serendipitous events – Molotch and Lester argued that news was produced in conjunction with the needs of those with access to them, driven by whomever engages in the event's promotion (as to whether or not the promoter is related to the event) and by the degrees of intentionality associated with the promotion work. Abandoning the notion that an objective world waits to be reported on by journalists and underscoring journalism's constructed nature, seeing news as purposive behaviour has pragmatic consequence, enabling the **routinization** of newswork.

News agency: an organization that supplies information to subscribing newspapers, journals, broadcasters and private or public entities for its processing as news. Serving clients in a local, regional, national or international area, news agencies – which are also called press agencies, news services, press associations and wire services – sell news and other types of informational output on a continuous and regularly updated basis. The majority of news agencies enter contractual agreements with the news media, as well as private and public corporations, individuals and institutions, to provide an informational stream of **hard news** and **soft news** from specified locations. News agencies not only collect information through their own reporting teams, they also involve **freelances** and **stringers**.

The initial news agencies were associated in the mid-1800s first with carrier pigeons and then with the telegraph, creating a new form of shared informational processing that could give newspapers reports from a broader geographic area even when they lacked the capacity to collect it on their own. Information today is transmitted globally to the computer screen through satellite, cable and internet. The largest early news agencies included the US-based United Press International (UPI) and the Associated Press (AP), the British-based Reuters, and the French-based Agence France-Presse (AFP), which together succeeded in installing a certain western territoriality over the shared information environment. That said, the agencies have been regularly transformed as competitive national, regional and global tensions made different kinds of entities more relevant at different points in time (Boyd-Barrett and Rantanen 1999). For instance, the German Deutsche-Presse Agentur (dpa) was only started after the Second World War in 1949, but today in many regions it remains the most frequently cited news agency. The so-called **alternative news** agencies – such as the Caribbean News Agency (CANA) – highlight regional issues in their circulation and distribution of informational output, while the movement in the 1990s into financial news forced an adaptation of Reuter's global role and created new competition with other primarily financial news agencies, such as the US-run Bloomberg News Agency. And finally **news aggregators**, portals and search engines – such as Google News and Yahoo! News – created alternative pathways to sharing that in many instances bypass the news agencies altogether.

Though the news agencies began as text-only services, they expanded during the late 1930s to provide wirephoto as well, offering the capacity for the first time to transmit images of distant events as they unfolded. This development helped consolidate **photojournalism** as a part of daily news, and photography became particularly prevalent during the Second World War, when agencies like the Associated Press Photos and Acme Pictures circulated still **pictures** of battles around the world. **Newsreels**, film and video had similar vagaries over time and space: begun by the now defunct Visnews and Worldwide Television News (WTN), which set them on the road to sharing visual information, today they are supplied primarily by Reuters Television and the Associated Press Television News (APTN) and exist alongside more retail-oriented television news operators like CNN, MSNBC, ITN and Sky Television. Those agencies servicing more than one medium of information relay tend to divide production across divisions, so that text, still photo and video are produced separately.

Although many expected the news agencies to go out of business with the rise of the internet, they have instead experienced a rebirth, displaying an impressive capacity to adapt to changing geographic alliances and technological imperatives. Today most agencies operate approximately 200 bureaux positioned around the world, where material is collected and then sent to the home office – usually London or New York – for processing and distribution worldwide. Critics maintain that the news produced by news agencies tends to be bland, lacking enterprise, homogeneous and predictable, but in crisis zones they still lead the pack in addressing stories missed by other news media and they still rank first in securing **breaking news**.

News aggregation website: an online news site which brings together on its main page various web-links to news reports (and related content) available elsewhere on the internet. Typically the web-link offers the headline of the report (e.g. 'Dust storm blankets Sydney, disrupts transport'), followed by the source (e.g. Reuters) and a time-stamp (e.g. 05:52). The Drudge Report site – where Matt Drudge has provided this service, interspersed with occasional items of gossip or rumour, since 1997 – is an early example which has served as a model of sorts for others (e.g. the Huffington Post). In the UK, NewsNow claims to be the country's oldest news aggregator. Google News, in contrast to these sites, is an example of an **automated news aggregator**.

News council/Press council: an organization that follows up on complaints about particular journalists or news organizations in order to safeguard and uphold standards of fairness in the news media. Set up in association with the emergence of a social responsibility theory of the press in the mid-twentieth century under the original title of 'press councils' (*see* **Four theories of the press**), news councils position themselves as external **ombudspersons** that ensure the fair and responsible operations of **newswork**. They vary, however, as to how they operate and which functions they provide. For instance, the British **Press Complaints Commission** is responsible for charges of problematic activity in newspapers and magazines but cannot deal with other media, while dozens of councils across Europe, Asia, Canada, Australia and Latin America regularly hear complaints, ensure a free flow of information, represent journalism in national and international forums, and support technical improvements. In the US, journalists and news organizations have shown considerable resistance to the establishment of a news council, viewing it as a potential green light for governmental intervention, though a National News Council did prevail from 1973 to 1983 in the midst of the Nixon-era attacks on the news media (after one decade it dissolved itself for lack of funds and media support). Four additional exceptions – in Minnesota, Washington, Hawaii and New England – also exist, the first of which, the Minnesota News Council, has been hearing complaints since 1971 before a non-profit forum comprised equally of journalists and members of the public. Seen as a prevalent example of a media accountability system, as classified by Bertrand (2000), news councils promote accountability and **professionalism** and help create consistency in ethical practices across news organizations. Critics maintain that they bear the potential for turning into instruments of **censorship** and for threatening the freedom of **underground** or **alternative journalism**.

News culture: the shared norms, values, beliefs, expectations, conventions, strategies, symbol systems and **rituals** shaping the ethos of journalism as an **interpretive community**. Implicit in the lived, everyday **routines** by which journalists engage in **newswork**, news culture drives journalism's distinctiveness from other modes of factual narrative and expression. Allowing for a wide expanse of journalistic forms, practices and epistemologies, the materiality of news culture underpins its negotiation in normative terms while, at the same time, including impulses that are counter-productive, contradictory and contrary to the declared ideals of journalism in the larger society. Recognizing journalism's various moments of creation, innovation, revision and repair, the taken-for-granted nature of news culture is most often called into question when its 'common-sense' assumptions are transgressed. In effect, this means that seeing journalism through a cultural lens strategically interrogates dimensions otherwise neglected by more economic, political or institutionally focused approaches (see also Zelizer 2005; Allan 2010).

News cycle: the period from one round of coverage to the next. Originating as a term denoting the number of hours between the publication of each issue of a newspaper, the news cycle refers to an operative temporal frame that differs across media but is upheld as a general rule for coverage which is broken to accommodate unfolding news. As **convergence** has blended the distinctions across media to a greater degree than before, with satellite and internet transmission reducing the temporal lag associated with transmission, the distinction between news cycles has dwindled.

Many news media today cover the news on a continuous or near-continuous cycle. Called the '24-hour news cycle' or the '**rolling news** cycle' and increasingly the rule of coverage since the early 1980s, this non-stop flow of news, which updates events almost instantly on a global scale, was slow in coming historically. News agencies until the end of the 1990s distributed stories with a morning or evening **slug**, which communicated to news organizations when the wire relay could best fit into their respective news cycles; in 2000 the agencies replaced that choice with the term 'BC' – both cycles – as coverage across news media became more continuous. Before then, news agencies regularly updated as a story broke, sending moment by moment (and usually sentence by sentence) wire additions to a given news report. Though most newspapers today update instantly and continuously through their online portals, historically they were organized with expectations of meeting a monthly, weekly or daily (24-hour) cycle. Even then, however, the expectation of meeting a cycle was accompanied by multiple accommodations to unfolding news, such as late editions on breaking stories or multiple editions with updated versions of earlier stories.

Newscasts today follow the 24/7 lead of CNN, but they were originally scheduled in given time slots (often hourly on radio and generally multiple times a day on television) and interrupted regular programming as news breaks occurred. Against these parameters, the news cycle for a given story historically differed across news media, so that a round of coverage on one story in print journalism might extend over 24 hours, while the same round of coverage on radio might last no longer than hourly updates. Each of the news media gravitated over time towards progressively shorter news cycles as technology made doing so possible. For instance, broadcast news moved from daily evening newscasts, to multiple short newscasts, to morning and evening shows and finally, bolstered by cable television, toward 24-hour a day news programming.

Today online technology has reduced the differences across the news cycles of respective media. It not only offers each of the other news media – print, radio and television – further opportunity to update instantly through converged sites (with the British *Guardian* becoming a web-first newspaper in 2007, for instance), but the internet also provides its own mode of continuous cycling on stories independent of other news media. Critics maintain that the move towards a continuous news cycle creates a rush to distribute the news at the expense of careful fact-checking or the provision of sufficient context, sourcing and editing. Critics also argue that the continuous news cycle may not produce novel news stories so much as recycle old ones.

News hole: the portion of a newspaper, journal or broadcast news programme that is available for news stories or **editorial** content. In referencing the amount of content a news organization needs to create in every publishing or broadcast **news cycle**, the news hole is discerned by deducting the area or airtime needed for sponsors, advertisements, **pictures** and the like and dedicating that area or airtime to news. Thought to reflect the empty spaces on the printer forms which remained after ads had been placed into the forms, the news hole rises and falls with the broader circumstances of the news organization. Tight financial constraints are one of the first developments that reduce it, thereby making it more difficult for reporters and **editors** to process reportorial material into news. At the same time, news organizations must fill up a requisite minimal news hole at each publishing or broadcast juncture. They do this by catering to known and proven venues for newsgathering, such as specialized and geographic **beats** and **patches**; **press releases**; developing newsgathering routines that hold back more timeless stories and pull them if the news hole unexpectedly grows; and archiving more timeless material such as pictures that can be appended to news stories as they unfold. News organizations remain on the lookout for other ways of making the spontaneous and unpredictable growth or reduction of the news hole manageable.

News management: attempts by government, state or military officials to influence the information presented as news. News management includes a range of actions designed to push coverage in certain ways, including shifting news agendas, timing the release of information, withholding media access and forcing journalists to remain 'on message' during **press conferences** or **briefings**. Less obvious than **censorship** or the outright control of journalists, news management nonetheless constitutes a problematic interference in the autonomous workings of journalism.

News net: a term referring to the role of news in imposing order on the social world. Coined by Tuchman (1978), the news net is seen as a social resource which implies a series of particular constraints or limits on the forms of knowledge which can be generated and called 'reality'.

Drawing on data gathered by participant observation and interviews with newsworkers over a ten-year period in the US, Tuchman documented how **news organizations** disperse a news net that intertwines time and space in such a way as to allow for the identification of 'newsworthy' events. If the news net is intended for 'big fish', then at stake in conceptual terms is the task of unravelling this 'arrangement of intersecting fine mesh (the stringers), tensile strength (the reporters), and steel links (the wire services) supposedly provid[ing] a news blanket, ensuring that all potential news will be found' (Tuchman 1978: 22). The bureaucratic threads of the news net are thus knitted together so as to **frame** certain preferred types of occurrences as 'news events' while, concurrently, ensuring that others slip through unremarked.

A news net stretched to encompass certain centralized institutional sites, ones where news is 'likely to be made today', reinforces a myriad of normative assumptions about what should constitute the public agenda. The problem of defining what counts as an appropriate news story is directly tied to journalistic assumptions about what the news audience is interested in knowing. Tuchman's (1978: 25) study discerned three general premises incorporated into the news net:

1   readers are interested in occurrences at certain localities and not others;
2   readers are concerned with the activities of only specific organizations; and
3   readers find only particular topics to be worthy of attention.

News on demand: the capacity to provide news through on-demand technology. Advances in digital hardware and software now allow news consumers to be reached virtually anywhere at any time through a number of devices, bringing with them the promise of allowing consumers to order news programmes whenever they want and in whichever personal menu they desire. Wireless technology, in particular, makes the delivery of news updates possible directly to mobile telephone handsets. Proponents argue that this positions consumers at the heart of the news media. Critics maintain that it decreases quality news because journalists become too oriented to the public as consumers.

News organization: a group of individuals committed to a shared bureaucratic project of gathering, processing and distributing the news in systematic ways. The term encompasses a wide range of organizational set-ups, ranging from multinational, globally competitive news corporations, at one end of the continuum, to grassroots, **hyperlocal** initiatives such as non-profit community news websites, at the other. In each case, an organizational emphasis stresses decision-making in the service of news production as well as the notion that news is the result of organizational strategies that themselves derive from a combination of occupational, professional, societal, political, economic and cultural tensions shaping what is reported, how and why. Factors influencing a news organization's operation include **ownership** characteristics, divisions of labour, allocations of resources (time, staff, money, technology), bureaucratic structures and **routines**, legal constraints, technological imperatives, occupational culture, staff expertise and training, ethical guidelines, **house style**, and perceived audience expectations, values and preferences, among others. The parameters by which news organizations work have been clarified by **ethnographies of news**, which seek to elucidate how organizational logics impact upon news **routines**, **rituals** and practices.

News values: a subjective set of criteria that journalists use to assess the **newsworthiness** of events or topics. Though rarely written down or codified, journalists are thought to invoke news values in deciding what merits attention as news. Mentioned since the early days of news, when a focus on journalists' selection processes targeted the relevance of value judgements in assessing what would draw attention, they are also temporally, spatially and culturally specific. Importance and proximity were noted as driving German newspapers as early as the 1600s, while Lippmann (1922) was first to draw attention to 'news value' as a judgement call among journalists. News values attracted particular attention in 1965, when Norwegian researchers Johan Galtung and Mari Ruge (1973) delineated 12 values in their study of three international crises: frequency, threshold, unambiguity, meaningfulness, consonance, unexpectedness, continuity, composition, references to elite people, references to elite nations, personification and negativity. They argued that the more an event or topic satisfied these values, the more likely it would be reported as news. Numerous scholars have updated Galtung and Ruge's list: Gans (1979), for instance, maintained that US journalists reflected a fundamental set of values in their news coverage, including ethnocentrism, altruistic democracy, responsible capitalism, small-town pastoralism, individualism and moderatism, as well as social order and its maintenance by national leadership. These values constituted what he called a **paraideology**, which journalists upheld by engaging in practices of value inclusion – upholding enduring values, taking stands, adopting unconscious opinions through word choice and making reality judgements – and of value exclusion – upholding **objectivity** and detachment so as to make claims to autonomous decision-making, disregarding implications and rejecting ideology outright. Still others argue that news values no longer have the same relevance, particularly due to the rise of new media, **citizen journalism** and **user-generated content**. In each case, news values provide at best a predictive estimation of the possible criteria that may drive news selection and production, but they cannot account for all that evolves as news.

Newsagent: a retail shop or store where newspapers and magazines are sold.

Newsboy/Newsgirl: an historical term to describe a young person who sells newspapers to passers-by, typically on a street corner. Historians suggest that the well-known shout 'Extra! Extra! Read all about it!' can be traced to the mid-nineteenth century in the US. Made particularly famous by the Newsboys Strike of 1899, when the newsboys of New York City, most of whom were homeless paupers, struck the presses of the *New York World* and the *New York Journal*, demanding compensatory wage, the strike met with limited success. However, popular lore held that it helped institute child welfare regulations the following decade.

Newsbreak: a news story that has just occurred or broken. Given the 24-hour **news cycles**, newsbreaks offer important high moments when the cycles converge around one particularly newsworthy event or issue that takes precedence over the others. Also called a newsflash, newsbreaks tend to freeze the news gathering activities associated with other simultaneous stories so as to focus efforts on **breaking news**. They often appear as single items that are displayed separately from the larger flow of news – a news bulletin that interrupts a scheduled broadcast programme or a runner across the bottom of a news organization's web page. Depending on the story, newsbreaks can sustain public attention for short periods of time, as when a local **crime** or **weather** upset forces the audience to change plans, or can take the form of short recurrent newsbreaks that funnel into one larger story, as when a health disaster strikes a community.

Newsgathering: the process of collecting information with the intention of turning it into news. Newsgathering involves multiple individuals in varied roles, including reporters, editors, copy editors, photographers and producers among others, all of whom work in tandem to turn "raw" information into a processed news story relative to the constraints of the medium in which it is being relayed. As the technologies of information retrieval have evolved, newsgathering has ranged across referencing the basic acts of collecting facts – and challenges associated with using tools of recording, gaining access to courts and crime scenes, and dealing with promises of confidentiality and **shield laws**, and the like – to different names for newsgathering practices in conjunction with the technology at hand. Examples include ENG (electronic newsgathering, a broadcasting acronym), SNG (satellite newsgathering), and DSNG (digital satellite newsgathering), which use mobile communications equipment for worldwide distribution. Though the right to gather news is not guaranteed by law, it is central to journalism's capacity to produce information.

News-grazing: a term describing the habit of consuming news from a variety of **sources**, rather than relying upon a single medium. Users of the term often employ it in a negative sense to characterize what they regard as a distracted, inattentive engagement with the news. Of particular concern in this regard are young people, many of whom are not in the habit of reading a daily newspaper, preferring instead to briefly access diverse sources, such as television, radio, magazines and the internet, in the course of a given day. Critics fear that news-grazers fail to sustain sufficient focus to become adequately informed about public affairs, and are thus more likely to feel disempowered or cynical than non-grazers.

Newspaper, emergence of: although handwritten notices about government affairs appeared in the days of Julius Caesar (who, in 59 BC, decreed that they be publicly displayed on a daily basis), questions regarding the processes which gave rise to the newspaper continue to attract considerable attention amongst historians of the press. Some have argued that the roots of the modern newspaper are most clearly discernible in the weekly news-sheets which originated in Venice close to the end of the sixteenth century (the first of which were still being written by hand). Called a *gazette* after the name of the coin (*gazetta*) used to pay for a copy, they typically consisted of a single sheet of paper folded over to form four pages. These gazettes reported on events from across Europe, largely of a political or military nature, mainly by drawing upon the accounts of travelling merchants and diplomats. As their popularity grew, they expanded in the range of their news coverage until, by the 1600s, they began to resemble a form broadly consistent with today's newspaper.

Similarly relevant here is the way the printing press facilitated the circulation of news throughout society. The first printing press was set up in England in 1476. Stephens (1988: 84–5) noted that 'each printed copy that marched off a press had a crucial advantage: it was an exact replica. Those thousands of readers would each receive the same story, with no *added* errors, distortions or embellishments.' Printed pamphlets or broadsides, which sometimes presented news narratives in the form of prose or a rhyming ballad, slowly replaced newsletters copied by hand by the start of the sixteenth century. Newsbooks followed next, the more sensational of which were often referred to as *canards*, providing several pages of news usually about the same topic. Items of public interest included news of state announcements, victories in battle, royal marriages, executions of witches and the like, as opposed to accounts of everyday events.

Disputes continue to surface among press historians regarding which publication deserves to be acknowledged as the world's first newspaper, with different titles from Germany, the Netherlands and Switzerland usually receiving the most attention. This controversy stems, in part, from disagreements over how best to define what constitutes a newspaper as distinct from other, related types of publication. In a European context, Smith (1979: 9–10) suggested that news publishing passed through four distinct stages over the course of the seventeenth century:

1 the single story (a 'relation' or 'relacioun'), usually published months after the event being reported;
2 a continuous series of 'relations' were brought together and published on a near weekly basis as a 'coranto' (the first in the English language appeared in Amsterdam in 1620);
3 the 'diurnall', which supplied a weekly overview of newsworthy occurrences transpiring over successive days; and
4 the 'mercury', a newsbook in which the journalist typically spoke in a personal voice, and the 'intelligencer', which addressed its audience in a more formal or official voice.

Throughout the 1600s, then, these and related types of publications spoke to an expanding audience as literacy levels improved. Available in towns and cities in bookshops and **coffee houses**, and sold in rural areas by hawkers and peddlers, they 'brought sex and scandal, fantasy, sensationalism, bawdiness, violence and prophecy to their readers: monstrous births, dragons, mermaids and most horrible murders; but they also brought items of news' (Craven 1992: 3).

The daily newspaper was fully established in Britain in the early eighteenth century. The first daily was the *Daily Courant*, launched on 11 March 1702 on premises 'next Door to the King's-Arms Tavern at Fleet Bridge'. Initially composed of a single sheet of two columns, it sold for one penny and offered its readers both domestic and international news. The *Daily Courant* was soon joined by a series of new dailies, amounting to multiple new papers by 1750.

Despite the severity of tax and libel laws, the sale of daily newspapers increased throughout the century, attributable, in part, to general population growth, the spread of literacy, the popularity of coffee houses, and the continuing expansion of networks of distribution. In the last case, the use of new roads in and out of London by stagecoaches and wagons, as well as the growing proficiency of the General Post Office across Britain, were particularly significant.

The first regularly published newspaper in the American colonies was *The Boston News-Letter*, established by the town's postmaster, John Campbell, in 1704. An earlier title, Benjamin Harris's *Publick Occurrences*, was closed after a single issue by the colonial authorities. Formerly a handwritten newsletter, this weekly newspaper relied heavily on European news obtained from the pages of various London publications. The country's first daily newspaper was not founded until 1783, when the *Pennsylvania Evening Post and Daily Advertiser* appeared in Philadelphia. Months after its launch the publisher, Benjamin Towne, was indicted as a traitor for having lent his support to the Tories during the city's occupation by the British. Journalism, as Schudson (1995: 45) argues, had become intensely political since the Stamp Act controversy had forced printers to choose sides in 1765. While some titles shied away from publishing any form of news that might be regarded as controversial, others made every effort to incite a revolutionary fervour among their readers.

By the close of the eighteenth century, the foundations were being laid for a newspaper press which, according to its champions, would come to represent to the world the epitome of democratic power, prestige and influence. Not everyone shared this view, of course, a point expressed rather forcefully in the words of one commentator writing in 1799:

> The American newspapers are the most base, false, servile, and venal publications that ever polluted the fountains of writing – their editors the most ignorant, mercenary and vulgar automatons that ever were moved by the continually rusty wires of sordid mercantile avarice.
>
> (Cited in Innis 1986: 158)

Differing opinions as to its proper role and deserved status apart, by the 1800s the ascension of the newspaper press as a vitally important forum for public discussion, debate and dissent was assured.

Newspaper circulation and readership: a newspaper's circulation is the average number of copies sold on a typical day; readership refers to the average number of people reading each copy. Though the terms are sometimes confused with one another, they are intertwined in their relevance for newsmaking. Circulation figures provide an indication of each newspaper's relative share of the market, although distortions can creep in where copies have been given away for free or sold at a reduced price in order to give the numbers an upward boost (see **bulks**). In any case, circulation is different from readership as more than one person typically reads a single copy of a given title. As a general rule, most industry calculations assume that between two and three people may be counted as readers per copy. Precisely how best to quantify a 'reading threshold' for a given newspaper, however, is itself hotly disputed. For some industry studies, 'reading' refers to the availability of a newspaper in a household, for others it means that some pages have at least been scanned, while others define reading as a thorough engagement with its contents (the reader's recollection of which may then be assessed the next day).

The most typical methods employed to collect data about newspaper audiences are **interviews**, conducted either face-to-face or over the telephone, and opinion surveys, usually involving a questionnaire circulated via the post. In addition, newspapers often survey their own readers by including a questionnaire for them to fill in and return, possibly in exchange for a chance to win a prize. A range of different groups have a direct interest in knowing more about the characteristics associated with a newspaper's readership. These groups include, first, the owners of the newspaper, its editors and marketing people. Secondly, groups which also have a vital stake in acquiring information about a newspaper's readers include advertising agencies, market research organizations and, of course, potential advertisers.

Newsprint: the paper on which **newspapers** are printed. Relatively inexpensive in comparison with higher-grade paper, it is increasingly made from recycled fibres.

Newsreader: the person who reads the news in a TV **bulletin** or **newscast**. The newsreader – the UK equivalent of the US news **anchorperson** – reads the news typically with the help of an **autocue** or **teleprompter**.

Newsreel: a compilation of various reports of news events, frequently from around the world, onto one film reel shown in cinemas prior to the main feature films. The first newsreel was *Pathé Fait-Divers*, screened in Paris in 1908 (later re-dubbed *Pathé Journal* as it travelled across the country). In 1910, *Pathé Animated Gazette* was shown in London, while the first US newsreel, *Pathé's Weekly*, began the following year. Of particular interest are the factors involved in establishing newsreels as a regular feature in cinemas, not least with regard to their capacity to inform captive audiences about a world far beyond their personal experience. The use of newsreels in the Great War raised disputes about authenticity (involving staging, fakery and propaganda), and most agreed they offered little by way of news value to rival newspapers. The 'golden age' of the newsreel in the 1920s saw it gradually consolidate its conventions (about ten minutes in length and containing seven or eight stories), thereby introducing a visually-led conception of news. However, it was during the Second World War that the newsreel achieved the high point of its journalistic influence, effectively relaying insights into distant events of considerable importance to cinema audiences. Of particular interest to researchers today are a host of issues concerning their attendant **news values**, questions of **censorship**, and varied pressures shaping their production and circulation, together with controversies about their reportorial integrity where the coverage of public affairs (such as the 'personalization' of politics) was concerned. Further scholarship has traced the slow decline of the newsreel in the face of its upstart rival, television news, following the Second World War. By the end of the 1960s, newsreels had disappeared from cinema screens in most countries. One exception was Australia, however, where they continued until 1975.

Newsroom: the space in a news organization where news is processed. The newsroom is the venue in which critical decision-making about a news organization's output takes place, and as the focal point of its activities often houses morning meetings, editorial meetings on **breaking news**, **assignment** meetings and other opportunities for gathering relevant personnel in a collective conversation about what the coming news output will look like. Usually bringing together a combination of **editors**, reporters, managers and executives, the newsroom reflects changes in technologies of news production.

Though the newsroom was originally an open reading room in European news organizations where newspapers were read, its evolving use responded to the growth of newspaper output, which not only required editors to help select and organize the news but also supported distinctions between the **editorial** and technical sides of operation. Largely in use since the mid-nineteenth century, the newsroom has also come to signify metonymically the operations of a news organization, and in this light newsrooms – mythologized as chaotic and energized places in which frenetic reporters and editors rush to process hot stories against a ticking clock – play a larger role in journalistic lore than in reality. In the operations of contemporary news organizations, seen against the ascent of new media, newsrooms in fact have become less central than they used to be. With increasing numbers of journalists in a news organization **multi-tasking** from multiple locations, often using online communication to do so, **convergence** is now driving much of its operations. Moreover, a 24/7 **news cycle** has come to replace the traditional temporal processing of news. Thus newsrooms no longer house the collective gatherings of yore with the same centrality, intensity or frequency.

Newsstand/Newsvendor: a small business displaying **newspapers** and **magazines** for sale to passers-by on the street.

Newswork: all of the varied journalistic roles associated with producing a news story. Newswork ranges across reporters, different **editors** and multiple kinds of production colleagues, all of whom are involved in the publication or broadcast of a news story at some point in the process from its start to finish.

Newsworthiness: having sufficient interest, importance or topicality so as to draw mention in the news. Reflecting a largely subjective and elusive evaluation as to whether or not journalistic attention is warranted, newsworthiness does not get decided by hard and fast rules but rather by intuitive judgement calls about the degree to which **news values** pertain. Having a 'nose for news' reflects the murky nature of what precisely constitutes news-worthiness. Often, it emerges in conjunction with past journalistic practice, where prior attention to certain kinds of events or topics increases the chances that similar ones will be deemed deserving at a later point in time. Some researchers maintain that preferred criteria of newsworthiness feature promi-nently in news **routines** because they help journalists to manage news flow better.

Newszak: a perceived tendency in journalism to retreat from investigative, 'hard' news reporting in favour of ever 'softer', 'lighter' stories. Coined by Franklin (1997), 'newszak' refers to a realignment of the **editorial** priorities of journalism in accordance with the dictates of the marketplace, where entertainment, **human interest** and the trivial have pushed aside informa-tion, the public interest and the serious. For Franklin, this transformation has profound implications for public information and democracy: 'Newszak understands news as a product designed and "processed" for a particular market and delivered in increasingly homogenous "snippets" which make only modest demands on the audience'(1997: 4–5). Given the intensification of market pressures to compete over these audiences – as well as to attract advertisers interested in reaching them – the increasing prevalence of **tabloid** journalism is hardly surprising. Moreover, to the extent that news becomes entertainment, there will be a corresponding decline in the availability of other kinds of news, not least foreign, parliamentary and **investigative reporting**.

Nut: a term for the **lead** paragraph of a news story. The nut also refers to the hard nut or essential elements (**Five Ws and H**) of the story.

O

Obit/Obituary: a type of news article or broadcast that announces the death of an individual and summarizes key points of his or her life. Drawn from the Latin word for 'pertaining to death' – *obituarius* – the obit is expected to provide a portrait of the deceased. It first appeared in the newsbooks of the seventeenth century and surfaced a hundred years after that in the US colo-nial press. Early obits were religious in nature, where pious lamentation and praise for the newly passed individual's moral merits were rife, but by the late 1700s obits began to include critical bits of character evaluation. By the middle of the following century, obituaries already occupied their own column, and when US President Abraham Lincoln was shot in 1865, his obituary arrived as a series of cables that were printed in full on the front pages of papers. Though obits tend to be given their own place in a newspaper or news broadcast and are tactfully crafted, they often elide the cause of death or problematic aspects of a person's life, as seen in some of the obituaries that circulated following the death of pop star Michael Jackson. The task of writing them is firmly situated in journalistic lore, by which either the most junior reporters craft them or an organization's veteran retirees are assigned the job. Writing obituaries includes both collecting details about people at the time of their death and, for more renowned individuals, preparing the articles ahead of time, particularly when death is expected due to illness. Though decisions on who 'deserves' to secure an obituary vary, they tend to reflect the most powerful, public and visible individuals who are notable for a wide range of positive – and negative – accomplishments.

Objectivity: detached, **unbiased**, value-free newsmaking. Long held as a central normative ideal of **professionalism** and **neutral journalism**, particularly in the US, and an ethos for much journalism around the world, the aspiration towards objectivity reflects a set of practices and ideas in relation to newsmaking that is presently undergoing increasing degrees of scrutiny. Objectivity supports notions of journalism as fair and **balanced** recordkeeping, ostensibly providing a disinterested and non-partisan mirror on public events and issues, rather than a **biased** or opinion-led perspective or slanted interpretation of them.

Schudson (1978) defined objectivity as the combination of a faith in facts, a distrust of values, and a belief in their segregation. It refers to both the process of newsgathering, by which journalists are supposed to aspire to **unbiased** practice, and the final presentation, by which the news copy should not privilege one side over another. Hackett and Zhao (1998) argued that objectivity serves multiple functions: it provides a general model for conceiving, defining, arranging and evaluating news texts and practices; it serves as a normative ideal about journalists' capacity to impart factual, accurate and complete information as well as offer a detached, **neutral**, **impartial** and independent stance on that information; it constitutes an epistemological stance and way of knowing the world through positivism and rationalist thought; it legitimates a set of newsgathering and presentational practices; it provides an independent institutional framework, with legal guarantees on free speech, a separation of editorial and marketing functions, and a code of ethics; and it actively shapes public discourse.

Objectivity has been easier to define than attain. Although it has been alternatively dated to the appearance of modern newspapers in the Jacksonian Era of the 1830s or to the rise of scientific positivism during the nineteenth century, today few believe in its absolute sustainability in contemporary journalism, arguing that total **neutrality** or absence of personal **bias** is impossible to achieve. Additionally, critics of objectivity maintain that its associated practices – reporting on only observable statements and actions, finding a presumed middle ground between polarized positions, revering stated facts even when they are wrong, losing sight of the bigger picture if it involves the assumption of interpretation – often steer journalists away from the truth and facilitate the normalization of the very things they are trying to correct. Most align a reduced belief in objectivity with its problematic performance as a prism for covering events. In believing that a news event can be reduced to observable actions and statements, journalists risk missing the opportunity to provide adequate explanatory context, not least with regard to the structural factors giving shape to the event in question.

Critics point out that what counts as objectivity is culturally specific, and can vary markedly across time, as well as national contexts. It remains more relevant to the 'serious', 'quality' end of the journalistic continuum than to the 'popular' end, for example, and figures more prominently in Anglo-American practice than in journalism elsewhere in Europe, where **partisanship** prevails, or in Asia, where authoritarianism and theocracy are prevalent. Moreover, the perceived decline of news organizations as autonomous **gatekeepers** in a more **convergent** digital world seems to be contributing to a displacement of objectivity as a reportorial ideal, with some commentators openly celebrating – while others condemn – the 'post-objectivity' associated with some forms of **citizen journalism** and **blogging**.

Objectivity as strategic ritual: a set of **routine** procedures adopted by journalists and news organizations to justify a claim to **objectivity** in news reporting as a means to ward off potential criticism. Journalists cope with everyday pressures by emphasizing 'objectivity' as a strategically defensive ritual, Tuchman (1972) argued, namely to enable them to 'minimize the risks imposed by **deadlines**, **libel** suits, and superiors' reprimands' where mistakes are concerned (1972: 662). In striving to manage these and related dangers, journalists follow strategies of **newswork** to identify 'objective stories', and also to gather and structure 'facts' in 'a detached, **unbiased**, impersonal manner'. In the event that factual accuracy cannot be verified in the usual way, further strategic procedures noted by Tuchman include: the presentation of conflicting possibilities ('the statement "X said A" as a "fact", even if "A" is false'); presentation of supporting evidence ('citing additional "facts", which are *commonly accepted as "truth"*'); the judicious use of quotation marks as a signalling device (e.g. interjecting someone else's opinion as supporting evidence); and structuring information in an appropriate sequence, carefully separating 'facts' from 'opinions' (e.g. by observing the **inverted pyramid** structure of **hard news** narrative). Tuchman thus concluded that 'news procedures exemplified as formal attributes of news stories and newspapers are actually strategies through which newsmen [and women] protect themselves from critics and lay professional claim to objectivity, especially since their special professional knowledge is not sufficiently respected by news consumers and may indeed even be the basis of critical attack' (1972: 676).

Objectivity, historical perspectives: in the years immediately following the close of the First World War in Europe, the necessary conditions were in place for a general affirmation of the tenets of 'objectivity' among both journalists and their critics. Popular disillusionment not only with state propaganda campaigns, but also with the recent advent of 'press agents' and 'publicity experts', had helped to create a wariness of 'official' channels of information. For those journalists alert to the danger of equating reality with official definitions of truth, the need for more 'scientific' methods to process facts was increasingly being recognized.

Over the course of the 1920s the ideal of 'neutral' reporting gradually became synonymous with the invocation of the 'public interest' for many news organizations. While in Britain this ideal tended to be left implicit to most definitions of journalistic practice, in the US it was formally enshrined as a professional standard by a number of different bodies. By way of example, in April 1923 the American Society of Newspaper Editors announced its 'canons' of journalism, the fifth of which read, in its entirety, as follows:

> Impartiality – Sound practice makes clear distinction between news reports and expressions of opinion. News reports should be free from opinion or **bias** of any kind.

> 1. This rule does not apply to so-called special articles unmistakably devoted to advocacy or characterized by a signature authorizing the writer's own conclusions and interpretations.

> (Cited in Roshco 1975: 46)

In other words, 'impartiality' demanded of journalists that they distinguish 'facts' from 'values' if their respective newspaper was to be recognized as a free arbiter of truth. As many of these journalists quickly discovered, however, such a commitment to 'value-free' reporting frequently had disturbing implications in professional terms. Specifically, many of the most passionate advocates of 'objective journalism' were the very editors and publishers intent on opposing the unionization of their newspapers. From this self-serving perspective, a journalist could hardly be a dispassionate, non-partisan observer while belonging to a 'controversial' organization like a union.

Interestingly, the near-obsession with 'objectivity' inherent in most US newspapers often encountered criticism from abroad. According to one historian, for example, the French 'condemned a worsening quality of journalism, which put facts before ideas, and attributed it to "Americanisation"' (Lee 1976: 231). Then again, in somewhat stronger language, the US press baron Joseph Pulitzer declared: 'In America, we want facts. Who cares about the philosophical speculations of our correspondents?' (cited in Chalaby 1996: 311). In any case, this appeal to 'objective', non-**'biased'** reporting was slowly becoming institutionalized, to varying degrees, throughout the 1920s in the growing professional culture of US and British (albeit to a lesser extent) journalism. Evidence of this gradual process of institutionalization is apparent in multiple factors, including more reporters specializing in distinct news topics (labour, science, agriculture, and so forth) using 'impersonal', fact-centred techniques of observation; a refinement of news interview conventions, leading to more aggressive questions asked of public figures (the interview itself being a relatively recent invention); more prominence of the by-lined news account; greater emphasis on new genres of 'investigative' and 'interpretative' reporting, the latter increasingly displaced from 'hard news' into political columns; a more pronounced reliance on quotation marks for source attribution; and improvements secured in the relative degree of autonomy from the day-to-day control of both proprietors and editors.

Each development spoke to public scepticism about the ideal of realizing 'the plain truth' on the pages of a newspaper. By dispensing with the language of truth in favour of that of 'objectivity', journalists underscored the necessity of discerning how 'the world out there' could be represented from an interested or **'biased'** viewpoint. That said, however, even if each and every statement of fact was to be subject to verification, the professionally validated rules and procedures of 'objective' reporting did not directly call into question the existence of absolute truth. 'Objectivity' demanded of journalists only that their role be delimited to one of facilitating the public's right of access to facts free from partisan values.

Off the record: an agreement between journalists and **sources** which stipulates restrictions on whether or not specific information can be used. Though definitions vary, most take it as a ground rule for information that is shared in confidence or not intended for publication/broadcast. In certain circumstances, journalists refuse to go 'off the record', namely because it constrains their ability to craft the news story as they envisage it. They then make every effort to have their source agree to go **on the record** or, failing that, strive to find an alternative source for the same information.

Office of Communications (**Ofcom**): the agency responsible for licensing commercial television and radio services in the UK. Ofcom answers to Parliament but is nonetheless independent of the government. Its main legal duties, set out in the UK Communications Act of 2003, include ensuring that the country has a wide range of electronic communications services (including high-speed broadband provision); high-quality television and radio programmes, appealing to a range of tastes and interests; viewers and listeners protected from harmful or offensive material; people protected from being treated unfairly in programmes (including where their **privacy** is concerned); and the radio spectrum utilized in the most effective way possible. Ofcom is funded by both fees from industry for regulating broadcasting and communications networks as well as grant-in-aid from the government.

Official Secrets Act: an Act drawn to prohibit the dissemination of information classified by the government as secret or vital to protect for national security interests. Several countries possess an Official Secrets Act, including India, Malaysia, New Zealand, the Republic of Ireland and the UK. However, the degree to which it is activated is questionable. For instance, journalists seldom find themselves testing the limits of the 1989 Act in the UK, and to date no journalist has been successfully prosecuted under it, although the 'chill factor' (fear of prosecution) can be significant. When tensions do arise, they frequently concern the official assumption that the government's interest and that of the nation are one and the same, and journalists tend to be disinclined to share this view. Significantly, no public interest defence is available for a journalist (or their sources, including **whistleblowers**) to plead. Abuses of this legislation by officials can lead to constraints on press freedom, including the stifling of dissent and, at minimum, a reduction in the transparency of governmental activities under scrutiny. Statutes of a similar nature to Official Secrets Acts exist in other countries, such as Australia and Canada. In the US, the Espionage Act of 1917, covering some of these provisions, has had its constitutionality contested in the courts on a number of occasions (including during the **Pentagon Papers** case in 1971).

OhmyNews: a South Korean 'online newspaper' that uses ordinary people to provide alternative news to the mainstream, conservative media while striving to ensure that the news site generates a financial profit. Launched in February 2000, OhmyNews has proved successful not only financially – rather unusually so for an online news organization – but also in journalistic terms within Korean society. The vast majority of stories appearing on the site – some 80 per cent – are written by ordinary citizens (about 70,000 to date) keen to try their hand at journalism. The content for the remaining 20 per cent of the newspaper is prepared by 65 staff writers and editors, some of whom cover major stories, while others assume responsibility for editing and fact-checking the material sent in by 'amateurs', such as students, office workers, police officers and shopkeepers.

The site's founding principle – 'Every Citizen is a Reporter' – is that participants email a news or opinion item (or blending of both) regarding whatever topic interests them. The overall **editorial** policy is fashioned to a significant extent by the emphases discernible in the collective response, which means in a practical sense that diverse publics shape the agenda. **Citizen reporters** are openly encouraged to identify stories that the mainstream media are not pursuing. The site's editors sift through the flow of items arriving each day (about 200 on average) to rank them on the basis of their relative **newsworthiness**, before making a judgement about where to place them in the hierarchy on the site.

Those items deemed to warrant priority are positioned on the top of the most prominent pages, while those of a more specialized interest are relegated to back pages (distinctions are made between 'basic', 'bonus' and 'special' items). Such decisions determine, in turn, the relative size of the payment awarded to the citizen reporter for his or her story. A highly valued item can earn as much as $20 (US), although a more typical sum would be a small fraction of that amount. Even for those employed as editors by OhmyNews (the majority drawn from the ranks of citizen reporters), the sense of reward is greater than the monies involved.

The news site's reputation for **investigative journalism** is hard-won. Editors interact with citizen reporters on discussion forums, answering questions but also negotiating story ideas, **angles** and possible **sources** to approach. Some critics argue that certain imbalances exist in this regard, not least with respect to gender and age, which impact on the nature of the items. Statistics gathered by the site indicate that about three-quarters of citizen reporters are male, and that the largest age group is made up of people in their 20s. Other critics complain that little pretence is made of **objectivity**; rather, citizen reporters typically make their personal point of view explicit, thereby inviting a more dynamic relationship with the reader than that derived from dispassionate forms of journalism. In the eyes of critics, this makes OhmyNews appear less **professional** than it should be, but its advocates consider this departure from the bland strictures of **impartiality** to be a virtue. Now firmly ensconced as a household name in Korea, OhmyNews averages about 2 million page views each day, with major stories sending those figures skyrocketing. OhmyNews International – an English-language site launched in February 2004 – aggregates news reports from 6000 citizens in over 100 countries.

Ombudsperson: a person who handles complaints on behalf of a news organization. Taken from the Swedish word for an appointee who investigates citizen criticisms of governmental maladministration, the ombudsman role (as it was initially known) has many alternative names that reflect its widespread positioning in news organizations as a go-between for the news organization and the public, among them 'reader's editor', 'mediateur' and 'reader's representative'. News organizations rely upon ombudspersons to reply to public complaints about the news coverage of particular events or topics, **editorial** policy and general practices of **newswork** and news presentation. Generally selected from the more veteran members of a news organization, the ombudsperson uses reader complaints to assess problems in news operation. Criticized for being little more than window dressing and for creating a bureaucratic wall between the public and the news organization's executives and editors, the ombudsperson role has nevertheless been seen as valuable because it enhances the news organization's ability to address public complaints, keeps news organizations responsive to public concerns and reduces the chance that complaints will escalate into **libel** cases.

On background: a prearranged agreement between journalists and **sources** which dictates how specific information can be used, usually involving granting **anonymity** to the source. Though definitions vary, background information generally cannot be attributed by name. Some maintain it can only be used **off the record** to enhance a journalist's understanding of an issue or event, while others claim it can be used without **attribution** in a news story, as in 'according to a high-ranking administration official'. Predicated on the premise that journalists are able to separate what they know from what they share with the public in a definitive fashion, the **assignment** of 'on background' to a meeting, exchange or briefing means that journalists and sources agree as to how much can be incorporated into a news story.

On diary: a pre-scheduled news event, which the journalist anticipates and has noted in his or her diary so as to cover it on the day of its occurrence. In contrast to an unpredicted or 'off diary' story, on diary stories are valued by news **editors** because they lend themselves to news **routines**, thereby allowing journalists and attendant resources to be deployed more efficiently. Examples include major speeches, **press conferences**, court trials, **photo ops** and so forth.

On spec: a news story prepared on speculation. On spec stories may or may not find a place in the available **news hole**, but they are prepared in case they can help close a gap under last moment **deadline** pressure.

On the record: a default arrangement between journalists and **sources** which presumes that all shared information can be incorporated fully into a news story. In the absence of declaring any other kind of arrangement – such as **'on background'** or **'off the record'** – a presumption of on the record prevails in exchanges between journalists and **sources**. Some exchanges may be on the record but go off-record for certain statements or details, but such agreements only come into effect if they have been declared explicitly by the source and agreed explicitly by the journalist.

Online news, emergence of: the emergence of the internet as a news provider is a highly contentious subject. Disputes continue to unfold regarding which website deserves to be acknowledged as the first news site on the global scene. This controversy stems primarily from disagreements over how best to define a news site as distinct from other related types of sites. Much of the early, experimental work was conducted by newspaper companies placing their news reports online, thereby blurring – some might say remediating – traditional categories.

Especially relevant here were the efforts of the Canadian national newspaper, *The Globe and Mail*. In 1979, it began publishing both in print and electronically on the same day, and also provided online access to a full text commercial database that included every story it had published over the previous two years. Whether or not *The Globe and Mail* is correct to claim recognition for these innovations as being world firsts – as it does on its webpages – depends, of course, on the agreed criteria for doing so. In the US, a collaborative effort between the *Columbus Dispatch* and CompuServe arguably produced the country's first online newspaper in July of 1980. Relevant here, however, is how few people at the time anticipated that the electronic edition of the daily would be read by people sitting in front of a personal computer in their own homes. By 1988, there were 10 newspapers online in Canada, and about 60 in the US, with the first online newspaper in the UK, the *Electronic Telegraph*, appearing in November 1994. Essentially, an online newspaper was little more than an electronic archive of the printed edition, and something of a challenge to navigate.

The potential of the internet as a news provider received a major boost in 1995. Historical accounts often note this as the year when users in the US 'fell in love' with the internet or, more to the point, the World Wide Web. If the web was three years old by then, its presence was slowly becoming a reality for increasing numbers of people due to the popular take-up of online services (the Microsoft Network or MSN was launched in July, and had acquired over 500,000 subscribers by the end of the year) using Netscape's refashioned browser software. Now it was possible to click a mouse to access information on a computer database directly on the web, as opposed to typing addresses such as 'Telnet 192.101.82.300' to retrieve it from the internet. The release of Microsoft's Windows 95 operating system in August was front-page news around the world, a clear sign that personal computing was becoming increasingly mainstream.

In 1995, news websites were typically little more than repositories of reports previously published elsewhere. In the aftermath of the Oklahoma City bombing on 19 April that year, however, the role of the internet in creating spaces for information to circulate was widely hailed as a landmark moment in online history. Worthy of particular attention at the time was the **immediacy** of the news coverage, as well as its volume and breadth. Minutes after the bombing, journalists and their editors at online news services rushed to post whatever information they could about the tragedy. News coverage of the ensuing judicial proceedings against the suspects held responsible for the attack saw *The Dallas Morning News* break precedent by posting a major story associated with the ongoing trial on the web, some seven hours before the newspaper went to press for that day's edition. Some commentators declared it to be a 'journalistic Bastille Day', seeing in the decision the sudden liberation of newspapers from the time-constraints associated with print, which meant that they were now empowered to break news straight away.

The **'scoop** heard around the internet', as it was aptly described at the time, was credited by some commentators with helping to chip away the rigid boundary separating newspapers from their online counterparts. Some of online journalism's strongest advocates sensed that progress was being made in the struggle for legitimacy. Indeed, advocates of the internet insisted that it had proved itself to be an indispensable news and information resource during the crisis. Critics, in sharp contrast, were sceptical about the value of news sites, arguing that they were slow to react, and in the main offered news that was otherwise available in evening newspapers or on television. Others pointed to technical glitches, observing that several of the major news sites had ground to a halt because they were overwhelmed with demand in the hours when they would have been especially valuable.

Nevertheless, for those in the newspaper industry, it was becoming increasingly obvious that they would not be able to compete with their internet rival where **breaking news** was concerned. Over the next few years, evidence to support this claim would be found in the online reporting of a number of tragic events, such as the TWA 800 crash, the Heaven's Gate mass suicide, and the death of Princess Diana, among others (see Allan 2006).

Op-ed: an abbreviated term for 'opposite the editorial page'. Op-eds are opinion pieces usually produced by non-journalists that appear within the routine outlay of a newspaper, magazine or broadcast news organization that separates news from opinion. Often thought to denote 'opinion-editorial', op-eds were generally assumed to have evolved during the 1920s in the *New York Evening World*, when the opinions of regular citizens came to be seen as having value. Op-eds denote authored opinion pieces offered by individuals who are not members of a news organization's editorial board but who provide commentary and analysis of current events and issues. Sometimes op-eds are written by public figures, politicians, celebrities, academics and journalists of other news organizations, while other times news organizations restrict them to 'citizen writers'. So as to ensure a steady stream of commentators, some news organizations create contributor boards, which collect individuals from a given community who are asked regularly to write opinion pieces.

Open source reporting: a type of journalism characterized by its relative 'openness' with regard to the diverse range of individuals (both 'professionals' and 'amateurs' alike) involved in helping to generate a news story. Most definitions resonate with the open source software movement, whose software code is generated by a number of people situated across the breadth of the internet in a collaborative effort to share their respective expertise. In journalistic terms, open source reporting can take a variety of forms. It may involve the professional journalist turning to citizen counterparts for help in writing a story, by providing information or double-checking facts (sometimes called **collaborative**, 'pro-am' or 'professional-amateur journalism'). It may also involve incorporating feedback from readers once a news item has been posted, namely to correct errors or to supplement points being made. The principal aim is to fashion new forms of connection between journalists and their publics, and thereby improve the quality of reporting on offer. Web journalist Dan Gillmor's concession – 'My readers know more than I do' – is widely held to be indicative of the guiding ethos of open source journalism.

Ownership: exclusive rights and control, conferred by a lawful claim or title of proprietorship, over a news organization. Issues regarding news media ownership may be identified at four interrelated levels of concern: *concentration*, involving the relative degree of diversity among the owners of companies in the media sector; *cross-media ownership*, as when one company might hold both newspapers and televisual stations, thereby raising potential conflicts of interest; *conglomeration*, by which a process of merger or takeover renders a news organization part of a company with financial stakes outside the media sector (once again, potential conflicts of interest are likely to arise); and *globalization*, when a news organization becomes part of an international company engaged in competition with other such companies in a range of different national markets.

P

Pack journalism: a type of journalism collectively practised by multiple journalists at one point in time, which produces uniform coverage. Thought to reflect a substitution of group-think for original thought or independent investigation, pack journalism occurs when journalists follow similar **tips**, rely on similar **sources**, or investigate similar settings in developing news leads and crafting from them full-blown stories. Originally coined by author Timothy Crouse in *The Boys on the Bus* (1973) in his discussion of the previous year's US presidential campaign coverage as an updated term for what was earlier called 'bandwagon journalism', pack journalism today can mean all modes of collective and uniform thought across news organizations, including collective judgement calls about which stories to feature as primary in the news relay of a given **news cycle**.

Page Three: the third page of the *Sun* newspaper (UK), where photographs of 'topless' (and, on occasion, nude) female 'glamour' models are routinely displayed. Easily the best-selling daily title in the country, the newspaper justifies the use of such imagery as a means of signalling its lively, 'cheeky' persona to the public. The feature's history may be traced back to Rupert

Murdoch's relaunch of the paper as a tabloid in 1969. Sexually suggestive imagery gave way to partial nudity the following year as a means to further boost circulation figures. Though efforts to emulate the strategy by the *Daily Mirror* were soon abandoned, they continued in the *Daily Star*. In 1986, MP Clare Short's campaign to have such imagery banned from newspapers was unsuccessful, despite attracting widespread support from the public. Rebekah Wade, the *Sun's* first female editor (2003 to 2009), disappointed critics by not dropping the feature, even though she had admitted publicly that it was offensive to some female readers.

Paparazzi: a term used to denote photographers who capture candid photographs or video unknown to their subjects while employing generally unethical or intrusive tactics. Contrasted with **photojournalists** who primarily aim to depict individuals in public places or expected private gatherings, paparazzi employ clandestine strategies to portray unknowing subjects who are usually engaged in mundane, sometimes intimate and often embarrassing actions – shopping, eating, quarrelling. While the term, associated with the Italian word for 'mosquito', originated in the 1960 Fellini movie *La dolce vita*, today it connotes all modes of unethical photography worldwide. The race to capture unwitting images of celebrities has produced problematic and often overblown tensions between photographers and their subjects. Princess Diana, for example, was presumed to have been hounded to her death by overly aggressive paparazzi.

Parachute reporting: the type of journalism that ensues when a reporter (or news team) is rushed to the scene of **breaking news** – most commonly in another country – to report on what is happening straightaway for the benefit of audiences back home. Advocates of parachute reporting usually justify it on the grounds that reporters can provide insights not otherwise furnished by wire or **news agency** reports. **Foreign correspondents** stationed abroad full-time would be more desirable, they acknowledge, but probably too expensive for most news organizations. Parachute reporting, by this logic, is better than none. Critics are sceptical, believing that the strategy typically has more to do with **infotainment** than **news values**. Moreover, they contend that the reports tend to be superficial, and all too frequently inaccurate; the journalist in question typically lacks adequate preparation, expertise or local contacts to provide a sufficiently in-depth treatment.

Paraideology: a term for the ideological nature of pressures shaping the news. Originally employed by Gans (1979) to describe the 'enduring values, conscious and unconscious opinions, and reality judgements brought to bear on the reporting process by journalists and editors' (1979: 203), paraideology – distinguished from more deliberate, integrated or doctrinaire renderings of ideology – was 'an aggregate of only partially thought-out values which is neither entirely consistent nor well integrated; and since it changes somewhat over time, it is also flexible on some issues' (1979: 68). Drawing in equal measure from impulses both within and beyond the news organization, paraideology constituted a form of ideology that remained in service of the professional ideals of journalism, and it was supported by a number of **news values** that he called 'enduring values': 'altruistic democracy', 'responsible capitalism', 'individualism', ethnocentrism, small town pastoralism, moderatism and the 'preservation of social order' by national leadership. Journalists engaged these values by following an intricate set of practices that allowed them to include or exclude ideological positioning, dependent on the circumstance. According to Gans, while a conservative conception of paraideology was more likely to be espoused by managerial figures in news organizations than by reporters, paraideology nonetheless gave expression in subtle, seemingly taken-for-granted ways to the evolving norms and values of the workplace and the **profession** more widely, thereby encouraging homogeneity and conformity. Comprising 'an untested and often untestable set of beliefs', its efficacy was illustrated 'by the fact that those who adhere to it do not conceive of it as ideology', Gans suggested. 'Like other empiricists working within a dominant paradigm, journalists believe themselves to be **objective**' (1979: 203).

Participant journalism: a type of journalism in which the reporter is an active participant in the events or issues being covered. Most closely aligned with **advocacy journalism**, in which journalists use **newswork** to take a stand on issues and events, participant journalists see themselves as agents of change and regard **neutrality** and **objectivity** as obstructions of good journalistic practice. Notions of participant journalism drew academic attention when Janowitz (1975) contrasted this mode of practice with **neutral** journalism, raising awareness that journalists could repair to multiple models of journalistic practice at one point in time. In the US context, for instance, it emerged largely with the early colonial press and experienced a rebirth in the **muckraking** era; it also attracted renewed interest in the 1960s when authority was more openly questioned (typified by efforts like the **Pentagon Papers**). More recently and globally, **alternative journalism** relies on intense degrees of journalistic participation in issues and events, **public journalism** is driven from a recognition that journalists act from within simultaneous roles as reporters and members of a larger civic community, and many discussions of **citizen journalism** emphasize its participatory qualities.

Partisan journalism: a type of journalism in which the news of events and issues is reported through an identifiable, predictable and consistent ideological prism. In taking on a particular vantage point through which to interpret the news, partisan journalism presents news with a **bias** that is consistent within the news organization but different from the multiple other news organizations with which it coexists and which are trying to achieve the same aim from their own vantage points.

Historically, partisan journalism typically appears during times of national emergence, because it helps consolidate the national consciousness of members of a given country. Ranging from India and continental Europe during the late eighteenth century to Japan and the US of the nineteenth, partisan journalism invigorates the **public sphere**. In media systems of a partisan nature, multiple newspapers exist in a given location, each targeting a particular share of the population that is drawn on political, gender, ethnic or economic lines and offering a variety of viewpoints on an issue or event. Most countries maintain partisan systems of journalism, and even the US, whose journalists today describe themselves as decidedly non-partisan, was partisan through much of the nineteenth century. However, early in the twentieth century, partisan journalism gave way to a politically **neutral** and **objective** commercial news media that acknowledged pluralism but drew from a broad social consensus between the major political parties (Schudson 1978). Because commercialism made multiple viewpoints anathema to generating as many readers as possible, partisan journalism was eschewed in favour of a more objective mode of recounting that could serve a larger reader population. Other developments – such as certain forms of press organization or political ideals that draw from consensual thinking – may also deter or supplant a partisan news media.

Proponents maintain that partisan journalism contextualizes political issues in a way that makes evident the structural patterns under seemingly random events and issues, and in so doing draws people into public involvement (as evidenced by the high voter turnouts and passionate political cultures in countries with partisan news media). Critics maintain that partisan journalism is dangerous, for it can degrade too easily into explicit propaganda, as evidenced in Nazi Germany and the former Soviet Union. That said, multiple developments of today's mediated landscape – the move from broadcast to cable news media, the embrace of **narrowcasting** and niche marketing, the ascendancy of **blogging**, the rise in **talk radio** – are all seen by many as a return to partisan journalism, even if mainstream journalists do not admit as much willingly.

Patch/Round: a British term for a distinct geographic or specialist area of coverage. The equivalent of a **beat** in US journalism, the patch or round reflects the assignment of a geographic reporter – to city hall, the courts, a World Cup tournament – or a specialist reporter to a topical area – local politics, crime, football – to a specific responsibility for coverage of a particular area on a regular, routine basis.

Pauper press: a British working-class press of the early nineteenth century. Broadly aligned with the **penny press** in the US, the pauper press emerged in Britain, where it attracted a largely working-class readership because of its commitment to delivering a form of journalism these readers wanted to see at a price that they could afford. An emphasis was placed on reporting news events which had a distinct 'human interest' **angle**, as they were perceived to possess a greater entertainment value. The pauper press, mainly made up of weekly titles, stood in marked contrast to the so-called 'respectable press'. Many pauper press titles, available for the price of a penny or two, actively campaigned for radical social change in the face of the Newspaper Stamp Duties Act which had been imposed with the clear intention of destroying them. Evading this politically motivated tax, which had also been extended to advertisements and paper, was a necessity if these titles were to retain their relatively cheap price.

Peace journalism: a type of **advocacy journalism** that forefronts reporting which facilitates the public consideration of non-violent responses to conflict and war. The term gained its present currency in the late 1960s, when Johannes Galtung coined it in response to what he saw as a prevailing negativity in war coverage (see also Galtung 1998). Still, efforts combining social movements and journalism to advocate the end of violence and war date back to the early nineteenth century in the US and elsewhere, when non-sectarian Christian periodicals associated with peace movements – such as *Calumet* or *Advocate of Peace* – advanced peace as part of their vision of a better society.

More recently, peace journalism is associated with multiple international peace movements that range across various post-Second World War nuclear disarmament positions. Focusing largely on the structural causation of conflict, peace journalism is conceived as an antidote to the contemporary mainstream coverage of war, which has tended to promote conflict and drama at the expense of understanding the deep-seated structural causes or outcomes of violence. Peace journalism suggests avoiding many of the dichotomies that characterize war coverage – between us and them, self and other, villains and victims, winners and losers – and focusing instead on shared problems and outcomes, on human rights abuses on all sides, on the use of more precise words and less pejorative adjectives to describe war-related actions and outcomes, and on a combined concern with visible and invisible effects of war-related policies. Driven largely by academic researchers, such as former journalists Jake Lynch and Annabel McGoldrick (2005), peace journalism today stretches across multiple academic and media training institutions, all of which advocate orienting journalists in a new direction when thinking about war and conflict.

Peg: the **angle** of a news story that makes it newsworthy. Also known as the story 'hook', a news peg refers to the aspect of an event that defines it as news and upon which it is possible to hang a news report, **feature** story, **editorial**, photograph, **cartoon**, and so forth. A suitable peg justifies the preparation of coverage. Pegs range across the most obvious and frequently visited topics of the news media – war, accidents, layoffs, indictments and extreme circumstances of most kinds. Journalists and prospective sources wishing to attract their attention are constantly on the lookout for pegs. The process by which a peg is identified is informed by **news values**.

Penny press: a type of newspaper that emerged in the nineteenth century US which drew together a working-class readership by orienting towards practices involving alternative economics, distribution, newsgathering and presentation than other newspapers of the time (*see also* **Pauper press**). The penny press has been credited with a slew of innovations in journalism, many of which remain integral features today: introducing cheaper modes of production by focusing on less expensive presentational features (charging one sixth the price for a paper – one penny – of that charged by other papers); generating mass market appeal that catered to the social lives of the common people rather than the interests of the political and commercial elites; selling the papers through newsstands and street hawkers instead of subscriptions; creating a new dependence on advertising as a way to generate revenue; recasting newsgathering routines to emphasize **scoops**, late-breaking stories and notions of timeliness; and favouring **tabloid**-like features – bold **headlines**, **human interest** stories, **pictures** and **sensationalist** content from venues not before covered, such as **sports**, **crime**, **local** and celebrity news.

Largely spawned from a rivalry between the publishers of two New York City papers – Benjamin Day of the *New York Sun* and James Gordon Bennett of the *New York Herald* – to secure the newly identified public's interest, the penny press was seen by many as so evolutionary in journalism that it has since been aligned with broadly scoped notions of what a newspaper should do in society. Though multiple scholars note that much of what was associated with the penny press was reflective of developments already in progress beyond journalism – such as the Industrial Revolution and its changes in technology that facilitated mass production and transportation, urbanization, the emergence of a democratic market society and growing rates of literacy (Schudson 1978) – many proponents credit the penny press with introducing the first paper that was commercial, popular, politically independent and modern into the journalistic landscape. Still others align the penny press with notions of democracy and equal access to the news, the emergence of the mass media, a surge in journalism's centrality in public life and the rise of modern news, and the limits and excesses involved in creating and sustaining a mass market.

Pentagon Papers: a top secret US Defense Department study that detailed the country's 20-year involvement in Vietnam. The study first appeared in the 13 June 1971 edition of the *New York Times* as a series of articles **leaked** by contributor Daniel Ellsberg to *Times* reporter Neil Sheehan. It offered an array of damaging revelations, prompting then President Richard Nixon's administration to intervene in hopes he could cease publication of further articles. Though Nixon was of the view that those behind the leaking of the study were guilty of felony treason under the Espionage Act of 1917, the *Times* withstood pressure and appealed against an **injunction** prohibiting the publication of classified material in the *Times* and the *Washington Post* all the way to the Supreme Court. The bitterly waged legal controversy was eventually resolved by the Court in June 1971, which ruled in a 6–3 decision that the injunction represented a form of **prior restraint** that was unconstitutional. Today the incident continues to be regarded as one of the most important legal cases concerning freedom of the press in the US.

Photo op: abbreviated term for photo opportunity. Photo op refers to an agreed time and place in which a certain individual or group is available to have their photograph taken by **photojournalists**. Those posing may be world leaders at a conference, sports figures before a match, or Hollywood celebrities on the red carpet. Also described as a photo-call, photos ops are particularly valuable to **paparazzi** and members of the **tabloid** press, who often present seemingly private photographs (e.g. celebrity couples 'caught' walking on the beach) which in effect have been set up beforehand as a staged photo op.

Photojournalism: the practice of incorporating **pictures** or images as part of news. Photojournalism has evolved through multiple stages connected to its reliance on various technologies, and news images have accommodated evolving technologies while accommodating their denotative (realistic or referential) and connotative (symbolic or generalizable) sides. Though prephotographic illustrations did appear in journalism before the middle of the nineteenth century, such as drawings that lampooned political adversaries in the **partisan** press of the eighteenth and nineteenth centuries, only after the development of early photographic technique in the mid-1800s did news **pictures** begin to proliferate as a more integral part of news. It was, however, a slow and uneven process. Though photographs were produced via woodblocks during the US Civil War in the 1850s and 1860s, they could not be distributed as news and were instead printed on stereocards and circulated individually.

Early illustrations appeared as wood engravings in the illustrated press of the mid-nineteenth century, featured by magazines like the *London Illustrated News*, *L'Illustration*, *Harper's Weekly* and *Frank Leslie's Illustrated Newspaper*. Known for producing images of dramatic events, the illustrated press featured visual coverage of fires, disasters, wars and celebrity sightings but due to the rudimentary state of photographic equipment at the time most coverage was provided by making engravings of drawings, not photographs. Action shots were unattainable. As technology became more user-friendly, photojournalism proliferated more and more as part of newsmaking. The arrival of more accessible cameras, the introduction of film, and the development of the halftone process were all critical stages in integrating photojournalism as part of news. By the 1890s daily newspapers began to include photographs reproduced through the halftone process alongside **cartoons** bearing didactic and moralistic messages on their front pages.

Photojournalism was well suited to documenting wide-ranging drama, strife and pathos, evidenced by the growing visual coverage of crime and disaster. At the same time, the picture essay developed as an important way to incorporate images as news. Though American photojournalist Jacob Riis had already published a photo essay in 1890 that documented the plight of the urban poor, the technological advances of the early 1900s – such as faster and smaller cameras – gave the picture essay new strength. Developed as their journalistic mainstay during the 1920s by two German illustrated magazines – the *Münchner Illustrierte Presse* (*MIP*) and the *Berliner Illustrierte Zeitung* (*BIZ*) – the ability to tell a story through a sequence of pictures provided a model that other picture magazines were encouraged to adopt later – *Life* and *Look* in the US and *Picture Post* in Britain (Goldberg 1986). Photographers continued to add new features to their toolbox, including flash bulbs, colour film, telephoto lenses and aerial cameras. The ascent of wire photo in documenting the fronts of the Second World War, particularly the liberation of the concentration camps, secured the image's status as a part of daily journalism to an even greater degree (Zelizer 1998). Television of the 1960s and cable of the 1980s further developed the centrality of images as part of journalism's record of public events and issues.

By the twenty-first century, digital cameras and the ability to rapidly produce scores of high-quality pictures, combined with web publishing, created a potentially infinite number of visual reporting junctures. Digital equipment rendered obsolete much of the old technological repository and its associated tasks, such as film storage, labs and editing tables. But despite the steady ascent in the prominence of the image, photojournalism has not always met with easy success within the ranks of journalism. Instead, images and their operators have been long treated as second-class citizens, adjunct to the words and reporters at their side.

Photoshop effect: the adjustment, correction or outright manipulation of digital photographic images in **photojournalism**, using Photoshop or related software packages. Controversial at times, the so-called Photoshop effect raises searching ethical questions about what constitutes acceptable, professional conduct. Disputes over what is permissible by way of alteration revolve, to some extent, over standards set down in relation to a pre-digital medium. That is to say, a language of film permeates normative descriptions of what sort of practical adjustments can be safely regarded as reasonable and appropriate. Techniques such as cropping, blurring, tinting, dodging or burning, once painstakingly applied through an elaborate set of procedures in a news organization's darkroom in order to accentuate the news photograph's intended significance (if not '**editorial** message'), can now be realized in a matter of minutes through a series of keystrokes and/or clicks of a mouse on a laptop computer in the **field**. Seemingly straightforward policy statements forbidding 'altering the content of news photographs' thus tend to gloss over the subtle ways in which images are routinely crafted in order to enhance their quality for better reproduction, thereby appearing to make what is really a question of emphasis into a stark either–or proposition.

Pics/Pix: an abbreviated term for photographs.

Picture: a photograph, film, drawing, video or other visual tool of relay that is incorporated into the journalistic record. Most closely associated with **photojournalism**, news pictures can be found across the various news media and are subject as much to the decision-making of journalists with little or no photojournalistic training as to that of trained photojournalists. Most media tend to gravitate towards news pictures in times of crisis, where they generally appear along formulaic lines (Zelizer 2010).

Plagiarism: using the language or thoughts of another in an unauthorized fashion without due **attribution** or credit while falsely presenting them as one's own original work. Long considered a cardinal sin and breach of journalistic **ethics** which regard plagiarism as akin to stealing, a charge of plagiarism is sufficient to force a journalist into multiple disciplinary measures, including suspension or termination of employment. Exacerbated by the internet, which makes it increasingly easy to 'borrow' material, plagiarism in journalism involves using information without crediting its **source**, copying passages from another reporter's writing or copying a novel idea or analysis of events or issues in the news from another reporter.

Platypus: a term for **photojournalists** expanding their skills beyond still photography to include video news production as part of their daily repertoire. Akin to the **MoJo** or **SoJo**, photographers are likened here to a platypus in metaphorical terms, namely as a blending of bird and mammal into one creature, to underscore how **multi-skilling** effectively blurs previously separate responsibilities. Critics are sceptical, pointing out that storytelling forms differ markedly from still to moving reportage.

Podcasts: digital media files – typically radio items but sometimes video – available to download either by computer or portable listening device. Podcasts allow 'old' media such as newspapers a means to connect with new audiences, and in this way enhance their 'brand' profile. Commonly thought of as a move away from push media and towards pull media, podcasting allows users to pull the bits of news stories that interest them. Newspapers such as the *Daily Telegraph* in the UK – which launched its daily podcast of news and features in November 2005 – seized on the idea as a means to encourage a culture of innovation in the newsroom. Podcasts differ from the relatively widespread practice of streaming audio files in that they are intended to be downloaded and played later at the user's convenience. Print journalists usually do the talking, with some podcasts offering a daily news summary, discussions of current affairs, or debates about public policy. Some provide weather reports, **sports** commentary, even **letters to the editor**, while various experiments with raw feeds direct from events – political debates, for example – are underway. In the main, however, their implementation tends to be seen as a practicable strategy to capture the attention of younger audiences on the move (sometimes dubbed 'the iPod generation') – people who may be otherwise disinclined to turn to a newspaper for their news.

Pool: the selection and organization of a small number of journalists into groups or 'pools', where they secure coverage as representatives for the larger journalistic community. Usually associated with visits to warzones while combat operations are underway, pools are organized by press 'minders', 'chaperons' or 'escorts' (e.g. military officials) seeking to exercise **news management** and control their processing of information. This information is shared equally among all journalists present so as to gain their co-operation, albeit at the expense of distinctive news **angles**. Usually associated with either large-scale events like political conventions or institutional settings like the White House, both of which might require organized coverage, pools require participating journalists to make their observations available to those who do not make it into the pool. While some journalists accept pools as necessary arrangements in circumstances which they would otherwise be banned from covering, others regard them as an invidious pact, in effect rewarding them with access in exchange for sacrificing their independence, as rules are set down with respect to their questions, interviews, travels, etc. Pools also facilitate **censorship**, the homogenizing of news reporting across news organizations, and cultivating of **pack journalism**. The turn towards **embedded reporting** during the recent Iraq war was an updating of the original pool system.

Popular journalism: a name given to journalism which is not high-brow or elitist. Popular journalism can refer to news that is widely loved and appreciated by large numbers of people, news that focuses on entertainment more than information, news that is mainly directed at the working class, news that is progressive rather than shielding the interests of the status quo, news that pokes an ironic, satiric or otherwise irreverent response to public events and issues, and news that displays simplified and often **tabloid** presentational forms. In each of these variations, what is clear is that the material of popular journalism is not the central material of the mainstream journalism of record.

Historically associated with the rise of the **penny press** (US) and **pauper press** (UK) in the early nineteenth century, popular journalism's commitment to reporting 'the news of the day' entailed a new, distinctive range of **news values**. In particular, the local **human interest** story was to be prized above all others, for it best represented the conditions of contemporary life as they touched the experiences of 'the masses'. These newspapers thus tended to restrict their coverage of party politics or issues of trade and commerce to matters of popular interest, electing instead to fill their pages primarily with news about the police, the courts, small businesses, religious institutions and 'high society'; they also played to the visual appeal of news from the streets and private households, especially suicides, fires and burglaries (Hartley 1992). As James Gordon Bennett, founder of the *New York Herald*, declared in the 11 May 1835 edition of that penny newspaper: 'We shall give a correct picture of the world – in Wall Street – in the Exchange – in the Police Office – in the Opera – in short, wherever human nature or real life best displays its freaks and vagaries' (cited in Roshco 1975: 32). Thus in presenting to their readers a 'gastronomy of the eye' largely made up of 'the odd, the exotic and the trivial', to use Carey's (1986: 163) terms, these newspapers expeditiously redefined what could and should qualify as news for 'ordinary people' in the context of their daily lives.

Post-mortem: a meeting held amongst journalists and/or editorial colleagues to discuss the relative success and/or problems with a specific newscast or project upon its completion. The aim of post-mortems is to learn from mistakes with a view to making improvements.

POV shot: a point-of-view shot as recorded by the (video or still) camera. POV shots typically reveal the visual (eye-level) perspective of the reporter or that of a news **source**.

Precision journalism: journalism which uses social and behavioural science research methods to analyse the news. Using methods like statistical models, quantification, hypotheses, probabilities, surveys and polls, precision or 'analytic' journalism offers a means of enhancing journalism's capacity to offer accurate information and counter anecdotal evidence with scientific formulations. Although early attempts to engage in precision journalism can be found in the early 1950s, when then-CBS correspondent Walter Cronkite used computer analysis of early returns to predict that Dwight Eisenhower would win the 1952 US presidential race, precision journalism in its contemporary recognizable form has been most directly associated with US scholar and former Knight-Ridder reporter Philip Meyer (1973). He saw it as a way to take public opinion measurement away from political and commercial inter-est groups and claim it for journalists. Often seen as a subset of **computer-assisted reporting** or 'database journalism', precision journalism was slow to spread among journalists and news organizations in the 1970s due to the need for access to mainframe computers. The growing prevalence of micro-computers in the 1980s and increasing levels of digitalization of official records enhanced its relevance as a scientifically rigorous approach to data.

Press agent: a **public relations** person who represents the interests of his or her client when negotiating on their behalf with a **news organization**. Such negotiations may occur when the client has a story to sell, as in **kiss and tell journalism**, or a reputation in need of repair or enhancement via positive coverage.

Press briefing: a regularly scheduled meeting between the spokesperson of a given institution (the White House, the United Nations, NATO) and journal-ists in which the **sources** offer **on the record** information for use by news organizations. Conducted as a Q & A session and usually held on a daily or weekly basis by recognized institutions, the press briefing does not typically occur in conjunction with evolving news though such events or issues are typically addressed during the briefing if they are concurrent. The briefing's predictable scheduling offers journalists a way to collect news in an ongoing fashion and **routinize** their newsgathering while providing sources with the opportunity to plant or otherwise share information about stories for which they want coverage. Critics argue that briefings offer new information only rarely, in that reporters ask questions that they know have little chance of being answered while officials do their best to avoid sharing information not ready for dissemination.

Press Complaints Commission (**PCC**): a British board that investigates public complaints about the news media. Set up in Britain in 1991 following a recommendation made by the Calcutt Committee, the PCC investigates com-plaints made by members of the public concerning the contents of newspapers and magazines, as well as the activities of news organizations. In addition to offering advice on **ethical** matters, it upholds a (voluntary) Code of Practice which defines acceptable standards of journalistic conduct. The service aims to be 'free, quick and easy', dealing with complaints – some 4698 of which were received in 2008 – within 35 working days. Critics contend that the Code, prepared by the editors themselves, lacks sufficient rigour to be effective.

Press conference: a meeting between **sources** and journalists that is usually scheduled in response to **breaking news**. One of the ways in which sources provide journalists with information, the press conference is usually held in conjunction with recognized organizations or institutions, such as the police or a local hospital, to share information about an unfolding news story. Though the most well-known and widely cited press conferences are attached to prime ministerial or presidential offices or to individuals managing a crisis, they in fact come in varying sizes, settings and topics. First established near the beginning of the twentieth century when newspapers began giving regular **assignments** to their reporters, they displayed a consistent progression towards publicness in the US. Press conferences given by the President are instrumental in this regard: President Theodore Roosevelt insisted on giving them a popular form, a trend further established by President Franklin Roosevelt, who established the Q&A format that most press conferences follow today. With the arrival of television in the 1950s, press conferences turned public and were televisually broadcast. President John F. Kennedy was the first to permit live cameras in the early 1960s. Though such a trajectory varies by country, press conferences remain a more frequent kind of sourcing practice in established democracies than in other political systems.

Press conferences are useful because they can give journalists access to individuals who might be difficult to locate, such as physicians treating a famous celebrity or police officers heading up a crime investigation, but their usefulness is qualified by the fact that the material distributed at a press conference is shared between rival members of a news corps who are present. They also constitute **public relations** devices on the part of sources, which can easily fail given the unscripted nature of the interchanges that take place between journalists and sources. Today's technological landscape has introduced additional variations to the traditional press conference, including convening press conferences which are limited to **beat** reporters, or sources communicating directly to the public through **blogs**, websites or live audio and video streams.

Press gallery: a space reserved for the use of journalists, enabling them to observe the formal proceedings of an organization, such as a parliament, court or legislative assembly.

Press kit: a package consisting of promotional and/or background materials that is provided to journalists by a **public relations** person seeking to influence the ensuing news coverage. Press kits might typically include a **press release**, photographs, fact sheets, biographies and **clippings**.

Press officer: an organizational spokesperson responsible for liaising with the news media on its behalf with a view to influencing news coverage in ways consistent with the organization's interests. Press officers perform a range of **public relations** tasks, such as conducting interviews or writing **press releases**, while also advising about broader media strategy.

Press release: a 'handout' or 'write-up' sent to **news organizations** free of charge in the hope that the material it contains will be used as news. Often written in the form of a seemingly **objective** news story, press releases aim to draw the attention of a reporter or **editor** so as to produce a news story consonant with the preferred **angle** it suggests. Arriving daily by post, fax and email, the more useful releases for journalists address meetings, notifications and agendas, but they remain among the most blatant attempts to publicize an organization's interests by influencing news media coverage. Press releases come from official sources such as governments or statutory bodies, commercial bodies seeking to advertise their wares, non-commercial bodies such as charities or pressure groups, and local organizations hoping to publicize their activities. **Public relations** firms, which are generally responsible for press releases, often employ former journalists to craft their releases in ways that will improve the chances of success. Though most press releases are trashed, some do find their way into news stories, especially in cases where dwindling reporting staffs and expanding **news holes** make near-instantaneous content useful (*see also* **Churnalism**).

Primary definers: the use of news **sources** by journalists to set down the initial terms of reference for an unfolding news story. Introduced by Hall *et al.* (1978) in their investigation of how **journalistic authority**, credibility and legitimacy restrict the range of possible definitions concerning what is at stake in reportorial terms, the notion of primary definers addresses the **routine** structures of news production, which typically serve to represent the 'opinions of the powerful' as consistent with a larger 'public consensus'. This issue of how claims made by **accredited** sources are recurrently 'over-accessed' to the detriment of alternative viewpoints is crucial. Sources who enjoy high status positions in society, this research suggests, will be more likely to have their definitions 'command the field' in any ensuing debate. Some critics have argued that greater attention needs to be devoted to source dynamics, however, to counter the media-centric nature of this keyword. Schlesinger and Tumber (1994) noted the importance of understanding the initiatives, tactics and strategies employed by sources to shape the reporting process and pointed out that the process was often hotly contested as sources struggled to compete with one another to define what is at issue.

Print run: the total number of copies printed of a specific edition of a **newspaper** or **magazine**.

Prior restraint: an attempt to prevent disclosure of information before it is publicized. Prior restraint occurs when a government seeks to intervene and prevent the publication or broadcast of a news item before it is made public (rather than seeking legal redress after the event). Seen as a mode of **censorship** and long regarded as a serious impediment to press freedom – see, for example, John Milton's *Areopagitica* written in 1644 – prior restraint is rarely justified by the courts. Indeed, in the US, the Supreme Court regards prior restraint, as a general rule, to be unconstitutional (hence the decision to allow the publication of the **Pentagon Papers** in 1971, for example). Today, prior restraint can take the form of an **injunction** or, more commonly, the threat of one.

Privacy: the quality of being secluded, concealed or hidden, and used in contradistinction from the publicness associated with exposure. Differing perceptions over what degree of privacy an individual is reasonably entitled to possess continue to generate considerable controversy within journalism. In the UK, the absence of privacy legislation setting out journalists' responsibilities is regarded as a virtue by advocates of press freedom, while critics insist that it makes unduly intrusive reporting difficult to restrict. In the US, the courts have traditionally recognized journalistic definitions of newsworthiness as a defence against complaints by individuals suing for unwanted publicity (i.e. that an invasion of privacy may be justified, in principle, so long as it is of legitimate public interest), although some commentators fear that this tolerance is gradually eroding. Where public figures are concerned, privacy rights can vary markedly from one national context to the next.

Professionalism: the quality, character, practice or conduct of being professional. Of particular relevance to those seeking to standardize the occupational roles involved in journalistic work, professionalism has taken on particular shape in various locations, and many have used the US example as a spearhead to considering the shape of professionalism elsewhere.

In the US, the notion of journalistic professionalism was valuable in the early 1900s for organizing a basically disorganized group of writers who wanted to become a more cohesive and consolidated unit. Claims to professionalism were thought to elevate the work of journalism, to standardize its practice and to protect its practitioners from formal attack. By the early twentieth century, the rise of commercialism pushed a commercial over **partisan** news media, and with it the Progressive Movement, helped to justify the development of a slew of projects associated with professionalism – the first journalism schools, codes of ethics, trade publications and trade groups like the American Society of Newspaper Editors (Schudson 1978). While considerations of journalism as a profession revealed the failed status of journalistic professionalism, in that the checklist of traits by which professions had been traditionally identified – including certain levels of skill, autonomy, service orientation, licensing procedures, testing of competence, organization, codes of conduct, training and educational programmes – were still only sparsely associated with journalism, at the same time professionalism in the US had other functions. Its status as an ideological construct gave journalists a set of cues about how to act in a given situation and bolstered claims to notions of **objectivity**, **balance** and **impartiality**.

Hallin and Mancini (2004) offered a comparative way to consider professionalism beyond the US case. Briefly, they analysed it alongside degrees of political parallelism, state intervention and media market development so as to illustrate different modes of diverging from an abstract notion of professionalism. Northern and central European journalism (democratic corporatist journalism) is highly professionalized and politically involved; Mediterranean journalism (polarized pluralist journalism) displays a weak level of professionalism and close ties to other political and social actors; US journalism (North Atlantic journalism) shows high levels of professionalism that depend on claims to journalistic objectivity and an abstention from politics. Critics argue that journalism's professional orientation has created its own problems, undermining recognition of journalism as a craft and further distancing journalists from the public they serve. Contemporary circumstances generate other obstacles to professionalization, including the increasing role of the internet in shaping journalistic work, the growing permeation of non-traditional journalists working in journalistic roles, and intensifying degrees of corporatization and politicization.

Professionalism, historical perspectives: current debates over whether or not journalism properly constitutes a fully-fledged profession, one with specialized rules of method and ethical conduct (like medicine, law or engineering), date back at least to the early nineteenth century. It was then that the term 'journalist' became widely used in the UK, although journalism itself was not held to be worthy of the efforts of a gentleman, let alone a gentlewoman, with the possible exception of editorial writers for *The Times*. Its gradual climb to 'respectable', if not prestigious, status encountered several difficulties along the way, such as a critique launched by the philosopher John Stuart Mill:

> In France the best thinkers and writers of the nation write in the journals and direct public opinion; but our daily and weekly writers are the lowest hacks of literature which, when it is a trade, is the vilest and most degrading of all trades because more of affectation and hypocrisy and more subservience to the baser feelings of others are necessary for carrying it on, than for any other trade, from that of the brothel-keeper up.
>
> (Cited in Elliott 1978: 177)

Appeals to professionalism have always been contested among journalists in the US. Some historians maintain that journalists began referring to their craft as a profession as early as the Civil War, while others eschew the idea of professional status altogether. Associated with the rise of the **penny press** in the 1830s, which started the practice of paying reporters, it was widely discussed by mid-century, when various social clubs and press societies were created as informal, shared spaces for journalists to meet and address their concerns about what was becoming – in the eyes of many – a 'profession'. These spaces were formally inaugurated after the Civil War with the opening of the New York Press Club in 1873. As the newspaper was redefined as a big business requiring financial investment on a large scale, journalists' formal claims to a professional status deserving of public esteem became widespread. Schudson (1978) noted that this status was contingent upon the public recognizing certain differences between the so-called 'old-time reporter' and the 'new reporter':

> The 'old reporter', according to the standard mythology, was a hack who wrote for his [*sic*] paycheck and no more. He was uneducated and proud of his ignorance; he was regularly drunk and proud of his alcoholism. Journalism, to him, was just a job. The 'new reporter' was younger, more naïve, more energetic and ambitious, college-educated, and usually sober. He was passionately attached to his job.
> (Schudson 1978: 69)

Concomitant with this shift from reporting as a provisional occupation like any other to a 'respectable, professional career' was a growing perception among journalists that they bore a responsibility to contribute to the general welfare of an increasingly democratic society. More specifically, the affirmation of a specific obligation to the reader was framed via a commitment to exposing the 'truth' about public affairs, regardless of the consequences and no matter how unpalatable.

Efforts to organize journalism as a profession in the UK unfolded differently, taking shape when the National Association of Journalists was founded in 1884 and became a royal chartered institute six years later. Its main aim, according to Elliott (1978: 175), was 'to achieve professional status for journalists by promoting the interests of journalists, raising their status and qualifications, supervising their professional duties and testing qualifications for membership'. An alternative definition of professionalism, this one based upon unionism, was mobilized in 1907 when the National Union of Journalists (NUJ) became the world's first trade union for journalists. Primarily concerned with enhancing the living conditions of its members, the NUJ fought for a national agreement on minimum wages which was eventually achieved in 1919.

In both countries, these and related developments gradually informed the notion of professional responsibility, linking it with the public interest. Further aspects indicative of its consolidation in the day-to-day **routines** of **newswork** include the ability to work under deadline pressure with speed and accuracy, knowledge of the law and ethical guidelines, or skill in **shorthand** and relevant **multimedia** technologies, as well as more formal markers such as membership in professional associations and/or a trade union.

Propaganda model of news: a theoretical model introduced by Herman and Chomsky (1988) to address how the commercial US news media are complicit in reinforcing the inequalities endemic to capitalist society. They argued that news organizations exhibit an institutional **bias** which broadly equates journalism with a range of 'propaganda campaigns' mobilized in the interests of the political and economic elite. The news media 'permit – indeed, encourage – spirited debate, criticism and dissent, as long as these remain faithfully within the system of presuppositions and principles that constitute an elite consensus' (1988: 302).

In seeking to demonstrate the extent to which journalists reiterate uncritically official positions of the state while simultaneously adhering to its political agenda, the features of a 'multiple filter system' are examined. Briefly, five component 'filters' of this model, each of which interact with and reinforce one another, are identified as follows:

1　the commercial basis of the dominant news organizations, by which the size and scale of the investment required to run major news outlets, the concentration and conglomeration of **ownership** and cross-ownership patterns, and the power and wealth of proprietors and managers all impact the news;

2　the influence of advertising, seen as the principal income source for commercial news organizations, on content;

3　the news media's over-reliance on government and corporate 'expert' **sources**, a symbiotic relationship between journalists and sources driven both by economic necessity and a reciprocity of interests;

4　the role of **flak** or negative responses to content as a means of disciplining news organizations, by which its production by individuals, officials and various advocacy groups often results in legal disputes and organized consumer boycotts and proves costly for news organizations; and

5　the role of the 'ideology of anti-communism' as a 'political control mechanism', an ideology which Herman and Chomsky (1988: 29) contended 'helps mobilize the populace against an enemy, and because the concept is fuzzy it can be used against anybody advocating policies that threaten property interests or support accommodation with Communist states [such as China or Cuba in the 1990s] and radicalism'.

Overall, then, only the 'cleansed residue', having passed through these successive filters, is pronounced 'fit' to call news. This is not to suggest, however, that the news media are monolithic in their treatment of controversial issues: 'Where the powerful are in disagreement, there will be a certain diversity of tactical judgments on how to attain generally shared aims, reflected in media debate' (Herman and Chomsky 1988: xii). Nevertheless, views which contest the underlying political premises of the dominant state discourse, especially with regard to the exercise of its power, almost always fall outside the parameters demarcated by the limits of elite disagreement. The 'filters' identified above thus reinforce these parameters in ways which make alternative news choices difficult to imagine, a process that 'occurs so naturally that media news people, frequently operating with complete integrity and goodwill, are able to convince themselves that they choose and interpret the news **objectively** and on the basis of professional **news values**' (Herman and Chomsky 1988: 2).

Pseudo-event: an event staged to draw public attention. Boorstin (1961) coined the term in his classic study, *The Image: A Guide to Pseudo-Events in America*, written at a time when social critics were concerned with what they perceived to be a crisis in standards and values in public life. As fears were expressed about the seemingly fabricated, inauthentic, frequently alienating nature of modern societies, journalism, together with political rhetoric, advertising, **public relations**, and the like, were complicit in the 'making of illusions which flood our experience' and in the construction of 'pseudo-events' – highly contrived occurrences taking place to satisfy the public demand for startling, important, vividly intriguing news. In a world where 'the shadow has become the substance', media celebrations of 'celebrity news' – in which celebrities themselves were human pseudo-events – were figuring all too prominently.

For Boorstin, pseudo-events were not spontaneous, but occurred because someone planned, planted or incited them for the purpose of being reproduced. He maintained that the 'rising tide of pseudo-events' washed away the traditional distinction between **hard** and **soft** news, and news events became little more than 'dramatic performances' (from **interviews** to **press conferences**, **leaks**, and self-promoting stunts) where everyone aims to follow a 'prepared script'.

Public interest defence: a legal appeal made by journalists to justify their reportage on the basis that it serves the public interest. Journalists accused of disclosing information unlawfully (such as with regard to **official secrets**, **embargoes**, **eavesdropping**, **privacy** or **contempt of court**) may plead in a court of law that they acted to provide the public with material about which it had a legitimate right to know. It can be difficult to distinguish the public interest from what the public might be interested in knowing.

Public/Civic journalism: a type of journalism that positions reporters as active participants in public life, namely as facilitators for public deliberation and participation in newsmaking. Starting as a movement in the US by academic Jay Rosen and journalist Davis 'Buzz' Merritt in the early 1990s in response to a perceived decline in public interest about civic life and loss of public trust in traditional journalism, public journalism – also called civic journalism – sought to reinvent the role of journalists as more actively fostering a vital **public sphere** and stimulating public deliberation (Rosen 2001). Seeing journalism and democracy as necessarily intertwined, public journalism takes as its charter inspiring the public to greater levels of civic engagement. Through an extensive training programme and seminars, including town hall meetings, focus groups, call-in sessions and brainstorming meetings, supporters of public journalism fostered the introduction of new presentational features to realize their aim. Examples include **framing** stories by using public response, following on public initiative in making story selection, and incorporating public feedback into the newsmaking process, all of which established a different kind of journalistic presentation (though news organizations incorporated its features in varying degrees). Critics argue that the differences between public and traditional journalism were more of emphasis than substance, and they debate both its theorization and methods of implementation. Many are sceptical of the conviction that journalism is capable of repairing a circumstance it helped to create (Glasser 1999). By the early 2000s, public journalism began to give way to **citizen journalism**, which relies on the public as active makers of news.

Public relations (PR): the management of the flow of information so as to improve a client's image. Practitioners of PR – sometimes called information officers or communications professionals – strive to ensure that the public image of a given individual, group, company or organization is presented in the best possible light. Efforts to promote or protect this image routinely lead to journalists being encouraged, through a variety of means, to reproduce a preferred message in their reporting. These include pitching or **spinning** information, distributing **press releases**, organizing **pseudo-events** or **photo ops**, developing news **angles**, offering financial inducements, and so forth. Journalists are expected to identify and resist PR strategies, and thereby counter their influence on coverage. Some critics are pessimistic, however, believing that news organizations are becoming so dependent upon ready-made PR source material as a cost-efficient means to fill their **news hole** that all too often a form of **churnalism** ensues.

Public Service Broadcasting (PSB): a type of broadcasting that receives all or some of its funding from members of the public, as evidenced by voluntary donations, fund drives, community support and/or licence fees. Driven by the desire to provide quality programming of an informative, enlightening or educational nature and presumed to operate independently of both the state and market, public broadcasting networks incorporate radio and TV and can be organized locally, regionally, nationally, or a combination thereof. The British Broadcasting Corporation (BBC), which introduced the national model of public broadcasting for radio in the 1920s, operates globally today; in Germany multiple public broadcasting systems were set up after the Second World War as an antidote to the monopolistic Nazi propaganda machine and operate on a regional basis; in the US public broadcasting stations are locally licensed, though many carry programming from the nationally based NPR (National Public Radio) and PBS (Public Broadcasting

System), with many public stations maintaining close ties to local institutions of higher education. Drawing from Enlightenment ideals and normative notions articulated in theories of social responsibility and public interest (*see* **Four theories of the press**), public service broadcasting sought legitimacy from multiple advisory commissions during the years following the Second World War, such as the US Hutchins Commission in 1947 or the British Royal Commission on the Press in both 1949 and 1977.

Though historically public broadcasting systems emerged as a nation-state's sole broadcasting enterprise and operated until the 1980s in most western countries as the chief mode of broadcasting, liberalization policies over new distribution technologies and changes in arguments over spectrum scarcity forced coexistence with more commercial networks in most places around the globe. Today public service broadcasting tends to operate alongside multiple larger and often more powerful commercial networks. One exception is the US, where commercial and public broadcasting systems coexisted from the beginning, albeit to the considerable advantage of the former over the latter. And indeed, though most public broadcasting systems claim non-profit status, most can and do embrace varying degrees of commercialism, as evidenced by on-air fund drives, advertisements permitted for certain programmes, partial sponsorship and/or the sale of related products (e.g. DVDs of previously broadcast programmes). Nonetheless, the charter of public service broadcasting remains clear: most systems are charged with providing news and current affairs programming that advances the public interest first and foremost.

Proponents of public broadcasting systems regard their role as an essential one for the health of democracy, not least as a necessary instrument for revitalizing 'rational–critical debate' in the **public sphere** (Habermas 1989). They maintain that these systems' primarily non-commercial ethos facilitates the provision of rigorous, high quality news and current affairs programming largely unencumbered by **market-driven journalism's** obsession with ratings and profit. Critics, in contrast, maintain that such quality is more of an aspiration than actuality, insisting that public broadcasters are more likely to be susceptible to government pressure to influence news reporting than their commercial rivals.

Public sphere: discursive forums in which public sentiment, attitudes and opinions are formed and articulated. Coined by the German sociologist Jürgen Habermas (1989), the public sphere serves as a space for public deliberation that under ideal conditions is situated between the realm of the state, on the one side, and the economic domain, on the other, creating a space for 'rational–critical debate' amongst citizens where 'a time-consuming process of mutual enlightenment' can take place for the 'general interest' and 'rational agreement between publicly competing opinions could freely be reached'

(1989: 195). This normative conception of open and free relations of communication facilitates people engaging in discussions about the conduct of
political life as equals.

Habermas contended that popular participation in the public sphere
reached its highest point in the nineteenth century, when a particular politics
of representation facilitated the formation and circulation of diverse opinions
and the opportunity to challenge the rationality of institutional decision-
making processes through mediation. In principle, access to the public sphere
was open to each individual willing to assent to the legitimacy of the 'rule of
the best argument'. Journalism, as a result, was charged with the crucial role of
ensuring that individuals could draw upon a diverse spectrum of information
sources to sustain their views, a responsibility placing it at the centre of public
life.

The maintenance of this critically reasoning public was dependent upon a
news media capable of lending expression to a richly pluralistic range of often
sharply conflicting opinions. This expression of views of a critical intent
vis-à-vis established authority relations was similarly contingent, in principle,
on discursive relations free of the coercion associated with power and privilege. Not surprisingly, Habermas conceded that these conditions were not
entirely fulfilled: formal rights could not be confused with actual, lived experiences of inequality. Even at the zenith of its inclusionary politic,
participation was restricted to relative elites, namely the propertied and educated (and thus primarily white males) members of society. Nevertheless, the
public sphere, to the extent that it facilitates the formation of public opinion,
makes democratic control over governing relations possible.

Habermas, however, offered a grim assessment of this prospect, contending
that the electronic media had become systematically implicated in the public
sphere's rapid state of decline over the course of the twentieth century.
Linking the disappearance of the public sphere with the commercialization of
mass communication networks, he believes that citizens today are excluded
from participation in public debates and decision-making processes in any
meaningful sense.

Puff piece: a derisory term for a news report or **column** that provides
primarily positive publicity for an individual, product or service. Puff pieces
tend to downplay or ignore existing negative evidence.

Pulitzer Prize: a prize for excellence in newspaper journalism. First awarded
in 1917, the prizes are announced in April each year by Columbia University,
New York, in honour of press proprietor Joseph Pulitzer, whose beneficence
made them possible (also awarded for letters and drama, education, and
travelling scholarships). The current number of awards covers 21 categories,
including meritorious public service by a newspaper or news organization,
investigative reporting, local reporting of **breaking news**, **editorial**

writing, **feature** writing, news photography, and **cartoons**. All material submitted to the Pulitzer Prize Board for consideration must originate from US newspapers or news organizations that publish at least weekly, are dedicated to original news reporting and 'adhere to the highest journalistic principles'. In December 2008, the Board announced that news organizations publishing on the internet exclusively would be eligible for consideration as well (entries made up entirely of online content may be submitted in all 14 journalism categories).

Put to bed: a phrase used to describe the moment when an edition of a **newspaper** or **magazine** is finalized and goes to press. Reflective of a series of metaphorical statements that reference journalism as a child in need of nurturing (Zelizer 2004), putting the paper to bed signals the moment at which journalists let go of their responsibility for it, and it is forwarded to the presses for printing.

R

Radical journalism: journalism committed to challenging the status quo by bringing about social change and thereby a redistribution of power in the interests of those exploited or oppressed by capitalism. The role of the journalist entails more than merely reporting on the world; radical journalism, advocates believe, contributes to changing the world in a politically progressive manner.

Radical journalism developed as an antidote to the rise of **objectivity** in the early decades of the nineteenth century, evidenced by the **penny press** in the US and the **pauper press** in Britain. Both were launched to secure a mass readership interested in the kinds of news which the more traditional, 'high-minded' newspapers largely neglected to cover. Governments of the day were fearful of the threat posed by more radical elements within popular journalism towards established relations of power and privilege, at the same time as the proprietors of the 'respectable' press wanted to reduce the competition for readership. Both groups therefore saw important advantages to be gained by restricting the ownership of newspapers to fellow members of the propertied class.

Two factors were significant here: first, advertisers were typically anxious to avoid any association with controversial publications. Second, they were willing to place their advertisements only with those titles which attracted an audience made up of people possessing the financial means to purchase their products. By this logic, the 'lower orders' of society inclined to support the campaigning press were, by definition, all but excluded. As a result, few radical titles could match the editorial content of their 'respectable' rivals. Nor could they afford to invest the capital required to stay up-to-date with the latest improvements in press and ink technologies. Consequently, far from inaugurating a new era of press freedom and liberty, this period witnessed the introduction of a much more effective system of press **censorship**: 'Market forces', Curran and Seaton (2003: 9) argued, 'succeeded where legal repression had failed in conscripting the press to the social order'.

Today the tradition of expressing dissent through radical journalism continues in a wide range of **alternative**, non-commercial news outlets, including newspapers (such as weekly Socialist papers) and magazines (relying on cover charges or subscriptions in the main), as well as via community access television and public radio provision. Radical journalism flourishes most effectively, however, on the internet, encompassing sites like **IndyMedia**, personal **blogs** and other internet links.

Radio news in the UK, emergence of: when the British Broadcasting Company (BBC) began its General News bulletins from London on 23 December 1922, it did not employ a single journalist to report the day's news. The cries of alarm expressed by newspaper proprietors about unfair competition from the wireless had been taken so seriously that a prescriptive injunction was inserted in the company's licence. BBC news reports were to be limited to summaries prepared by a consortium of news agencies (Reuters, the Press Association, Exchange Telegraph and Central News) and then broadcast only after 7.00 p.m., so as to minimize potential harm to the sales figures of the daily press.

Improvements in this situation were achieved only gradually, even though John Reith, the managing director-general of the BBC – later the Corporation's first director-general from 1927 to 1938 – repeatedly petitioned the postmaster-general to reduce the restrictions on news coverage. In 1924, for example, he wrote a letter requesting 'permission to handle controversial subjects, providing we can guarantee absolute impartiality in the act' (cited in Scannell and Cardiff 1991: 27). His request was flatly denied; 'controversial' matters continued to be prohibited for fear of their potentially dangerous influence on public opinion.

About two years later, during the General Strike of May 1926, the BBC was provided with a remarkable opportunity to proclaim its independence while demonstrating its willingness to obey government instructions. With almost all of the newspapers temporarily closed due to the strike, the public turned to the wireless for reports on the crisis; the BBC responded with up to five bulletins a day, most of which included some of its own material. At stake was the BBC's political loyalty, an issue framed in terms of its capacity to uphold the tenets of 'responsible' reporting in the name of 'impartiality'. As Reith wrote in a memorandum to Prime Minister Stanley Baldwin, the BBC could be trusted to endorse the government's position against that of the trade union movement. In his words: 'Assuming the BBC is for the people and that the Government is for the people, it follows that the BBC must be for the Government in this crisis too' (cited in Burns 1977: 16–17). Government ministers were therefore given direct access to BBC microphones in order to advance their definitions of the crisis, while voices from the opposition parties and the trade unions were virtually silenced. Many listeners disgruntled with the 'one-sided' radio coverage took to using the term BFC (British Falsehood Corporation) to express their indignation.

This 'baptism of fire' for the BBC, as it was later characterized by some newspaper commentators, underlined how the direct line of state control under the legal authority of the Wireless Broadcasting Licence translated into **self-censorship**. At the same time, however, the strike proved that a national audience could be created for broadcasting. In the words of Hilda Matheson, writing in 1926 as the first head of the Talks Department: 'The public and wireless listeners are now nearly synonymous terms' (cited in Curran and Seaton 2003: 114). In the years immediately following the General Strike, Reith sought to further enhance public trust in the BBC's 'authentic impartial news'. He recognized that a greater degree of independence would have to be established for the company from direct government surveillance, even if the use of such pressure was the exception rather than the rule. His efforts were largely in vain, although he did achieve some success in redefining the BBC as a national service in the public interest. By January 1927, when the BBC had achieved Corporation status by Royal Charter, an earlier time slot of 6.30 p.m. had been secured for the news bulletins. Further concessions had also been won with regard to the use of live '**eyewitness** accounts', especially with sporting contests and public events, such as the coronation of 1937.

Still forced under its licence conditions to avoid any controversial programming, which included Parliamentary proceedings, the Corporation nevertheless began to grant itself more latitude in the imposition of **self-censorship** despite the postmaster-general's veto power. The government's confidence in the BBC's willingness to be respectful of the limits of its 'independence' was slowly reinforced, and the ban on controversial broadcasts was lifted in 1928. There was also at this time a growing sense that the mutual interests of the Post Office, the newspaper proprietors and the press agencies inhibited the introduction of the more interesting and informative news formats offered by broadcasting systems in other countries.

By the end of 1934, changes were under way to turn BBC News into an independent department, a move designed, in part, to further encourage public confidence in its corporate ethic of neutrality. The separation of News from the Talks Department was linked, in part, to charges of '**bias**' being made against the latter department. If newspaper commentators framed the new division as the BBC's 'Answer to Tory Suspicions of Radicalism', within the Corporation 'it was seen as a result of a sustained campaign by the right-wing press against alleged BBC "redness" (Scannell and Cardiff 1991: 118). Also under way at this time was a gradual shift to embrace more accessible, if not popularized, norms of reporting, particularly with respect to questions of style, tone and format. In 1936, the journalist Richard Dimbleby, who would later be recognized as perhaps the most influential radio reporter ever to work for the BBC, proposed a radical redefinition of what should constitute radio news:

> It is my impression, and I find it shared by many others, that it would be possible to enliven the News to some extent without spoiling the authoritative tone for which it is famed. As a journalist, I think I know something of the demand which the public makes for a 'News **angle**', and how it can be provided. I suggest that a member or members of your staff – they could be called 'BBC reporters or BBC correspondents' – should be held in readiness, just as are the evening paper men [*sic*], to cover unexpected News for that day. In the event of a big fire, strike, civil commotion, railway accidents, pit accidents, or any other major catastrophes in which the public, I fear, is deeply interested, a reporter could be sent from Broadcasting House to cover the event for the bulletin.
>
> (Cited in Scannell and Cardiff 1991: 122)

This construct of a public audience for the bulletins demanding a 'news **angle**' and 'deeply interested' in catastrophes (perhaps regrettably so in Dimbleby's eyes) undercut previous conceptions of the BBC's audience. Moreover, it brought to the fore the issue of what type of newscast would be best suited to presenting the news. Interestingly, 1936 would also see the BBC undertake its first rudimentary forms of audience research.

The BBC's self-declared responsibilities *vis-à-vis* the listening public were posited within the dictates of government influence, notwithstanding its occasional assertion to the contrary. For this and related reasons, it would be years before Dimbleby's vision was realized. In the meantime, the news bulletin's authoritative claim to impartiality relied almost exclusively on material acquired via the news agencies, even in those instances where the newer forms of technology made 'on the spot' reports possible. Deviations from this general pattern would occur only rarely until the outbreak of war, clearly the most important of which was the live radio and TV broadcast of Prime Minister Neville Chamberlain's return to London from his meeting with Adolf Hitler in Munich. Still, when Britain declared war against Germany in September 1939, the BBC possessed only a tiny staff of reporters, of whom one was Dimbleby, to call into action.

Radio news in the US, emergence of: it is difficult to say precisely when radio news broadcasting began in the US. This is partially a problem of defining what constitutes a fully fledged newscast, but also a recognition of how dispersed the array of different radio stations was compared with a centralized BBC network (a situation aptly described by one commentator as 'chaos in the ether'). News had been relayed by 'wireless telegraphy' since the earliest experimental broadcasts, but the audience was almost entirely restricted to 'ham' or 'amateur' operators who happened to be listening in on their crystal sets with earphones. One early event of note was the decision made by a Detroit newspaper, the *News*, to announce the returns from the local, state and congressional primary elections on 31 August 1920. The next day's edition of the newspaper declared:

> The sending of the election returns by the Detroit *News* Radiophone Tuesday night was fraught with romance, and must go down in the history of man's [*sic*] conquest of the elements as a gigantic step in his progress. In the four hours that the apparatus, set up in an out-of-the-way corner of the *News* building, was hissing and whirring its message into space, few realized that a dream and a prediction had come true. The news of the world was being given forth through this invisible trumpet to the waiting crowds in the unseen market place.
>
> (Cited in McLauchlin 1975: 111)

A number of interesting points emerge here, not least of which is the configuration of the public sphere as an 'unseen market place'. Rather tellingly, and in sharp contrast with notions of public service broadcasting developing in Britain and elsewhere at the time, this commercialized rendering of the audience for radio underscored its profit potential.

Historians typically identify a scheduled broadcast made in Pittsburgh on 2 November 1920 as deserving particular attention. That night, station KDKA (operated by the Westinghouse Corporation) went on the air to relay news of the Harding–Cox presidential election returns, an event which attracted thousands of wireless enthusiasts. The broadcast, using a 100-watt transmitter, took place in a shack built on top of one of Westinghouse's taller buildings as a temporary studio, and to help fill the gaps between returns, broadcasters used a hand-wound phonograph. The resultant 'radio mania' sparked by this 'national sensation' spread far and wide, sparking sales of receiving sets to about 100,000 by 1922 and over half a million in 1923. By 1925, 'five and a half million radio sets were in use in the US', 'nearly half the number in use in the world' (Stephens 1988: 276).

It was the financial imperative of increasing radio equipment sales which led the manufacturing companies to introduce regular forms of programming on their stations. KDKA was soon joined in broadcasting news bulletins by a number of stations situated across the US. The station WJAG in Nebraska, owned by the Norfolk *Daily News*, was arguably the first to inaugurate a daily noon-time news broadcast on 26 July 1922, while the New York *Tribune* aired a daily fifteen-minute news summary via WJZ beginning on 3 February 1923 (Danna 1975). It was typically the case that these stations derived the content for these bulletins from newspaper accounts, namely because it was cheaper for the announcers to read 'borrowed' extracts than to employ reporters to generate news.

By the early 1930s, the public was becoming accustomed to the idea of this new medium as a 'hard' news channel. NBC, with Lowell Thomas, had been the first to launch a fifteen-minute newscast five times a week in 1930, with the other networks following in step by 1932. Aspects of what was becoming distinctive about radio news were highlighted by various news events, such as the kidnapping of the infant son of Charles and Anne Morrow Lindbergh in New Jersey on 1 March of that year. Charles Lindbergh was a world famous aviator, the first person to fly solo and non-stop across the Atlantic Ocean on 20–21 May 1927. Reporters with NBC News were among the first to learn of the kidnapping, yet the network evidently refused to broadcast the story because it was judged 'too sensational'. This decision was reversed hours later as NBC joined other stations in clearing its evening schedules for several days as news flashes brought fresh details to light (the child's body would not be discovered for about ten weeks). The sheer volume of the news reports was unprecedented, leading some then to argue that it represented 'perhaps the greatest example of spot news reporting in the history of American broadcasting' (cited in Bliss 1991: 31). In their relentless coverage of the story, radio journalists were seeking to out-manoeuvre their newspaper rivals so as to be recognized as the best sources of information for a public desperate for the latest revelation. And they succeeded.

Election night in 1932 also provided radio with the opportunity to show how easily it could **scoop** the press by reporting election returns swiftly and comprehensively. For the newspaper industry, this was the last straw. The public's growing interest in radio news programming worried industry executives, who were anxious about the competition for audiences that it posed, particularly where advertising revenues were concerned. Nor had the broadcasters' practice of selectively 'lifting' news from the press escaped their attention. If initially they were satisfied with on-air credit for being the source of the news items (many of which were produced via the wires services they effectively controlled), in the aftermath of the election the situation deteriorated to the point of an all-out 'press–radio war'. In April 1933 the Newspaper Publishers' Association, the principal organization of newspaper executives, together with the major news wire services, sought to bring any further encroachment on their profitability to a halt through a variety of tactics, including advertising fees for printing daily radio schedules on their pages, intimidating the sponsors of radio newscasts into placing their advertisements exclusively in the press, and denying broadcasters access to wire service bulletins.

Before 1933 came to a close, however, the combatants in the 'press–radio war' agreed to a compromise. The so-called Biltmore Agreement meant that radio stations such as those operated by NBC and CBS could broadcast only two five-minute newscasts per day (one at 9.30 a.m. and another at or after 9.00 p.m.) in order to 'protect' both morning and evening newspapers; were to ensure that only news summaries provided by the Press–Radio Bureau were used (which began on 1 March 1934); had to refrain from engaging in their own newsgathering activities; and, finally, were to avoid including advertisements in newscasts, although sponsorship of commentary was permitted. This arrangement did not hold for very long, primarily because independent ('non-chain') stations, many of which were locally based, began to gather and report their own news. Moreover, the news agency Transradio also stepped in to fill the 'news blackout gap' left behind by the Associated Press, United Press and International News Service. In about a year's time, the main tenets of the Biltmore Agreement were openly transgressed to the point that it was rendered defunct. Other attempts to limit radio news would be launched by print media groups throughout the 1930s, but none would prove successful.

Raw feed: broadcast material sent from the **field** to the **newsroom**, where it is processed by an **editor** prior to broadcast. In online news, raw feed refers to news distributed directly from the source to the outside world without the mediation of professional journalism. Typical sites involving raw feed include social networking sites like Facebook, MySpace, Flickr or **Twitter**.

Raw footage: video footage that has been shot for purposes of a news report before it has been properly processed and edited for broadcast. Raw footage also applies to material sent to a news organization by **citizen journalists** (*see also* **User-generated content**), prior to formal verification of its suitability.

Re-ask: a repetition of questions posed during an **interview**. A re-ask occurs in broadcast news or **documentary** when the journalist conducting an interview repeats her or his questions over again, taking care to pose them in the same way as initially performed in front of the camera. This footage is then edited together with the original recording, when the camera was focused on the interviewee, so as to produce the impression of a fluid (visually seamless) conversational exchange.

Really Simple Syndication (RSS): a computer program that monitors a webpage (via its server) for changes or updates and, when alterations appear, alerts its subscribers accordingly. The version of RSS likely to be familiar today emerged from Microsoft in 2005 (XML file format), but several formats have appeared over the years, including sending the updated content, or a summary or headline link to it. In all cases, RSS saves the user the effort of regularly checking individual websites for new items. Most news sites offer an 'RSS feed' for free. 'Subscribe to our feeds to get the latest headlines, summaries and links back to full articles – formatted for your favorite feed reader and updated throughout the day', states the RSS page on NYTimes.com.

Remote: any location outside the newsroom where the news is gathered and/or presented. In television news, a live remote is typically regarded as a visually compelling contribution to what may be otherwise a routine studio-based segment.

Reporter: one who gathers information for its recounting as news. In early newspapers, the printer himself collected information from clippings and occasional correspondence, but by the 1830s this function was taken over by salaried individuals known as reporters. Contrasted with correspondents, who wrote long, elaborated and often opinionated accounts about business, trade and politics from generally distant places, reporters acted like stenographers who gathered accounts of interest from local institutions such as the courts and police. In Barnhurst and Nerone's (2001) view, as time went on, reporters gained more prestige, privilege and an authorial voice, and the distinction between reporters and correspondents diminished. Nonetheless, reporters remain associated with an ability to report the facts in their accurate unfolding, not interpret them nor opine about them.

Retraction: a news organization's withdrawal of a previously published or broadcast fact, claim or statement, or all (or part) of a story. Ordinarily a retraction is accompanied by a formal statement of disavowal – possibly in recognition of a mistake having been made, or due to legal pressure by an aggrieved party – in order to help repair possible damage to the organization's reputation for accurate reporting.

Right of reply: a principle delineating every individual's right to respond to any criticism made of them. The BBC, for example, notes in its editorial guidelines: 'When we make allegations of wrong doing, iniquity or incompetence or lay out a strong and damaging critique of an individual or institution the presumption is that those criticised should be given a "right of reply", that is, given a fair opportunity to respond to the allegations before transmission.' Most news organizations recognize this right as a matter of ethical responsibility, but few countries have sought to enshrine it in law.

Rim editor: slang for the ordinary rank-and-file copy editor. Rim editors discern details like the size of stories and headlines, the font and size of required captions, the presence of **pull-out quotes** and the precise formatting trims necessary to make the news story fit its available space.

Ritual: day-to-day actions, procedures or strategies associated with the forms and practices of **newswork**. Journalists are socialized into upholding certain rituals prescribed by professional norms, values and traditions, yet tend to see them as simply consistent with performing their job properly. Adherence to ritual is observed for pragmatic purposes, and in the knowledge that departures from it risk the charge of arbitrariness. Processing the news is a **routine** accomplishment made easier by respecting rituals that confer upon it rational priorities and predictable qualities, especially where the mediation of compet-ing truth-claims is concerned (*see* **Objectivity as a strategic ritual**). Rituals afford those upholding them a sense of shared solidarity, identity and in-group cohesion, which similarly helps to explain their persistence over time. Elliott (1980), for instance, argued that rituals constituted rule-governed activity for managing symbolic content that encouraged the formation of collective identity.

A second definition pertains to news consumption as a ritualized activity, whereby the habit of following the news (such as reading a daily newspaper or listening to radio news at breakfast time) is regarded as a meaningful occasion or marker-point in everyday life. Ritual in this context points to the social uses of news, that is, the varied purposes its negotiation helps people to fulfil on a regular basis (e.g. a personal sense of reassurance or security in the face of unexpected, possibly threatening events taking place in the world).

Rolling news: television news broadcasting around the clock in a 24-hour **news cycle**. Typified by CNN, BBC News, Al-Jazeera, France 24 or STAR News, rolling news offers an ongoing engagement with news events as they unfold. Critics maintain that the demands of **immediacy** are such that **foreign correspondents**, in particular, are less inclined to engage in **investigative reporting** in the **field**. Rather, once an appropriately 'authentic' backdrop has been secured for a 'live shot', such journalists are often reduced to reading news copy largely written for them by producers (drawing on news agencies, state officials, and so forth) back in the studio.

Rooftop journalism: a term for an emergent practice associated with satel-lite television technology whereby war reporters file dispatches from the relative safety of a distant rooftop rather than from the scene of battle. 'The truth is that good old-fashioned journalism is no longer possible in today's war zones', former BBC correspondent Martin Bell (2009), a critic of the practice, argued. 'Hence the rise of rooftop journalism, in which sharply dressed reporters address the camera from inside fortified compounds. They may be near the scene but they are not at it' (see also Matheson and Allan 2009).

Routine: a recurrent, systematic practice which journalists uphold so as to accomplish **newswork** within relatively stable parameters. Ranging from meeting **deadlines** to following a news organization's **style** guide, news routines offer journalists a way to ensure that their work gets completed under unpredictable, pressured, rapidly evolving and often tension-ridden working conditions. Famously described by Tuchman (1978) as a way of managing the unexpected, the news routine gives journalists a way to control their workload while attending to the news organization's expectation that the news will be produced in an efficient and seamless fashion. Unable to anticipate the uncertainties associated with news, journalists instead **typify** it into categories of its use – such as **hard/soft news**, **spot**/developing news or continuing news – thereby rendering themselves better able to predict how to cover its unfolding: **spot news**, for instance, requires an immediate reallocation of resources in a way that is not necessitated by developing news. Though news routines may differ across medium, technology and news organization, they accomplish fundamentally similar aims by allowing journalists and news organizations to organize the production of news more efficiently. They also constitute one of the most prevalent and often unexamined constraints on journalistic innovation.

Running order: a term used in news broadcasting for the sequence to be observed in the arrangement of news reports in the line-up. Alterations to the running order may be made right up to the moment of broadcast, depending on a host of logistical (and not always journalistic) considerations.

S

Satellite telephone: a mode of relay between the field and the newsroom via an orbiting satellite. Increasingly popular with **foreign correspondents** from the early 1990s onwards, this type of mobile telephone relays its signal from the **field** to a distant **newsroom** via a satellite connection. Satphones, as they tend to be called, have become increasingly powerful and portable, consistently proving their value to reporters covering war, conflicts and crises – not least when terrestrial telecommunication networks are absent or inoperable.

Satire: a form of verbal and visual expression which employs ridicule, sarcasm, irony or derision to expose or denounce vices, foibles and other irregularities. Though widely associated with comedic or humour-generating modes of expression, in journalism satire is most commonly used to target particularly biting problems of a political, social, economic or cultural bent. Found in early forms in the 1700s English newspaper *The Spectator* and using a host of expressive forms such as parody, exaggeration and caricature, satirical writing and drawing have been most often found in magazines and journals – including the British *Punch* (now defunct) and *Private Eye* or the Canadian *Frank* – where they are thought to be 'safely' separated from bona fide news content. Satire dates to the earliest days of modern journalism: US reporter-turned-author Mark Twain/Samuel Clemens published multiple journalistic hoaxes and was reported to have been challenged to duels because his satire was taken by newspaper readers as truth; British and US news organizations regularly run hoaxes on April Fool's Day, following an example set by the *Boston Post* when it urged readers in the 1840s to look for pirate treasure in the pouring rain; the **cartoons** of Thomas Nast in *Harper's Weekly* grounded the corruption of New York City politician Boss Tweed in legendary ways in the late nineteenth century.

Satire also runs across the diverse technological platforms offered by different media. Comic strips, such as Al Capp's *Li'l Abner* and Gary Trudeau's *Doonesbury*, established themselves as predictable satirical voices on events like the Great Depression and the Vietnam War, respectively, while cover **cartoons** of *The New Yorker* regularly ruffle public sensibilities, as seen in the uproar over the magazine's controversial cover portrayal of US President Barak Obama and his wife Michelle. Satire has driven television shows like the Canadian *This Hour Has 22 Minutes*, the British *That Was the Week That Was* or the Australian *The Chaser's War on Everything*. Online journalism produces platforms like the US website *The Onion* and India's *Faking News*. The most widely known contemporary examples of television news satire are Comedy Central's *The Daily Show* and *The Colbert Report*. Spawning notions of **fake news** to ridicule US political figures through a news-like format, both TV programmes show the extent to which satire has established itself as an integral part of the journalistic landscape. Some reports even suggest that the US public learns more from such platforms than they do from mainstream news, though critics maintain that satire is often misinterpreted as real by both other news media and audiences.

Science journalism: a type of journalism dealing with science and, to a lesser extent, technology as a distinct realm of newsworthy events. Though the emergence of science journalism as a reportorial genre has yet to be fully documented, it can be found worldwide.

In Britain, science journalism emerged alongside broader trends informing the popularization of science and technology, and journals in the mid-1800s such as the *Quarterly Journal of Science*, *Scientific Opinion* and *Nature*, serial periodicals like *Popular Science Monthly*, *Hardwicke's Science-Gossip*, *Pearson's Magazine*, *Tit-Bits*, *Cassell's Magazine*, *Knowledge: An Illustrated Magazine of Science* or even 'Science Jottings' in the *Illustrated London News* promoted science and its appreciation in the interest of modernity and social progress. Each title similarly helped to configure interested 'lay' communities of readers, enthusiastic to hear the latest news about scientific developments, innovations and curiosities. In the years following the First World War, science news eventually evolved into a recognizable genre, facilitated in part by the growing professionalism of 'objective' reporting methods. It was regularly featured in newsreels in the cinema, as well as on the fledgling BBC wireless network from its start in the 1920s. By the late 1930s, an increasing number of newspaper journalists were formally associated with science reporting as specialist correspondents, with individuals such as J.G. Crowther of the *Manchester Guardian* and Peter Ritchie Calder of the *Daily Herald* helping to lead the way. Growing momentum led to the formation of the Association of

British Science Writers in 1947, which enriched debate about working practices and ethical standards. Television's arrival brought with it science-centred programmes, such as *The Sky at Night* in April 1957, followed by the science documentary series *Horizon* in 1964.

Science journalism underwent a similar process of gaining legitimacy in the US. In addition to mainstream publications, the public could turn to specialist titles, such as *Scientific American, Popular Science Monthly, National Geographic* and *Popular Mechanics*, which were intent on helping readers meet the challenges of 'self-instruction in science'. Relevant here is LaFollette's (1990) examination of the science coverage produced in the country's family magazines between 1910 and 1955. She contended that science reporting contributed to a 'climate of expectations' whereby science – along with scientists – were celebrated in glowing terms, with articles assuring readers that a future of endless progress beckoned. As in Britain, however, it was during the 1920s when especially formative developments were set in motion, such as the founding of the Science Service, a syndicated news service, which became the exemplar of the ideals to be emulated by major newspapers. Set up with the financial support of newspaper publisher E.W. Scripps in 1921, it supplied news and feature material to more than one hundred newspapers by the 1940s. In the years to follow, as news organizations slowly began to add full-time science reporters to their staff (such as Waldemar Kaempffert and William Laurence, both of the *New York Times*), science journalism gradually consolidated its evolving forms and practices into a recognizable news **assignment** or **beat** specialism.

By the 1960s a marked shift of orientation was apparent in science journalism in the UK and US, as well as in other national contexts. Sharper, more aggressive types of science reporting emerged, employing an increasingly sceptical, even critical stance. The publication of Rachel Carson's *Silent Spring* in 1963 was a case in point. Recent decades have seen this trend continue, with some commentators expressing the fear that science is likely to be recognized as newsworthy only to the extent that it is perceived to be potentially harmful or dangerous. More optimistic accounts point to how the internet is transforming what counts as science news, not least by affording spaces for citizen scientists to actively engage – mainly via **blogs** – in a democratization of scientific discourse. At a time when news organizations are under budgetary pressure to trim or reduce specialized areas of reporting such as science, these online spaces may prove to be increasingly significant for science journalism.

Scoop: an exclusive news story. Scoops are stories of distinct value to the journalist and news organizations, because the exclusivity they provide also offers prestige and stature. Scooping the competition figures centrally in journalistic lore, where assumptions about agility, resourcefulness, improvization and quick thinking support notions of good journalism.

Scoops can involve the disclosure of secret information, being first on a **breaking news** story, or offering a new track to already presented news coverage. *Scoop* is also the title of a 1938 book by British novelist Evelyn Waugh.

Scrum: impromptu occasions in which journalists physically and informally surround a prospective **source** while demanding answers to questions.

Self-censorship: situations in which journalists voluntarily censor themselves. Arguably the most insidious form of **censorship**, self-censorship occurs when the journalist or editor decides not to pursue a particular dimension to a news story for fear that to do so will engender harmful repercussions.

Sensationalism: journalistic coverage which caters to lurid or exaggerated presentational parameters. Sensationalism is most often used as a label for certain kinds of news content, such as titillating stories of **crime**, scandal, disaster and accidents, though it also refers to the sensory overload it encourages in the public within a setting that gravitates more broadly towards presentational restraint. Often linked to the desire for organizational profit and the associated desire to capture audiences through **infotainment**, sensationalism has generated multiple debates at various points in time: for example, in response to the US **penny press** of the 1830s, to the **yellow journalism** of the nineteenth century, to the **tabloid** news magazine shows of the twentieth and to reality television of the twenty-first. Typical sensationalist features of journalistic presentation include attention-grabbing **headlines**, shocking 'if it bleeds, it leads' coverage, or **paparazzi** photographs capturing celebrities or known figures engaging in inappropriate activities. Though proponents argue for the usefulness of sensational journalism, suggesting it helps maintain clear moral boundaries for the public by showcasing what is not acceptable, others contend that it is harmful. In their view, it contributes to a 'dumbing down' of the **news culture**, undermines public engagement with issues in the news, violates public taste and decency, and erodes civic values, among other concerns.

Shield laws: US laws providing protection for journalists from being compelled to violate their agreement with a confidential **source** not to disclose information, such as the source's identity or unpublished notes or out-takes, collected in the newsgathering process (and protection for sources from being required to provide such information as well). Shield laws are seen as necessary safeguards to the free flow of information, enabling informants or **whistleblowers** to share information without fear of retaliatory action while, at the same time, enabling reporters to publish such information without fear of disclosing the identity of their informants. First implemented in 1886 in the state of Maryland and now recognized in 49 US states, no federal shield law exists at present, though it has been discussed numerous times. One of the most recent cases involved former *New York Times* reporter Judith Miller, who spent 85 days in jail in 2005 for refusing to divulge to federal prosecutors which of her sources had outed CIA agent Valerie Plame. Not only does the language of state shield laws vary, with California providing journalists with immunity from being held in contempt of court, but the degree to which shield laws protect **bloggers** and those not gainfully employed by a recognized news organization (e.g. **freelancers** or **citizen journalists**) remains unclear.

Shorthand: a formal system for note-taking, which relies on the journalist learning a range of symbols and abbreviations in order to transcribe a source's words accurately and proficiently as they are being spoken. Examples include the Pitman, Teeline and Gregg systems, among others.

The significance of the practice of shorthand as part of the journalist's **craft** has been recognized by historians. Smith (1978: 162) noted that shorthand gave reporters their 'true mystery' by separating the correspondent from the reporter and giving the reporter an aura of neutrality as he or she stood between event and reader. By the end of the nineteenth century, journalists increasingly recognized that a knowledge of shorthand was desirable if the rudimentary standards of **objectivity** were to be upheld as being representative of **professionalism**.

Shovelware: a derogatory term for news 'shovelled' from one medium to another. When a newspaper places print copy on its news website without altering it in any way, critics accuse it of shovelling copy or pushing shovelware.

Sidebar: a column of supplementary information situated to one side of the principal (or mainbar) news report in newspapers, magazines and webpages. Originally associated with the **human interest** dimension of a major news story, sidebars now include any additional material that is not sufficiently or explicitly developed in the main story but can sustain its own spin-off in a smaller treatment. Also called box-outs or panels, sidebars are often presented as standalone pictures, informational graphics such as tables, charts, diagrams, graphs or maps and feature briefs, with anecdotal leads, descriptive writing and multiple quotations that help the public see events or issues in concrete terms. Facilitated in the 1980s by a larger move in newspapers towards more user-friendly **layout** and design, sidebars are supported by a broader perception that readers increasingly require visual aids, background context, and extrapolated **angles** to understand news stories better.

Skybox: an attention-grabbing **teaser** appearing on the front page of newspapers that promotes an inside **feature**. Skyboxes usually appear at the top of the page, above the **flag** or logo, and tend to be accompanied by an image.

Slander: an instance of **defamation**, in which a false and damaging statement has been relayed in a transitory form (usually oral or spoken words).

Slander usually involves the damaging of an otherwise good reputation that an individual or group is entitled to possess.

Slug: a catch phrase to indicate the story content as a news story moves through production. Also called a 'catch line', the slug facilitates easy identification of each story and helps organize its processing from story idea to finished relay.

Social control: the mechanisms by which the actions of individuals are brought into line with those of the group. First discussed in journalism by Breed (1955), social control delineated how the newsroom functioned as a system of social power, where publishers set policy and reporters followed it. More specifically, Breed examined the extent to which publishers enforced journalists' conformity by imposing institutional authority and sanctions; promoted feelings of obligation and esteem for superiors; encouraged upward mobility in the newsroom; discouraged conflicting group allegiances; emphasized the agreeable nature of **newswork**; and underscored news itself as a value. Breed maintained that the norms of social control were unwritten yet followed willingly by journalists wanting to exist in a conflict-free environment strongly shaped by reference group formation. Critics maintain the study was purely functionalist, where journalists acted only according to normative behaviour and existed only alongside other journalists. Proponents meanwhile credit it for drawing a context around journalism that highlighted social constructions of authority and power.

Soft lead: an introduction to **soft news** items or **feature** articles. In contrast with the **hard news lead**, soft leads adopt a style more akin to a soft news item or feature article, emphasizing vivid, dramatic personal information in their introductory paragraphs.

Soft news: news that is primarily interesting rather than important. Juxtaposed with **hard news** – important news that the public needs to know – soft or **human interest** news is more likely to be seen as news of secondary importance that people are interested in learning about. That is, it lacks the seriousness and/or timeliness typically associated with the demands of the 24-hour **news cycle**. Soft news is regularly disparaged by hard news journalists, some of whom fear its prevalence is indicative of **news values** more firmly aligned with **infotainment** or **tabloidization** than with proper reporting. In any case, few would dispute that the boundaries between hard and soft news continue to blur.

Sot: abbreviated form for sound on tape. In sots, the sound is accompanied by a visual view of a person speaking, usually during a **stand-up**.

Soundbite: a brief recorded statement, usually by a public figure, distilled from the original footage and presented as part of a broadcast news report.

Usually no more than one or two phrases or sentences, the soundbite draws journalistic attention because it is perceived to be catchy, memorable or significant. Also spelled 'soundbyte' (and alternatively called 'sound clip', 'sound on tape' and **actuality**), it is valuable for journalism because it encapsulates an important or interesting **angle** of a news story and/or can be used to enliven or clarify the broadcast coverage. The soundbite is similarly useful for those speaking because it offers guides to **editors** about which part of a speech, statement or dialogue can best advance the speaker's broader message.

Largely thought to have emerged as a response to the rise of an orientation towards image management in the media, the duration of the soundbite is perceived to have reduced over time, hovering in the US at 43 seconds in the late 1960s but shrinking to under 10 seconds by the late 1980s. The soundbite has also produced its own practices, in that contemporary public figures tend to be carefully coached to produce quotable statements which are clear, remain on point and can be easily picked up by the news media. Critics of soundbites argue that they have stripped public and political discourse of its complexity and nuance, and that they advance simplistic responses to complicated problems and circumstances. This problem has since been addressed, to varying degrees, by news organizations in Britain and the US.

Source: the originator of the information that is processed into news. Sources are critical to successful journalism, providing the early kernels of **raw** information that are transformed into a news story. Embodied in people (such as **eyewitnesses**, routine informants or individuals with opinions to share via **vox pops**), documents (such as **press releases** or archival material) and organizations (such as officials conducting **press conferences** or experts giving **interviews**), sources are thought to reflect a wide public spectrum of positions but in fact represent a narrow swathe of the **public sphere**.

Pioneering studies conducted by Sigal (1973) and Gans (1979) in the US found that the majority of news sources were high-ranking officials and members of elites. Little appears to have changed in the years since then. That said, in contrast with early scholarship on sourcing practices suggesting that either the source or the journalist wielded the power in the relationship, contemporary scholarship on sources sees them as having a symbiotic relationship with reporters, exchanging positive media exposure or publicity with useful information. Gans pointed out that the value of the exchange was assessed through corresponding notions of source suitability and availability. With each party perceived as having much to give and gain in making news, sourcing practices are now thought to reflect a mutually dependent and advantageous set of interactions.

Sources and sourcing practices differ across cultures: Latin American sources tend to use journalists to aggressively tweak their political rivalries, Japanese reporters join formal associations called Kisha clubs that determine which sources a reporter can access, and Italian journalists actively choose sources who will better advocate their cause. Sources and sourcing practices also routinely include an expansive set of interchanges, including punditry, political consultants and **spin**. Sources and sourcing practices have also recently come under a critical public eye, appended with terms like 'feeding frenzy' and 'attack journalism' to signify what is thought to be aggressive and inappropriate behaviour. Proponents say sources offset journalism's media-centricity, underscoring the fact that **journalistic authority** has limits.

Spectacle: an event processed as news because of its visually compelling nature. Such events tend to be unusual, dramatic and controversial, thereby resonating most strongly with **soft** or **human interest** news. Critics argue that spectacle-led reporting is becoming increasingly prevalent because of its perceived commercial appeal, much to the detriment of quality journalism. Some conceptions elaborate upon work on spectacle by Guy Debord, by situating ensuing forms of reporting within popular culture as a realm of spectacle.

Spheres of consensus, controversy and deviance: a conception of the journalist's world as comprising three regions, each governed by different standards of reporting. Proposed in a study of Vietnam War reporting by Hallin (1986: 116–18), these regions, themselves an elaborated model of the **public sphere**, include:

1   the *sphere of consensus*, which addresses social issues typically regarded by journalists and most of the public as beyond partisan dispute and non-controversial, and where journalists assume roles of advocates and celebrants of consensual values;
2   the *sphere of legitimate controversy*, which includes social issues framed by journalists as the appropriate subject of partisan dispute – such as controversies which unfold during electoral contests or legislative debates – and where journalists follow norms of **objectivity** and **balance** in their coverage; and
3   the *sphere of deviance*, which reflects the political actors and views which journalists and the societal mainstream reject as unworthy of being heard, and where the pretence of journalistic **neutrality** falls away as news organizations perform the work of boundary maintenance by exposing, condemning and excluding from the public agenda those who violate or challenge the political consensus.

Hallin argued that these three news spheres were fluid and changeable, though the model suggested that 'gut instincts' about **source** credibility were politicized: the further a potential source is from the political consensus, the less likely a source's voice will gain media access.

Spike: a term for deciding against broadcasting or publishing a news story. In journalistic slang, to spike a news story is to 'kill it'. Its origins can be traced back to the early days of newspapers, when copy rejected as unusable was literally pierced with a metal spike affixed to the editor's desk.

Spin: the interpretation or slant through which a news event or topic is approached. Drawn from a sporting metaphor referencing the baseball pitcher's spin of the ball, spin recognizes the primacy of **interpretation** over **objective** fact in the processing of news and public opinion. Recognizing that those who can spin the news to their advantage are able to wield a stronger grasp of public opinion, spin usually involves a series of strategic actions that are designed to include the control of negative perspectives, the slanting of a favourable **bias**, and often outright lying to ensure that a story runs in a desired fashion. Those who work spin are sometimes called 'spin doctors', a term drawn in the late 1970s from **public relations** with reference to the active working of a slant placed on a news event or topic. Though spin in some form was provided early on by political counsellors or advisers, contemporary invocations of spin doctor tend to have increasingly negative connotations, not least in the eyes of those fearful that the strategic and forceful insertion of **bias** into the news will manipulate public opinion.

Splash: a major story prominently displayed on a newspaper's front page **above the fold**. Splash signifies a news organization's corralling of its central resources so as to focus on a news story.

Spoiler: the prior publication or broadcast of a rival news organization's exclusive story. The term arises when one news organization succeeds in publishing or broadcasting details about a rival organization's **scoop** or exclusive, thereby spoiling – or at least undermining – the impact that might have been engendered otherwise. The term 'spoiler' is also used when a newspaper or magazine review forewarns the reader that certain details about the cultural text under scrutiny (film, book, television programme, play, etc.) are about to be revealed in the next paragraph or two. This 'spoiler warning' allows readers to decide whether or not they wish to continue reading the review, the risk being that information presented may spoil their surprise or enjoyment of the text later on.

Sports journalism: a form of reporting devoted to covering organized, competitive games of interest to the news organization's target audience. Widely regarded as one of the most important features of any news provision, namely due to the intense passion it engenders in fans (and in advertisers seeking to reach them), sports journalism has been slow to gain recognition for journalistic integrity.

Critics inside and outside journalism have been dismissive of its status as 'serious' reporting, likening sports journalism to a 'toy department' within the news media. In marked contrast with the **Fourth Estate** ideal, it has been chastised for being entertainment-driven **soft news** of little consequence, with its practitioners effectively serving as fawning cheer-leaders for the sports they cover (Rowe 2004). This marginalized status in the newsroom has been reinforced, in turn, by relatively poor pay over the years, making its reporters more susceptible to various forms of compensation on offer by teams (such as gifts and travel expenses) in exchange for sympathetically partisan coverage. Examples of scandals involving teams which were broken by general – as opposed to sports – reporters were frequent, such as when match-fixing failed to trouble a cosy relationship. Gambling, for instance, is a problem that persists today, with a recent US study asserting that 40 per cent of sports reporters admit to betting on sports themselves (Strupp 2009).

Recent years have seen matters improve considerably, however, with much greater emphasis placed on analysis and critique, in general, and more in-depth off-the-field investigation, in particular. Still, challenges remain, one of the most insidious of which concerns the (usually) subtle pressures brought to bear by the corporate convergence of sports teams and media companies owned within the same conglomerate. Others point to the implication of sports news in broader trends towards celebrity-driven **tabloidization**, and thereby a revealing example of the 'dumbing down' of journalistic standards. Here the growing role played by sports **public relations** is often cited, with its increasingly sophisticated strategies for influencing reportage in line with the wider political economy of the sports industries.

Historical studies point out that sports first entered newspapers through the Sunday editions of daily papers in the early 1800s, followed thereafter by special sports journals, in the UK devoted to specific sports like horse racing, cricket and water sports and in the US to baseball and boxing. As newspapers recognized that sports coverage could appeal to a general rather than elite public, the **penny papers** began soliciting sports coverage in the 1830s, though they were slow to compensate the individuals who provided it. For instance, Henry Chadwick, the first baseball reporter known for developing the baseball box score for the *New York Herald*, was reportedly not paid for his efforts till the late 1850s. Moreover, early sports journalism lacked an identifiable reportorial standard. Though early journals like the British *Sporting Life* and American *Sporting News* were instrumental in helping to establish sports, such as the early baseball leagues at the turn of the twentieth century, many reporters engaged in boosterism for their own teams. Early sports journalism bore an affinity to the communities supporting the papers, and, upholding values like teamwork and fair play, supported the widespread sentiment that amateur sports could be used to cultivate youth participation and the enforcement of desirable social norms. Over time, though, the professionalization of sports won out, and an emphasis in the news on professional sports heroes and large-scale athletic events involving high stakes, extensive resources and widespread media exposure – such as the World Cup, Super Bowl and the Olympics – pushed aside the community aspects of early sports coverage.

Sports journalism has also gone hand in hand with its adjacent technologies of relay. The telegraph, for instance, developed as a medium alongside the wireless transmission of the 1899 America's Cup races, which Guglielmo Marconi saw as a showcase for his new invention and which the *New York Herald* recognized as a valuable investment when it bankrolled Marconi's trip from Italy to the US for the event. Boxing and baseball were long seen as embracing a symbiotic relationship with radio, which created instant audiences for the athletic spectacles each sport produced. Football, golf and car racing each underwent transformations in the sport so as to better accommodate television relay. Today sports coverage ranges across mainstream journalism, where it has also been energetically taken up by specialist journals such as *Sports Illustrated* and the French *L'Equipe*, special radio programming like all-sports **talk radio** stations, and television **niche broadcasting** such as ESPN and Eurosport that make sports coverage available around the clock. Certain kinds of sports – such as some of the 'extreme sports' formats – developed primarily with the possibility of television relay in mind. With the ascent of the internet, **blogging** and **citizen journalism**, new forms of sports journalism are moving in the direction of increasing instantaneity and interactivity (Boyle 2006). Experiments in **immersive journalism** – such as implanting technology that will turn an athlete's participation into virtual reality for the audience – highlight groundbreaking ways in which journalism and athletics continue to be intertwined.

Spot news: news that occurs unexpectedly and unfolds at the moment of – or near to its – presentation. Often used as another term for **breaking news**, spot news refers to news as it happens 'on the spot' demanding immediate **eyewitness** attention. Because spot news unfolds generally without prior notice, it involves fast and high-pressured decision-making, high stakes, unpredictable circumstances and the reallocation of resources within a news organization.

Stand-up: typically a head and shoulders shot of a reporter standing in front of the television camera, reporting from the scene of a news event. Also called a 'piece-to-camera', a stand-up is characterized by a reporter looking straight into the camera and making direct eye contact with the imagined viewer. In addition to lending a sense of **immediacy** to a news story and a claim to **eyewitness** status, stand-up footage also can be employed to introduce a report or to round it off by invoking closure.

Stereotype: standardized 'mental pictures' which symbolically reinforce certain normative assumptions about people, groups or institutions (or, indeed, entire countries) through over-simplification. Credit for introducing the term is often given to US journalist and commentator Walter Lippmann (1922), who in his book *Public Opinion* described a stereotype as a 'picture in our heads' shaping our imaginations in ways that are difficult to resist.

Lippmann was alert to their dangers, but he also believed that they could be used responsibly as a 'short cut' by journalists striving to make complex points more straightforward to grasp. In more cases than not, however, a journalist's deployment of stereotypes, far from being harmless or 'just a bit of fun', may contribute to the cultural reproduction of prejudice or discrimination.

Stock shot/File footage: material shot earlier which has been preserved and stored to be used at a later point in time to illustrate an event for a broadcast news report. Used both for historical purposes and because a current shot is not available, stock shots are carefully organized in a **morgue** or library in order to ensure that they are readily accessible under **deadline** pressure. Use of this material should be duly acknowledged onscreen (e.g. with a 'library pictures' or 'archive footage' label in the corner of the screen) so as to avoid misperceptions that it is current material.

Story: a **narrative** by which the unfolding of public events or issues is relayed as news. The focus on the story as a way of explaining what journalists produce when they gather and present the news obscures a basic tension in much journalism: the better the storyteller, the weaker the journalist (Bird 1992). Storytelling is thought to be antithetical to the process of producing **neutral** and **objective** news reports, and in like fashion thinking of news as stories has often been opposed to thinking of news as information, though both offer alternative but complementary emphases on critical aspects of news relay. And yet the notion of the news story suggests a fundamental epistemological way of knowing the world that has remained central to an understanding of journalism. Additionally, different kinds of news stories populate journalism: **hard news** emphasizes the timely, important and novel; **soft news** the interesting, touching and heartfelt.

Stringer: a part-time or non-staff employee of a news organization, who is paid in proportion to his or her published or broadcast work. Stringers are often employed to report on events associated with a particular **beat** – law or education, for example – or a particular geographic location, where their value derives from the fact that they are usually well-versed in the specialism that they take on. Often doubling as **local news** reporters who boost their income by selling material to other news organizations, stringers are of particular import when responsible for a news organization's coverage of a geographic location. Because they are local specialists, they know the local language, customs, and lie of the land usually better than the news organization's own correspondent and thereby ease a potentially steep learning curve for journalists being **parachuted** to the location for the coverage alone. Additionally, in an age when **foreign correspondents** are becoming less financially viable for cash-strapped news organizations, stringers often lead the way in covering areas otherwise falling through the **news net** when crisis strikes, such as during times of war, terrorism or natural disaster.

Style/House style: the manner of expression typical of journalistic prose. Style refers to a usually informal set of features by which the news is delivered and includes the word choice, sentence structure and syntax typical of news presentation. Style differs slightly by medium, referring to typeface, font size and other graphic features of newspapers and journals, to delivery style, logos and other visual and audio features of broadcast news, and to characteristic features of interactivity in online news. Style also differs by time period, in that since the evolution of news, style has changed with the evolving circumstances of newsgathering and presentation. Though early modes of journalistic style involved elaborated and highly descriptive prose, one of the most referenced news styles is that associated with the **inverted pyramid**, by which the most important information in a news story comes first as journalists aspire to answer the **five Ws and H** in their initial paragraph of prose. Style differs by news organization, with many developing their own style-guides or house style.

Most news style tends to strive for a serious tone of delivery that speaks in clear, simple, succinct and intelligible language about **objective** truths to the largest possible audience, and reporters tend to prefer short words over long ones, active verbs, clear attribution, a dispassionate voice, few adjectives, and anecdotes or illustrative examples over abstract concepts. Adam (1993) argued that news style tends to be generally plain, routinized, uniform, consistent, impersonal and official, written through the perspective of a hidden anonymous third person. In contrast, some news organizations strive for **sensationalist** delivery, others for an ironic glimpse of news events, and still others for an impassioned engagement with the news and a polemical delivery of its key events. In most cases, news style aims to deliver a comprehensive, fair, accurate and **balanced** delivery of the news, but some news organizations push for a style that may not include all these attributes. Specific news styles are often outlined in a house style book that is shared among all members of a news organization.

Subedit/Sub: an **editorial** role performed under the supervision of the principal or senior **editor** of a newspaper or magazine, involving the correction of copy prior to publication. Tasks for the subeditor may include ensuring conformity to **house style**, double-checking of facts for **accuracy**, or the adjustment of syntax, grammar and spelling for clarity and felicity of expression. Typically a 'chief sub-editor' will oversee the work of other 'subs'. Journalists who prepare their copy in such a way as to reduce the amount of effort involved for subs in processing it may find it enhances their reputation within the **news organization**.

Sunshine laws: a US state or federal statute providing citizens, including journalists, with due access to government meetings and records. The notion of 'sunshine' is associated with shining light on official decision- and policy-making, thereby promising openness and transparency. Other countries offer similar rights of access, often in open records or meetings law (*see also* **Freedom of information** legislation).

Supermarket tabloid: a weekly **tabloid** publication devoted to the worst excesses of **sensationalist** reporting, often deliberately blurring the line between fact and fiction so as to generate outrageous stories. A modern day version of the scandal sheet, supermarket tabloids share with magazines a distribution strategy based on supermarket outlets. 'News' items tend to revolve around **pseudo-events** and celebrities, often amounting to little more than salacious gossip from unnamed sources (e.g. 'a friend of the Hollywood star claims …'), or ridiculously improbable tales about ordinary people (e.g. 'SEX-CHANGE WOMAN MAKES SELF PREGNANT! … Scientists confirm "first of a kind" case' is one item that appeared in the *Sun*, owned by American Media Inc.). Many readers are aware that such 'news' reporting is unlikely to be true, but nevertheless enjoy assuming an 'as if' stance whereby they read between the lines to try to fathom where the fact/fiction divide lies. Supermarket tabloids are no strangers to legal controversy, routinely finding themselves defending accusations of **libel**, though efforts to improve reportorial quality – and thereby avoid costly litigation – have been made in recent years. Several noteworthy **scoops** have been achieved (e.g. the *Enquirer*'s 2007 report that US politician John Edwards had conducted an extramarital affair, which he initially denied but later admitted at the cost of his Presidential ambitions), although various questionable strategies (e.g. paying sources for tips or information) remain firmly in place.

Syndication: a service by which journalistic material is made available simultaneously to subscribers for use in their publication, broadcast or website. Such services, which may include news, **features**, **editorials**, opinion **columns**, **photojournalism**, advice, **cartoons** and clip **art**, usually charge an annual fee to a news organization or work on a per item basis. The Reuters News Agency, for instance, syndicates its news wire to multiple newspapers, broadcast and cable stations, and internet portals such as Yahoo!, while Independent Network News was a syndicated evening news programme that ran in the New York City area in the 1980s and was shown nationally on independent stations.

T

Tabloid: a term referring to a particular style of journalism, which presents the news in a popular, simplified, sensational, titillating, emotional or easily accessible fashion. Though tabloids emerged at slightly different points across the globe (in Britain during the first decade of the twentieth century and in the US during the following decade), their introduction articulated a tension associated with what the tabloid signified: did it reflect the legitimate desires and voice of the people or did it represent a vulgarization of public sentiment (Bird 1992)? That tension has been resonant ever since.

Originally a term used in the late 1800s as a trademark for what was being marketed as a small, concentrated pharmaceutical product (combining 'tablet' and 'alkaloid'), 'the tabloid' was initially invoked in conjunction with news by British Lord Northcliffe to describe his new paper, the *Daily Mail*, in 1896, which he touted as being more compact in size and concentrated in tone than the conventional **broadsheet**. The paper, vertically folded, was about one-half the size of a horizontally folded **'broadsheet'** title. The first tabloid in the US – similarly small and concentrated, the *New York Daily News* – appeared in 1919. Over time, the original distinction about compact size was altered, and tabloids are now so labelled for a variety of attributes – including their presentational style, tone, content selection and presumed audience. Alternatively dichotomized as a distinction between entertainment and information, **soft** and **hard news**, **human interest** and public affairs, and **infotainment** and edutainment, and contrasted with the elite, high-brow or quality news media, the tabloid's features cohere around a distinctive mode of selection and presentation. **Sensationalist** content, such as a focus on crime and celebrity, numerous **pictures**, or bold and catchy headlines are one such distinction; another is a terse presentational **style**; yet another is a largely working-class audience presumed to be more interested in entertainment than information. On television, tabloid journalism and **talk shows** are expected to cater to more simplified and accessible impulses of presentation and selection than their more elitist counterparts. The active bidding for information that takes place is seen as anathema to good ethical journalistic practice.

Sparks (2000) notes that the tabloid is distinct in three main ways – in its topical emphases, paying more attention to sports, scandal, popular entertainment and the personal lives of celebrities and ordinary people than politics, economics and society; in its prioritizing of entertainment over information; and in its catering to shifting boundaries of taste which push **talk radio** shows, confessional television **talk shows** and reality TV as a way of catering to a populist tone and rightist content. Though today's information environment reveals more blending of tabloid and non-tabloid elements than may have been the case in earlier times and studies have shown that tabloids provide substantial information to otherwise politically inattentive individuals, critics nonetheless hold the tabloid as partly responsible for the overall decline of journalism's stature.

Tabloidization: the process of taking on the attributes of a **tabloid**. Tabloids include an embrace of sensationalist content (such as a focus on crime and celebrity, provocative photographs, or bold and catchy headlines); a premium on entertaining as opposed to informing; and informal modes of expression ('tabloidese' or everyday vernacular, 'straight talking') and presentation (visually compelling forms of layout). Sometimes colloquially referred to as 'dumbing down', debates about tabloidization typically draw attention to a perceived realignment of **broadsheet** (factual, worthy, respectable, upmarket) conceptions of **news values** with those associated with populist interests (emotive, superficial, prurient, downmarket). This perceived shift in priorities, with its negative impact on informed, serious coverage of public affairs, is said to be most readily discernible in newspapers, but also becoming increasingly apparent in news broadcasting. In addition to conflating **hard** and **soft** news – thereby privileging scandal, **pseudo-events** and celebrity over and above politics and economics – information is said to be merging with entertainment into **infotainment** indicative of **market-driven journalism**. Moreover, much is made of how editorial commentary appears to be flourishing at the expense of **investigative journalism**. Critics observe that employing a commentator with views on the news is often more cost-effective than hiring a journalist to generate news in the first place. While this apparent trend is arguably most pronounced in the western news media (*see also* **McJournalism** and **Murdochization**), research suggests that it is gaining momentum as it circulates the globe.

Tagline: a line of text delineating authorship that is positioned at the end of a news story. Though the tagline tends to be regarded as synonymous with the **byline**, in online news (or **blogs**) authorship is more likely to appear at the end rather than start of a news item (or post). Taglines may also contain a sentence or two of biographical information about the journalist or writer. The term is also used to refer to a short phrase or slogan intended to project a positive image for a news organization's brand identity (e.g. 'All the News That's Fit to Print' in the case of the *New York Times*).

Talk: spoken broadcast discourse embedded in social interaction. News talk ranges from the words performed by a **newsreader** or **anchor** using an **autocue**, across the exchanges between a reporter in the studio and one in the **field**, to the turn-taking dialogue of a news interview where a **source** is questioned on-air. Whether scripted or unscripted, news talk is linguistically stylized, observes tacit rules and **rituals** in accordance with the format of delivery, and typically strives to impart a sense of **immediacy** within an ethos of **professionalism**.

Talk radio: a format of radio programming that is built around the free flow of unscripted talk between host and guests on topical issues in the news that day. Often structured around the exchanges between one host and multiple guests (who change from show to show), talk radio shows tend to have their own programmed and repeated time slot, to which audiences relate through an identification of the kinds of discussion that characterize each show. Though the expression of political opinions and their ensuing debate have been part of radio's evolution since the early 1920s and some kind of listener–participant format has been active since the 1940s, politically oriented talk radio in the US took flight in the 1990s with the repeal of the FCC **Fairness Doctrine**. Talk radio in its present form evolved in the mid-2000s as a way to cut the costs of radio programming, with talk being cheaper than music, for example, let alone news provision. Many talk radio shows are recognized for offering decidedly conservative (and, in rarer instances, liberal or progressive) discussions of news and **current affairs**.

Talk shows: television broadcast shows that combine live, unscripted talk between a host and multiple guests with some kind of news, informational or **current affairs** orientation or **angle**. Often called 'chat shows' in the UK and originally associated with comedy, talk shows combine what appears to be free flowing and spontaneous talk with ritualized and often highly structured behaviour on the part of participants, providing a visible attempt to blend news and entertainment. Originally programmed with the start of television when they were confined to late night or early morning hours, long-standing examples include *The Oprah Winfrey Show*, *The Tonight Show*, *Meet the Press*, and in Ireland the longest-standing talk show, *The Late Late Show*. Many early hosts were trained as journalists, including Oprah Winfrey, Geraldo Rivera, Barbara Walters and Phil Donahue in the US. Contemporary talk shows, however, have broadened considerably, and they range today across multiple programmes, take on a variety of formats and are regularly scheduled in prime time. Some provide objectified public affairs programming or veer to highly politicized content, others focus on celebrity lifestyles and interviews, and still others target sensationalized topics, bizarre behaviours and dysfunctional relationships. Their effects are debated: critics argue that they reinforce public cynicism, loneliness, isolation and alienation, while proponents contend that they promote social integration and political engagement.

Teaser: a short statement or segment intended to grab the attention of the broadcast viewer or listener. Teasers provide information about a forthcoming item in the **bulletin** or **newscast**. A typical example: 'When we come back [from the commercial break], a story about a boat that refuses to float.'

Telegraph, influence on news: the introduction of the electric telegraph in the 1840s is typically cited by newspaper historians as a crucial factor in the emergence of journalistic **objectivity** as a **professional** ideal, one based on the presentation of 'unvarnished facts'. Credit for the world's first telegraphic patent belongs to two British physicists, William F. Cooke and Sir Charles Wheatstone, who together in 1836 created a prototype system. The first fully working version was patented the following year by Samuel F.B. Morse in the

US. It would take about another six years, and a substantial financial invest-ment from the US Congress, before an experimental telegraphic line was ready to be tested before the public. This successful demonstration, which took place on 1 May 1844, relayed the news from Baltimore that the Whig Party had nominated Henry Clay for President and Theodore Frelinghuysen for Vice-President to an anxious Morse waiting at the other end of the line in Washington, DC. Later that same month, Morse used his sending device in the Supreme Court chamber to tap out the first official telegraph message, 'What hath God wrought?' The second message was 'Have you any news?'

Four years later, six New York newspapers organized themselves into a monopolistic co-operative to launch the Associated Press (AP), a wire service devoted to providing equal access for its members to news from one another and, more importantly, from sources in distant sites covering, for example, the Mexican War and later the American Civil War. News reports, which had previously travelled by horse, boat and less frequently carrier pigeons, took on an enhanced degree of timeliness which had far-reaching implications for the redefinition of a public sphere. This point was underscored by James Gordon Bennett of the *New York Herald* when he commented on the significance of the telegraph for the political **public sphere**:

> This means of communication will have a prodigious, cohesive, and conservative influence on the republic. No better bond of union for a great confederacy of states could have been devised ... The whole nation is impressed with the same idea at the same moment. One feeling and one impulse are thus created and maintained from the centre of the land to its uttermost extremities.
>
> (Cited in Stephens 1988: 227)

The news values of newspapers were thus recast by a new language of 'dailyness', one which promoted a peculiar fascination for facts devoid of 'appreciation' to communicate a sense of an instantaneous present.

Debates regarding the strictures of non-partisan, factual reporting took on a new resonance as the AP began to train its own journalists to adopt different norms of reporting. This included the **inverted pyramid** structure of news accounts, as unreliable telegraph lines made it necessary to compress the most significant facts into a summary **lead** paragraph. Moreover, because newspa-pers with different political orientations subscribed to its service, the **impartiality** of the AP's 'real time' news accounts became a further selling feature. 'Opinions' were left for the client newspaper to assert as was appropri-ate for their 'political stripe'. In the words of the head of the AP Washington bureau, an individual who had worked for the service since its inception:

> My business is to communicate facts; my instructions do not allow me to make any comment upon the facts which I communicate. My dispatches are sent to papers of all manner of politics, and the editors

say they are able to make their own comments upon the facts which are sent them. I therefore confine myself to what I consider legitimate news. I do not act as a politician belonging to any school, but try to be truthful and impartial. My dispatches are merely dry matters of fact and detail. Some special correspondents may write to suit the temper of their organs. Although I try to write without regard to men or politics, I do not always escape censure.

(Cited in Roshco 1975: 31)

These emergent conventions of wire service reporting, apparent not only in a 'dry' language of facts but also in the routinization of journalistic practices, helped entrench the tenets of objectivity as a reportorial ideal.

In Britain, the first news received by telegraph appeared in a newspaper on 6 August 1844 in the form of a telegram from Windsor Castle announcing the birth of Queen Victoria's second son. This development set in motion a series of events which would enable news to travel at breathtaking speeds. By the early 1850s, British engineers had succeeded in stretching a submarine telegraph cable across the English Channel to France, as well as one between England and Ireland. It would take several attempts before a viable transatlantic telegraph connection was established, but in 1866 a British steamship laid down a submarine cable between Valentia, Ireland, and Heart's Content, Newfoundland. It was the first of 15 such cables that would be laid by 1900. Using combinations of terrestrial and submarine cables, Britain was linked by the early 1870s with South-East Asia, China and Australia, and later Africa and South America. Most of the information transmitted along these lines was of a commercial nature, often consisting of financial data like forecasts about commodity trading. Various governments were also quick to exploit the technology, primarily for political (and, as in the case of the Boer War, military) advantage. News of interest to the public made up only a small part of the messages, but its significance for how newspaper organizations 'covered' the world was profound.

'Telegraphic journalism', as it was sometimes called at the time by commentators, dramatically transformed how newspaper readers perceived the world around them. The 'latest telegrams' rapidly became a regular feature of most dailies, creating a sense of immediacy that made 'news' and 'newspapers' synonymous. Just as was the case with their counterparts in the US, British journalists placed a greater emphasis on processing 'bare facts' in 'plain and unadorned English'. Each word of a news account had to be justified in terms of cost, which meant that the more traditional forms of news language were stripped of their personalized inflections. This development was particularly pronounced with 'foreign' news, for which public demand was growing, especially with respect to the British Empire, in direct relation to increases in the costs associated with providing it. Of the mid-century daily newspapers, only *The Times* was willing and able to meet the expense of an extensive network of correspondents and 'stringers' to telegraph news from around the world. For its rivals, an alternative source of foreign news were the daily reports relayed by the European **news agencies**, the most important of which for British newspapers was Reuters, followed by Havas of France and Wolff of Germany. Considerable pride was taken in communicating the essential facts of 'hard' or 'spot' news ostensibly free from the distorting influences of personal opinion.

Teletext: a television service, usually available free of charge, offering regularly updated news and information on a specific television channel throughout the day. Content takes the form of rolling lines of text, which the individual can choose to access via interactive menus such as News, Sports or Weather.

Television news in the UK, emergence of: Britain's first experimental television programme was transmitted from Broadcasting House in London on 22 August 1932. News made its appearance on 21 March 1938 (a recording of **radio news** presented without pictures). **Newscasts** would not become a daily feature on television, however, until the launch of the BBC's *News and Newsreel* on 5 July 1954. While the 7.30 p.m. programme had been heralded as 'a service of the greatest significance in the progress of television in the UK', critics expressed their keen disappointment in its failure to make compelling use of visual material. By June 1955, the title *News and Newsreel* was dropped in favour of *Television News Bulletin*. The ten minutes of news was read by an off-screen voice in an 'impersonal, sober and quiet manner', the identity of the (always male) newsreader being kept secret to preserve the institutional authority of the BBC, to the accompaniment of still pictures (as the title suggests, the news was then followed by a **newsreel**). Only in the final days leading up to the launch of its 'American-style' rival on the new commercial network, ITV, did this practice change, and then only partially. In the first week of September 1955, the BBC introduced the faces of its **newsreaders** to the camera, but not their names. The danger of 'personalizing' the news as the voice of an individual, as opposed to that of the Corporation, was considered to be serious enough to warrant the preservation of **anonymity**. This strategy, which had its origins in radio, arguably communicated an enhanced sense of detached **impartiality** for the newscast, and would last for another eighteen months (the policy of anonymous newsreading would continue for BBC radio until 1963).

The Television Act (1954), introduced by Winston Churchill's Conservative Party government after two and a half years of often acrimonious debate, led to a commercial rival being established. At 10.00 p.m. on 22 September 1955, ITN made its début on the ITV network. In contrast with the BBC's anonymous newsreaders, its 'newscasters' were given the freedom to rewrite the news in accordance with their own stylistic preferences as journalists, even to the extent of ending the newscast with a 'lighter' item to raise a smile for the viewer. Editor Geoffrey Cox was well aware, though, that the advantages to be gained by having newscasters who were 'men and women of strong personality' (who also tended to be 'people of strong opinions') had to be qualified in relation to the dictates of the Television Act concerning 'due **accuracy** and **impartiality**'. Given that ITN was a subsidiary company of the four principal networking companies, lines of administrative authority were much more diffuse than was the case in the BBC or, for that matter, in the newspaper press. Still, pressure from the networking companies to increase the entertainment value of the newscasts was considerable. The news agenda was similarly shaped by a principle of impartiality which dictated that analysis and interpretation were to be scrupulously avoided in both the spoken news and film report segments of the newscast. However, expressions of opinion could be included in the newscast through studio interviews. These 'live' segments facilitated a stronger sense of **immediacy**, for spontaneous or 'off the cuff' remarks added a degree of excitement that might have otherwise been denied in the name of editorial fairness or **balance**. Perhaps more to the point, though, they were also more 'cost-efficient' than film reports.

By 1956, the BBC had elected to follow ITN's lead. In seeking to refashion its television newscasts to meet the new 'personalized' standards of presentation audiences were coming to expect, the Corporation began to identify its newsreaders by name. It also emulated ITN by allowing them to use **autocues** in order to overcome their reliance on written scripts. Further technological improvements, most notably in the quality of film processing, similarly improved the visual representation of authenticity. That said, however, the question of whether or not to use dubbed or even artificial sound to accompany otherwise silent film reports posed a particularly difficult problem for journalists anxious to avoid potential criticisms about their claim to impartiality. Much debate also ensued over what circumstances justified imitating ITN's more informal style of presentation, particularly with regard to the use of colloquial language, to enhance the newscast's popular appeal (previously BBC news writers had been told to adopt a mode of address appropriate for readers of the 'quality' press). ITN had also shown how the new lightweight 16mm film camera technology could be exploited to advantage in the **field** for more visually compelling images (complete with the 'natural sound' of **actuality**) than those provided by the newsreel companies with their bulky 35mm equipment. Indeed, through this commitment to 'bringing to life' news stories in a dramatic way, as well as its more aggressive approach to pursuing **scoops** (exclusives) and **beats** (first disclosures), ITN was stealing the march on the BBC with respect to attracting a greater interest in news among viewers.

Television news in the US, emergence of: television news, which first appeared in the US during the 1930s on several experimental stations, did not get fully under way until after the Second World War. The first regularly scheduled network newscast to adopt the characteristics familiar today was *The CBS-TV News with Douglas Edwards*, which appeared in a fifteen-minute slot each weekday evening beginning in August 1948 (newscasts would not be lengthened to half an hour until September 1963). It was sponsored by the car manufacturer Oldsmobile. NBC was next with *The Camel News Caravan* beginning in February 1949, sponsored by Winston-Salem, makers of Camel cigarettes. Advertisements formed a part of each newscast, and in the case of *The Camel News Caravan* went even further. The newsreader, John Cameron Swayze, sat at a desk to read the news, a packet of Camel cigarettes and an ashtray (the word 'Camel' on its side in clear letters) strategically placed beside him. Further sponsorship 'distortions' took many forms, as Barnouw (1990) elaborated:

> Introduced at the request of the sponsor, they were considered minor aspects of good manners rather than news corruption. No news personage could be shown smoking a cigar – except Winston Churchill, whose world role gave him special dispensation from Winston-Salem. Shots of 'no smoking' signs were forbidden.
>
> (Barnouw 1990: 171)

The pace of the newscast was brisk, with the 'breezy, boutonniered' Swayze moving it forward each day with the line 'Now let's go hopscotching the world for headlines!' before bringing it to a close with his customary 'That's the story, folks. Glad we could get together!' Rival newscasts followed shortly thereafter on the ABC (formerly NBC's 'Blue Network') and DuMont networks (the latter collapsed in 1955).

Most of the editors and reporters who found themselves working in television news had backgrounds in either newspapers, the wire services or radio news organizations. Such was likewise the case for the producers and production people, although they also tended to be drawn from wire service picture desks, newsreels and picture magazines. The significance of these disparate backgrounds is apparent in the types of debates which emerged regarding how best to present news televisually. In essence, the television newscast represented a blending of the qualities of radio speech with the visual attributes of the **newsreel**. With little by way of precedent to draw upon, a number of variations on basic newscast formats were tried and tested during these early years.

If the techniques of radio news provided a basis for anchoring the authority of the voiceover, it was the newsreel which supplied a model for the form that television news might take. Aspects of this model included 'the fragmented succession of unrelated "stories", the titles composed in the manner of front page headlines, and the practice of beginning each issue with the major news event of the day, followed by successively less important subject matter'

(Fielding cited in Winston 1993: 184). Newsfilm items tended to be the principal component of the newscast (video tape was first used in network news in 1956), although switches to reporters in other cities were by now a regular feature. The performative role of the **anchorperson** – or, more accurately, 'anchorman' as women were almost always denied this status – was also firmly established by the mid-1950s.

By 1954, television had displaced radio in the daily audience figures for usage of each medium. Newscast formats had become relatively conventionalized from one network to the next by this time, although the question of how journalistic notions of **impartiality** and 'fairness' were to be achieved in practical terms was the subject of considerable dispute (*see also* **Fairness Doctrine**). The determined search for ever larger ratings figures, due to the higher sponsorship revenues they could demand, made television news increasingly image-oriented in its drive to attract audiences. An emphasis was routinely placed on staged events, primarily because they were usually packaged by the news promoters behind them (whether governmental or corporate) with the visual needs of television in mind. News of celebrities, speeches by public figures, carnivals and fashion shows made for 'good television', and such coverage was less likely to conflict with sales of advertising time. Significantly, then, the very features of television news which some critics pointed to as being vulgar, banal or trivial were often the same ones which advertisers believed created an appropriate tone for the content surrounding their messages. Pressure was recurrently brought to bear on the networks to ensure that their viewers, as potential consumers, would not be offended by newscasts presenting the viewpoints of those from outside the limits of pro-business 'respectability'.

Television news magazine: a type of television programming that combines multiple brief segments, each of which focuses on a different news story. Generally focusing on **soft** rather than **hard news** via stories about **crime**, celebrities and social trends, television news magazines became popular in the US in the late 1970s. Seen as an answer to the disappearing commercial network **documentary** that was later further sidelined by the ascent of cable news, the news magazines offered an antidote to the broadcast networks' waning fortunes by focusing on material that was relatively inexpensive to produce and that gave reporters a chance to produce longer stories than could be accommodated on the nightly news programmes. Though some version of TV news magazines could be found as early as the 1950s, the pioneering US network news magazine was *60 Minutes*. In Campbell's (1991) view, the programme, which opened on CBS in 1968, functioned by taking on one of multiple possible **narrative** frames, promoting journalism as therapy, mystery or adventure, for example, with journalists assuming roles consonant with the programme's frames. Its enduring popularity – it still ranks among the top **TV news** magazines – prompted other broadcast networks to start similar programming, such as ABC's *20/20* and NBC's *Dateline*, though the most recent trend has been to use the TV magazine format to service increasingly **tabloid** material.

Thirty/–30–: a convention used by journalists to signal 'end of story' for their news item when typing **copy**. Represented in different ways, such as –30–, XXX and </30>, thirty is long associated with the evolution of the **newspaper**, though its precise origins remain unclear.

Throw: situations in which an individual (journalist or presenter) passes responsibility for delivery to someone else during a **newscast**. Whether ad-libbed or scripted beforehand, examples of throws include: 'Over to you Christine, reporting live from Beijing', 'And now I will hand you back to Zena in the studio' or 'Here is Sally with a traffic update.'

Tip: idea or information of use to a journalist or **editor** concerning a possible news story (or one in preparation), most likely provided by a **source**.

Trade press: material produced by, for and among journalists that usually focuses on journalistic practice in some form. Historically, as journalism worked its way from a **craft** orientation to aspirations of being a **profession** during the late nineteenth century, many who considered themselves acting journalists began to share their perspective on being a journalist with others in the same circumstance. Professional journals such as *The Journalist, Editor and Publisher* or *British Journalism Review* began to air issues relevant to practising journalists, and they addressed with increasing regularity the nature, function and role of journalism as it modernized. Later, as journalism schools began to evolve, they too produced their own journals, as with the *Columbia Journalism Review*, and today a set of trade journals, papers and magazines offer industry-specific titbits of information, job listings, and a place to address ongoing issues of concern to journalists. Dedicated websites and **blogs** have become active as a virtual trade press of sorts, such as the Project for Excellence in Journalism which regularly collects and processes articles on journalistic practice.

Travel journalism: a popular form of **lifestyle journalism** that focuses primarily on the relative merits and shortcomings of various holiday destinations. A long-standing feature of newspapers, often in its own section or supplement since the 1970s, travel journalism offers a degree of escapism for readers curious about exotic locales. Travel journalism has often been said to be at least as much about the traveller (his or her personal journey through life, so to speak) as the trip itself. In addition to detailed descriptions about what a visitor may expect to encounter, usually vividly represented in photographs, reportage typically provides practical advice and tips, with online news sites actively encouraging readers to share their experiences as well. The unapologetically consumer-focused nature of the coverage has long attracted criticism by those sceptical that it actually constitutes journalism *per se*. Others point to the extent to which **public relations** officers work behind the scenes to inflect what is reported in line with commercial interests. Indeed, it is common practice for travel companies to offer to underwrite the travel expenses incurred by journalists in exchange for positive treatment, a symbiotic relationship that more reputable news organizations reject outright or – at the very least – disclose in the account. In any case, travel journalism is called upon to garner advertising revenue from what is a major industry, which also explains why so little of the ensuing coverage is critical in tone or investigative in reach. In the event of 'proper news' emerging, the story is likely to be repositioned as a **hard news** item elsewhere in the newspaper.

The capacity of travel journalism to expose individuals to more locations than they are able to experience personally and to generate interest about those locations has been its central appeal for many years. From the early nineteenth century onward, travel journalism adapted to the evolving technologies associated with ocean liners, trains, electricity and the telegraph so as to provide information to the public about distant lands. For instance, the premier issue of *North American Review*, published in 1815, brought news of Paris to Americans, while *Scribner's Monthly* ran regular features on European cities a few decades later and the British *Queen* made its travel column 'The Tourist' – offering women advice on foreign travel such as dress and manners – a regular feature. For many news organizations in the US, correspondence from Europe took on added value in the mid-1800s when the so-called 'springtime of nations' produced a series of revolutions across the European landscape and employed travel writers already on hand to provide eyewitness reports of what was happening.

As travelogues, diaries, letters and articles appeared increasingly across the European press during the nineteenth century, tourism became more and more a pastime of the middle class and not just the aristocracy, thereby establishing a link from the outset between journalism and tourism's popular spread. For instance, British journals increasingly used the travelogues of private citizens, as in *Picture Postcard* or *World Wide Magazine*'s incorporation of anecdotal narratives of individuals engaging in leisure activities like sledging and cycling across eastern Europe. By the late 1890s, both American and British journals and newspapers began to employ reporters to travel and write of their escapades, and *Queen*, *The Saturday Evening Post*, *MacMillan's Magazine*, *Travel* and *Atlantic Monthly* regularly published travel memoirs and travelogues for pay.

Travel journalism developed in even greater strides from the late 1800s to early 1900s as further changes in technology and lifestyle made travel ever more accessible in many places around the globe. Improved and faster technologies of transport (including the automobile and the aeroplane) and enhanced demographic and economic growth (such as increased wealth and more leisure time) continued to transform travel from a privileged occupation of wealthy elites into a popular leisure activity. In Britain during the second half of the nineteenth century travel destinations became a way for journals to segment their target reading communities, though the blurred boundaries between travel journalism and travel literature reflected a broader mix of journalism and literature at the time, and identifying destinations for travel helped push tourism further as a potential leisure activity for the growing middle class. By the beginning of the twentieth century, a tourism industry had begun to develop in various places worldwide, with guidebooks, travel agents and group tours creating a rich and varied setting on which travel journalism could focus. Multiple journals like *Ladies Home Journal*, *Cosmopolitan* and *Colliers* emerged with regular features attending to tourism, and journals devoted exclusively to the topic began to appear, such as *National Geographic*. By using photos to generate interest in distant territories from 1896 on, the journal gave foreign countries a visible shape, a success story later followed by other magazines like *Travel and Leisure*. Through it all, travel journalism was central to the burgeoning interest in distant lands, and its modes of visual representation – building on an earlier reliance on stereocards and travel posters – depicted what remote locations looked like. Individual journalists – like Lowell Thomas on American radio from the 1930s or Charles Kuralt, whose *On the Road* programme solidified US television's entry into travel news – also reflected a growing interest in geographic and cultural diversity that translated into the continued growth of tourism.

Today, the ascent of new media facilitates the incorporation of **user-generated content** by the tourism industry and makes travel journalism an opportune topic for **bloggers** interested in writing of their travels and disseminating them. Contemporary travel journalism is also less celebratory than its earlier forms and more consumer-oriented, as today's reporters use their platforms to warn of abuse in the tourism industry, advise about dangerous destinations and counsel on how best to secure value for one's money. Nonetheless, critics maintain that travel journalism still runs a particularly strident risk of boosterism, by which the connections between the tourism industry and travel writers can become overly close and mutually supportive, often to the detriment of the public.

Truth: the display of fidelity with the real world. One of the principles of good journalism, truth is approached by journalists not as an absolute entity but as a practical objective to be realized in newsmaking practices. Truth refers to the capacity to report things as they 'really are' and rests on multiple adjacent values, including conformity with the facts, **accuracy**, and veracity of claims. It emerges through the journalist's ability to assemble and verify facts and to collect them in an account that approximates in a reliable and credible fashion some unfolding of action in the real world.

Twitter: a social networking service which allows participants to share short messages (maximum 140 characters in length) on the internet. Described as a form of micro-**blogging** by some, messages or 'tweets' from **eyewitnesses** to news events have been heralded for their contribution to the reporting of **breaking news**. Twitter's status as a form of journalism was widely debated in the aftermath of the hostage crisis in Mumbai in November 2008, when the role played by **citizen journalists** using the micro-blogging service to relay vital insights warranted much comment in news accounts. Some commentators maintained that Twitter deserved praise as a useful means to gather information during a crisis, while critics questioned its value as a trustworthy news source in its own right.

Two-Shot/2-Shot: a term for **television news** footage or **documentary** shots in which two people appear in the same shot. Two-shots typically refer to an over-the-shoulder shot of the reporter situated in front of the interviewee who is facing the camera.

Two-source rule: the maxim that a journalist should scrupulously confirm each and every fact in a news story with at least two **sources** before publishing or broadcasting it.

Two-way: an on-air **interview** between the news **anchorperson** or **newsreader** in the studio and a journalist in the **field**.

Typification: a term for news classifications whose meanings reside in the ways they are used. Coined by Tuchman (1978), news typifications enable the routinization of newswork because they turn classifications related to practical tasks confronting journalists into facilitators that speed work along in an acceptable manner. Drawn from research on the social construction of reality, typifications offer available courses of action and provide solutions to practical problems. Distinctions between **hard news** and **soft news**, for instance, rest on practices related to scheduling: soft news items tend to be non-scheduled and their date of dissemination is generally determined by the news organization, while hard news items either occur unexpectedly (such as a fire) or are pre-scheduled (such as an awards ceremony). Tuchman identified three further distinctions within hard news: distinctions between **spot news** (news that occurs suddenly and must be processed quickly) and developing news (news whose details take time to unfold) are made because they help redirect the allocation of resources in conjunction with the technological strengths and limitations of the medium at hand, rendering the same news event defined as spot news for television and as developing news for the print media. The typification of continuing news, or news which produces a series of stories on the same topic, enhances the journalist's ability to predict how the story will take shape in different technological environments. Though each typification overlaps with the others, they nonetheless turn what had long been thought of as inherent qualities of the news event itself into a series of newsmaking **routines**.

U

Unattributed source: a type of sourcing practice in which a **source** is quoted or paraphrased in a news item by a journalist who has agreed not to divulge his or her name. A departure from the usual rules of **attribution**, unattributed sourcing is displayed in statements like 'A close friend of the musician revealed that ...' and is driven by circumstances in which a source agrees to talk only on condition of **anonymity**, usually from fear of repercussions. Several major stories have been made possible because of such agreements, including 'Deep Throat' from the **Watergate** scandal. Critics contend that the practice is ethically dubious (not least due to the risk that inaccurate or malicious claims may be put into public circulation), complicates any attempt to hold journalists accountable for what they report, and encourages lazy, superficial journalism.

Underground press: publications that challenge mainstream media priorities and conventions and may be of subversive intent. While often associated with the counterculture politics of the 1960s in various western countries, the history of the underground press is intertwined with that of **censorship**. Examples of underground publications emerge in situations in which individuals and groups seek to gather and distribute news and information considered objectionable, or otherwise undesirable, by those in power.

User-generated content (**UGC**): content provided by ordinary **citizen journalists** that is processed into news. Variations of 'user-generated' reporting are evolving, with types of content including **eyewitness** accounts, digital photographs, video, audio files, comments on news items and so forth. Whatever the content in question, the UGC phenomenon is now firmly entrenched, and still growing at a remarkable rate. Reasons for its appropriation by news organizations include the fact that it is relatively cheap to gather and process, a key consideration when financial resources for reporting are under pressure, and it is popular with members of the public.

Still, there are certain risks for news organizations intent on drawing upon UGC. One such risk concerns the need to attest to the **accuracy** of the material (text, image, media file, etc.) in question, given the potential of hoaxes being perpetrated. Steps have to be taken to ensure that it has not been digitally manipulated or 'doctored' so as to enhance its news value, and to attest to its source in a straightforward manner. A further risk is that rights to the content may be owned by someone else, raising potential problems with respect to the legality of permission to use it. While users turned citizen

photojournalists may provide the BBC with their images free of charge, for example, they may seek to retain the copyright, enabling them to sell the rights to them to other news organizations (Sky TV, for example, reportedly offers £250 for exclusive rights to an image). Evidently within BBC television news, **editors** believe that trust is the central issue where gathering material from members of the public is concerned. For individuals to send their work to the BBC, as opposed to rival news organizations (especially when the latter will offer financial payment), they have to share something of the Corporation's commitment to public service.

V

Viewspaper: a critical term for **newspapers** which prioritize opinion over and above news. Often associated with **advocacy journalism**, the term was first used in June 2007, when British Prime Minister Tony Blair chastised the *Independent* for being a 'viewspaper', critiquing it as 'the idea of journalism as views not news', lacking adequate '**balance**', and for assessing '[t]hings, people, issues, stories [as] all black and white. Life's usual grey is almost entirely absent.' In his response, then editor Simon Kelner pointed out that the *Independent* is 'avowedly a viewspaper, not merely a newspaper', before adding that it 'was not established as an antidote to the idea of journalism as views, but as an antidote to proprietorial influence and narrow political allegiance'.

Viral: adjective describing a video clip of a news story posted on the internet that achieves sudden, widespread popularity amongst web users. A clip that has 'gone viral' is typically posted on sites like YouTube and may have been drawn from a **newscast** or consist of telephone camera **footage** shot by a **citizen journalist**.

VJ (video journalist): broadcast journalists who **multi-task** across reportorial, editorial, camera operator and/or sound operator roles, comprising a one-person crew to cover the news. First used in the early 1990s by US cable news organizations, video journalists were seen as a way of rendering **newswork** less expensive for the organizations charged with its production and of making journalists less obtrusive in the field. Though VJs raise questions about the absence of checks and balances in the newsmaking process, today they are used by most large broadcast **news organizations**.

Vlogger: a **blogger** posting video-based news or commentary on the internet. Also called vid-blogging, vloggers post video logs or vlogs.

Voiceover: words narrated by journalists or others working from prepared notes over either video footage of a news event or an audio recording of

actuality sound. Voiceovers typically explain the footage or recording's significance for the benefit of the viewer or listener.

Vox pop/Streeter: a practice by journalists that offers an informal index of public or popular opinion as represented through brief on-the-spot **interviews** with ordinary people. Taken from *vox populi* (Latin for 'voice of the people'), vox pops usually last no longer than 30 seconds. Though the practice does not claim to deliver a representative sampling of opinion from a particular location – often the street, hence the terms 'streeter' or 'man on the street' interview – it does provide a diversity of viewpoints, usually in response to the same question being posed to each person selected.

W

Walkthrough: slang for a rehearsal of a **newscast** (or portion thereof) in order to help ensure that it unfolds properly during the on-air broadcast.

Wapping dispute: one of the most bitterly fought strikes in British newspaper history. The Wapping dispute began in January 1986 when about 6000 employees of Rupert Murdoch's News International (publisher of *The Times*, the *Sunday Times*, the *Sun* and the *News of the World*) sought to resist new working conditions being imposed by managers. These conditions included demands that the unions agree to accept a no-strike clause, an end to the 'closed shop' (where employees were required to be union members), more 'flexible' working arrangements, and the introduction of 'new technology' (replacing 'hot-metal' with electronic printing methods) in the name of cost efficiency. A further demand was that employees agree to move from **Fleet Street** to a new printing plant in Wapping, East London. Faced with the threat of losing their job, most journalists accepted the new terms, while others, particularly the printers, refused and formed picket-lines to demonstrate. The strikers sought to stop buses delivering workers to the plant, which led to arrests and many injuries. News International, with the benefit of strong police and government support, was able to ensure uninterrupted production of all four newspaper titles. By the time the strike was settled in its favour in February 1987, other news companies had decided to follow its departure from Fleet Street and emulate its printing practices.

War journalism: journalism associated with the waging of war and conflict. War journalism has long been associated with imperialism, and the war correspondent developed as British newspapers needed on-site reports of distant colonial wars during the nineteenth century. As additional major wars unfolded that required journalistic address, it was further consolidated as a central journalistic responsibility. Early forms of war reporting were provided by soldiers or travellers, who transmitted their accounts with considerable delay by horse or ship, but their accounts were often erroneous, overly biased and misguided. As the separation of war reportage from the governments waging war grew distinct, the need for journalism intensified; its viability became more attainable once the telegraph made it possible to report from distant battlefields in the late nineteenth century.

Debates over who constituted the first war correspondent continue apace, with candidates including the Dutch painter Willem van de Velde observing naval conflict in the 1650s, Henry Crabb Robinson covering the Peninsular War in 1808, correspondents associated with the Mexican War of the 1840s, and William Howard Russell covering the Crimean War (1853–6) for *The Times* of London. Though their accounts were often partisan, they nonetheless established a gateway for a 'golden age' of war reporting between the two world wars (Knightley 1975). Once radio ascended in the 1920s and 1930s and wire-photo made it possible to transmit images of wartime alongside words, war reporting took on an intensified immediacy, evident during both the Second World War and the Korean War. The arrival of television had direct effect on the reporting of the Vietnam War and the wars that followed.

Most discussions of war reporting bear a decidedly western bias. Related to the prosecution of war and its reportage have been questions of **censorship**, with governments seeking to control the flow of information. Correspondents reporting on the First World War, for instance, were highly censored, while those covering the Second World War were moderately controlled if they reported for democratic nations, and strictly controlled if they reported for totalitarian ones. Other related practices associated with wartime reportage include press **pools** and **embedding** reporters with military units. One of its recommended antidotes is the **journalism of attachment**.

While the role of war correspondent has long been associated with a certain romantic lore, in **actuality** it is beset by an array of problems associated with allegiance, responsibility, **truth** and **balance**, among others. Covering war often entails encountering conditions of an entirely different order than anything ordinarily associated with **newswork**. Images of the war reporter as adventurer or risk-taker, in the optimum sense, or as daredevil, fortune-hunter or rogue, in the negative, help to fuel their celebration in novels, films, plays, and other **fictional representations of journalism**. Similarly implicit here, however, is the notion that war reporters somehow 'do journalism' better, that their experiences are more authentic, engaged and noteworthy than those of other kinds of journalists. And yet, it is their very commitment to some rendering of national identity, even patriotism, that is likely to engender a change in journalistic work. It may entail a migration towards vague word choice, the absence of a broader perspective, the lack of explicit images, even the wearing of flag pins. When journalists under everyday conditions are seen to have strong sentiments for family, friends or community, they are often taken off the story that involves them. When their sentiments for country are seen as strong in wartime, they are rarely removed from the story; rather, the expectation, at least in some quarters, is that they will simply change how they conduct themselves as journalists.

War reporters face an additional responsibility of working through trauma that is associated with crisis in general. Invested in the best of cases with clarifying what is often undecipherable to distant publics, journalists play a key role in moving whole populations from trauma to recovery. Serving as conveyor, translator, mediator and meaning-maker, journalists do more than just relay information as they are called upon to assume a far broader range of tasks, none more important than contributing to the reconfiguration of identities, both individual and collective, that have been temporarily shattered. Given these considerations, it was not surprising that so much of the coverage of the September 11 attacks, for example, focused on the key question of trauma and its aftermath (see Zelizer and Allan 2002). Both the popular and **trade presses** (those publications written by journalists for journalists) ran stories detailing symptoms of stress, with reporters on the scene regarded as being particularly at risk. Questions arose not only concerning the ways in which trauma altered ongoing journalistic roles, but also about whether journalists themselves were capable of accomplishing what the broader collective expected of them during a crisis.

War reporting, in short, demands that notions of what constitutes good journalistic practice be realigned on the basis of different criteria than would typically seem appropriate, criteria thrown into sharp relief – at times violently so – by challenging circumstances (see Allan and Zelizer 2004; Matheson and Allan 2009). At the same time, war reporting's positioning as a litmus test for journalism also rests on an understanding of its capacity to influence public perceptions. Journalists are expected to function variously during war: to be present enough to respond to what is happening, yet absent enough to stay safe; to be sufficiently authoritative so as to provide reliable information, yet open to cracks and fissures in the complicated truth-claims that unfold; to remain passionate about the undermining of human dignity that accompanies war, yet **impartial** and distanced enough to see the strategies that attach themselves to circumstances with always more than one side. In these and related ways, then, war reporting reveals its investment in sustaining a certain discursive authority – namely that of being an **eyewitness**.

This act of witnessing, of seeing for oneself the heart of the story, encapsulates the larger problem of determining what counts as truth in the war zone. Being there suggests that the violence, devastation, suffering and death that inevitably constitute war's underside will somehow be rendered different – more amenable to response and perhaps less likely to recur – just because journalists are somewhere nearby. And yet, the experience of a reporter's being there, so important for distant publics eager for news of a war-torn region, is shaped quite systematically by a weave of limitations – political, military, economic and technological, among others – that together may curtail the experience in drastic ways. Anecdotal evidence from a range of wars bears this out, whereby a journalist's capacity to be present was limited, undermined or even denied altogether when the battleground was placed off limits, the military barricade went up, the cameras broke down, or sources refused to talk. Moreover, a journalist's sense of citizenship, even patriotism, may call into question his or her perceptions of how best to conduct oneself as a reporter. All too often, journalists encounter those who demand to know: are you with us, or are you against us? It is at this point that individual journalists determine for themselves what their role should be, knowing that their *ad hoc* decision may have profound implications for how their audiences come to understand the nature of war and the consequences for its victims. In so doing, they know that even the most basic expectation of journalists in wartime – being there – is rarely realized entirely in the way they may have wanted, given the exigencies with which they must cope.

Warblog: a type of blog dealing with the so-called war on terror. Warblogs emerged during the weeks following the attacks of September 11, 2001. Taking as their focus the proclaimed 'War on Terror', **blogs** devoted particular attention to the perceived shortcomings of the mainstream news media in informing the public about possible risks, threats and dangers. Warbloggers were divided between those who favoured US and UK military intervention in the Middle East and those who did not. In both cases, however, they stressed their dissatisfaction with what they deemed to be the apparent biases of the mainstream news coverage of the ensuing conflict in Afghanistan. For pro-war bloggers, a 'liberal **bias**' was detectable in much mainstream journalism, leading them to call into question the patriotism of well-known reporters and news organizations, while bloggers opposed to the war were equally convinced that mainstream journalism, with its over-reliance on sources from the Bush administration, the Pentagon and other military sources, pro-war think tanks, and so forth, was failing to provide fair and **balanced** coverage. Many were able to show, with little difficulty, how voices of dissent were being routinely marginalized, when they were even acknowledged at all. Warbloggers of either persuasion, then, sought out **alternative** sources of information from across the web in order to buttress their preferred perspective.

Though difficult to generalize, most warbloggers posting from Iraq seemed motivated to share their **eyewitness** experiences of the conflict so as to counterbalance mainstream news media coverage. The work of CNN correspondent Kevin Sites was a case in point, who, in addition to filing his television reports, wrote 'behind the scenes' features for CNN.com and maintained a multimedia blog that provided personal commentary about the events he witnessed, various photographs and personalized audio reports.

Especially noteworthy was the eyewitness reporting attributed to the warblog of 'Salam Pax' (a playful pseudonym derived from the Arabic and Latin words for peace), a 29-year-old architect living in middle-class suburban Baghdad. Of the various English-language warblogs posted by Iraqis, perhaps none attracted a greater following than Salam's *Where is Raed?* (dear_raed.blogspot.com), which began to appear in September 2002. His motivation for blogging was later explained as a desire to keep in touch with his friend Raed, who had moved to study in Jordan, and in the months leading up to the initial 'decapitation attack', to use his turn of phrase, the blog contained material ranging from personal – and frequently humorous – descriptions of everyday life to angry criticisms of the events around him. It was to his astonishment, however, that he discovered that the international blogging community had attracted such intense attention to his site. As word about *Where is Raed?* spread via other blogs, e-mail, online discussion groups and mainstream news media accounts, the warblog began to regularly top the lists of popular blogs. For Salam, this attention brought with it the danger that he would be identified – a risk likely to lead to his arrest, possibly followed by a death sentence. As he would later reflect, 'I was telling everybody who was reading the weblog where the bombs fell, what happened [...] what the streets looked like.' While acknowledging that the risks involved meant that he considered his actions to be somewhat 'foolish' in retrospect, nevertheless he added: 'it felt for me important. It is just somebody should be telling this because journalists weren't' (cited in Church 2003; see also Matheson and Allan 2009).

Watchdog journalism: a form of journalism that seeks to hold public institutions accountable by tracking and investigating their activities. Seen as the opposite to lapdog journalism, watchdog journalism draws from aspirations that journalism acts as a surrogate for the public in that it has a critical role to play in keeping the **public sphere** vibrant and the body politic healthy. Keeping a close watch on political, economic and other public institutions is an important way to achieve those ideals. A particularly prevalent ethos of the news media in certain areas of the world – Waisbord (2000), for instance, discusses its centrality in South America – watchdog journalism includes the display of an ongoing scepticism and commitment to investigate institutional life beyond a single news story; the maintenance of a rapport with the public through readers' letters and other encouragement of audience feedback; features showing that the news organization investigates itself through an **ombudsperson**'s column or reader's advocate; and declarations attesting to the transparency of its own news mission.

Watchdogging: the monitoring of news reporting for quality. Beginning from the premise that the news media should perform a **watchdog** role in functioning democratic societies, watchdogging involves keeping a close eye on possible abuses of power by government or corporations. Usually performed by ordinary citizens using internet resources, watchdogging is credited with helping prevent powerful interests from exercising undue influence over news organizations and for stopping published or broadcast errors from going uncorrected. Citizen-led watchdogging may also be directed at public figures and institutions, double-checking claims they make in news reports.

Watergate effect: the enhanced reputation widely accorded to journalism in the aftermath of the Watergate scandal in the 1970s. When two investigative journalists working at the *Washington Post* – Bob Woodward and Carl Bernstein – were credited with toppling the Nixon administration on August 9 1974, it was believed to have engendered a highly beneficial impact on public perceptions of journalism as a laudable profession, not least amongst young people considering possible careers. A film based on Woodward and Bernstein's book describing their reporting of the scandal – *All the President's Men* (released in 1976) – enjoyed both popular and critical acclaim, similarly helping to secure the celebrated place of Watergate in journalistic memory. Critics maintain that the importance of the Watergate effect has been overblown (Schudson 1992) or reconstructed over time (Zelizer 1993).

Weather journalism: journalism focusing on changing weather conditions, including summaries and forecasts as well as advice and warnings about appropriate responses. Though weather journalism became an integral part of news in the mid-1800s, when the telegraph and the development of meteorology helped make weather generally **newsworthy**, its incorporation by the various news media over time generated different modes of coverage. When relayed as part of **radio news**, weather journalism takes the form of brief and continuous updates, while its incorporation as television, print and online journalism depends on highly visual **graphics,** key among them the weather map. Weather journalism has also taken on different demeanours around the globe. For instance, personalized weather forecasting became popular in the 1950s, shortly thereafter rendering the 'weatherman' a feature of British broadcasting who first appeared in a live, five-minute segment on BBC television in January 1954. At the same time, US broadcasting veered towards a light-hearted and sometimes silly relay of weather information, whose weather forecasters employed costumes, tricks and other gimmicks when covering the weather. In 1982, the US-run Weather Channel reflected a growing trend towards **narrowcasting** and niche cable marketing, and its 24-hour a day programming soon thereafter extended to weather networks and websites in the UK, France, Germany, Canada and Latin America. Recognizing the value of immediate weather forecasting for attracting audiences, most online news sites today include some coverage of weather-related issues.

Whistleblower: someone who discloses confidential information to the press, usually motivated by a desire to direct public attention to a perceived wrong, crime or injustice. Several noteworthy news stories have originated from individuals whose place inside an organization has afforded them access to otherwise secret or classified information (the role of the covert informant 'Deep Throat' in the **Watergate** scandal was a famous example). Whistleblowers usually wish to remain **anonymous sources** of information, not least for reasons of their personal safety, thereby relying on the journalist to follow conventions of **unattributed sourcing** and uphold the principle of 'protecting their source' to safeguard them from reprisals. Recent years have seen several countries introduce measures to provide legal protection for whistleblowing.

Wikinews: an online site where citizen journalists independently report the news on a variety of current events. Self-titled 'the free news source you can write', Wikinews represents one of the most developed ventures of reader-written news in **citizen journalism**. Computer programmer Ward Cunningham is widely credited with creating the first wiki-software in 1995, when his 'writeable web page' program was thought to acquire the term 'wiki' from the Hawaiian phrase 'wiki wiki' (meaning 'quick'). In 2001 internet entrepreneur Jimbo Wales applied the 'wiki' concept to an online encyclopedia he called Wikipedia, which offered editable pages that enabled any user to post an item, edit or correct anyone else's item or vote for it to be removed and whose changes were recorded for viewing and could be easily reversed or improved upon by the next person. The nascent news service Wikinews followed as an offshoot soon after.

Wikinews is an initiative of the non-profit Wikimedia Foundation, its parent organization, based in St Petersburg, Florida. Wikipedia operates by drawing upon the energies of dedicated volunteers, financed through donations as no online advertising is allowed to appear. Committed to developing free, open content for the public in a manner that is ideologically 'neutral', the Wikipedia project strives to overcome the digital divide of information inequality and is guided by transparent decision-making, where posted entries are never complete and remain open to revision and elaboration by anyone at any time. For better or worse, there is no 'deference to experts', as everyone enjoys equal status within a larger process of 'collective intelligence'. By March 2005, the English version of Wikinews had reached 1000 pages, a solid presence but easily overshadowed by Wikipedia, with its millions of entries in over 200 languages. The wiki ethic at the heart of Wikinews invites a particular type of relationship with its volunteer journalists, or 'wikinewsies' as they are sometimes called, that revolves around their continued goodwill, reliability and – even though most post anonymously – shared accountability.

In contrast with **IndyMedia's** political agenda or **OhmyNews's** encouragement of subjective opinion, Wikinews plays a more traditional journalistic role. Mutual trust and co-operation are the key 'checks and balances' guiding the conduct of Wikinews. Given that it is impossible to determine who has posted a particular entry or altered someone else's, the site remains vulnerable to those seeking to deliberately compromise its integrity as an **alternative news source**. Of particular import for Wikinews is its policy for users when referring to points of fact. Specifically, all sources used for information must be cited and verifiable, at least in principle, by someone else, and in original reporting field notes must be presented on the article's discussion (Talk) page. Disputes over points of fact and interpretation are inevitable, of course, as the site's policy guidelines readily concede in its discussion of '**neutral point of view**' (**NPOV**). But by encouraging users to be patient and polite with one another, it offers specific tips for resolving problems.

Advocates laud the way in which Wikinews allows its users endless scope to pursue stories that matter to them. Critics consider the wiki format to be irreconcilable, by definition, with the 'brand' of a news organization based on **accuracy**, remain sceptical about its viability as a business model, point to gaps in its coverage – identifying important stories that escaped Wikinews attention – and complain that too many items are rewritten news stories from elsewhere (see Allan 2006).

Wires: slang for **news agencies**.

Y

Yellow journalism: a form of journalism driven by **sensational** and flamboyant coverage, degrees of misrepresentation and self-promoting, profiteering tactics. Originating in the US during the late 1890s as part of a battle for readers between Joseph Pulitzer's *New York World* and William Randolph Hearst's *New York Journal*, yellow journalism was developed as a way to draw more readers with sensational content, garish **pictures** and bold **headlines**. As innovations in print technology and the ascent of advertising made it possible for publishers to attract a larger **readership**, the two papers began experimenting with novel strategies, reducing the price of the papers and introducing sensationalistic presentational features, such as hyperbolic language, coverage of romance, scandal and **sports**, large **headlines** and copious illustrations. Popular lore holds that the name 'yellow journalism' originated in a comic strip in the papers which featured a child in a yellow nightshirt – 'The Yellow Kid' – and the analogy was drawn in 1887 by the *New York Press* as a derisive term for the two battling newspapers. Yellow journalism was also associated with unethical journalistic practice, and it was largely held responsible for driving the Spanish–American War with its melodramatic coverage and profiteering tactics to draw readers. Its most famous, though unconfirmed, story involved the artist Frederick Remington telegraphing Hearst to say that all was quiet in Cuba. Hearst was said to have responded, 'You furnish the **pictures** and I'll furnish the war.' Though yellow journalism died out shortly after the turn of the century, some of its techniques still remain, including banner **headlines**, coloured **cartoons** and comics and graphic **pictures**.

Z

Zinger: a **human interest** item placed at the end of a **bulletin** or **newscast** in order to leave the viewer or listener with an upbeat, strange-but-true or wryly amusing story (sometimes called a 'sweetener'). Used to wrap up the broadcast, zingers, which are one type of **bagger**, are often good place-fillers. They are usually created by a designated staffer whose responsibility is to establish a repository of such stories for the moments they can be accommodated.

References

Adam, G.S. (1993) *Notes Toward A Definition of Journalism*. St Petersburg, FL: Poynter Institute.

Allan, S. (2006) *Online News: Journalism and the Internet*. Maidenhead and New York: Open University Press.

Allan, S. (2010) *News Culture*, 3rd edn. Maidenhead and New York: Open University Press.

Allan, S. and Thorsen, E. (eds) (2009) *Citizen Journalism: Global Perspectives*. New York: Peter Lang.

Allan, S. and Zelizer, B. (eds) (2004) *Reporting War: Journalism in Wartime*. London: Routledge.

Barnhurst, K.G. and Nerone, J. (2001) *The Form of News: A History*. New York: Guilford.

Barnouw, E. (1990) *Tube of Plenty*, 2nd edn. New York: Oxford University Press.

Becker, H.S. (1967) Whose side are we on? *Social Problems*, 14(3): 239–47.

Bell, M. (1995) *In Harm's Way*. Harmondsworth: Penguin.

Bell, M. (1998) The journalism of attachment, in M. Kieran (ed.) *Media Ethics*. London: Routledge.

Bell, M. (2009) The death of news in Afghanistan, *Guardian*, 10 September.

Bertrand, J.C. (2000) *Media Ethics and Accountability Systems*. New Brunswick, NJ: Transaction Press.

Bird, S.E. (1992) *For Enquiring Minds: A Cultural Study of Supermarket Tabloids*. Knoxville, TN: University of Tennessee Press.

Bliss, Jr, E. (1991) *Now the News*. New York: Columbia University Press.

Boorstin, D.J. (1961) *The Image: A Guide to Pseudo-Events in America*. New York: Vintage.

Bourdieu, P. (1998) *On Television and Journalism*, translation by P.P. Ferguson. London: Pluto.

Boyd-Barrett, O. and Rantanen, T. (eds) (1999) *The Globalization of News*. London: Sage.

Boyle, R. (2006) *Sports Journalism: Context and Issues*. London: Sage.

Breed, W. (1955) Social control in the newsroom, *Social Forces*, 33: 326–55.

Briggs, A. (1970) *The War of Words, Volume III: The History of Broadcasting in the United Kingdom*. London: Oxford University Press.

Bromley, M. (2006) One journalism or many? Confronting the contradictions in the education and training of journalists in the United Kingdom, in K.W.Y. Leung *et al.* (eds) *Global Trends in Communication Research and Education*. Cresskill, NJ: Hampton.

Burns, T. (1977) *The BBC: Public Institution and Private World*. London: Macmillan.

Campbell, R. (1991) *'60 Minutes' and the News*. Urbana-Champaign, IL: University of Illinois Press.

Cappella, J. and Jamieson, K.H. (1997) *Spiral of Cynicism: The Press and the Public Good*. New York: Oxford University Press.

Carey, J.W. (1986) The dark continent of American journalism, in R.K. Manoff and M. Schudson (eds) *Reading the News*. New York: Pantheon.

Carey, J.W. (2000) Some personal notes on US journalism education, *Journalism*, 1(1): 12–23.

Chalaby, J.K. (1996) Journalism as an Anglo-American invention, *European Journal of Communication*, 11(3): 303–26.

Church, R. (2003) Interview with Salman Pax, CNN International, Transcript Number: 100302cb.k18, 3 October.

Clayman, S. and Heritage, J. (2002) *The News Interview*. Cambridge: Cambridge University Press.

Cohen, S. (1972) *Folk Devils and Moral Panics*. London: McGibbon and Kee.

Condit, C.M. (2004) Science reporting to the public, *Canadian Medical Association Journal*, 170 (9): 1415–16.

Craven, L. (1992) The early newspaper press in England, in D. Griffiths (ed.) *The Encyclopedia of the British Press*. London: Macmillan.

Crouse, T. (1973) *The Boys on the Bus*. New York: Random House.

Curran, J. (1978) The press as an agency of social control: an historical perspective, in G. Boyce, J. Curran and P. Wingate (eds) *Newspaper History*. London: Constable.

Curran, J. and Seaton, J. (2003) *Power Without Responsibility: The Press and Broadcasting in Britain*, 6th edn. London: Routledge.

Curran, J., Douglas, A. and Whannel, G. (1980) The political economy of the human interest story, in A. Smith (ed.) *Newspapers and Democracy*. Cambridge, MA: MIT Press.

Danna, S.R. (1975) The rise of radio news, in L.W. Lichty and M.C. Topping (eds) *American Broadcasting: A Source Book*. New York: Hastings House.

Davies, N. (2008) *Flat Earth News*. London: Chatto and Windus.

Dennis, E. (1984) *Planning for Curricular Change: A Report on the Future of Journalism and Mass Communication Education*. Eugene, OR: School of Journalism, University of Oregon.

Eason, D. (1986) On journalistic authority: the Janet Cooke scandal, *Critical Studies in Mass Communication*, 3: 429–47.

Elliott, P. (1978) Professional ideology and organisational change: the journalist since 1800, in G. Boyce, J. Curran and P. Wingate (eds) *Newspaper History*. London: Constable.

Elliott, P. (1980) Press performance as political ritual, in H. Christian (ed.) *The Sociology of Journalism and the Press* (Sociological Review Monograph 29). Keele: University of Keele.

Entman, R. M. (1993) Framing: towards clarification of a fractured paradigm, *Journal of Communication*, 43 (4): 51–8.

Ettema, J. and Glasser, T. (1998) *Custodians of Conscience: Investigative Journalism and Public Virtue*. New York: Columbia University Press.

Fishman, M. (1980) *Manufacturing the News*. Austin, TX: University of Texas Press.

Franklin, B. (1997) *Newszak and News Media*. London: Arnold.

Franklin, B. (2005) McJournalism: the local press and the McDonaldization thesis, in S. Allan (ed) *Journalism: Critical Issues*. Maidenhead and New York: Open University Press.

Galtung, J. (1998) High road, low road: charting the course for peace journalism, *Track Two*, 7(4) (December).

Galtung, J. and Ruge, M. (1973) Structuring and selecting news, in S. Cohen and J. Young (eds) *The Manufacture of News*. London: Constable.

Gans, H. (1979) *Deciding What's News*. New York: Vintage.

Gitlin, T. (1980) *The Whole World is Watching: Mass Media in the Making and Unmaking of the New Left*. Berkeley, CA: University of California Press.

Glasgow University Media Group (1976) *Bad News*. London: Routledge and Kegan Paul.

Glasgow University Media Group (1980) *More Bad News*. London: Routledge and Kegan Paul.

Glasser, T. (1999) *The Idea of Public Journalism*. New York: Guilford.

Goldberg, V. (1986) *The Power of Photography*. New York: Abbeville Press.

Graber, D.A. (1980) *Crime News and the Public*. New York: Praeger.

Habermas, J. (1989) *The Structural Transformation of the Public Sphere*, translated by T. Burger with F. Lawrence. Cambridge, MA: MIT Press.

Hackett, R.A. and Zhao, Y. (1998) *Sustaining Democracy? Journalism and the Politics of Objectivity*. Toronto: Garamond.

Hall, S. (1973) The determinations of news photographs, in S. Cohen and J. Young (eds) *The Manufacture of News*. London: Sage.

Hall, S., Critcher, C., Jefferson, T., Clarke, J. and Roberts, B. (1978) *Policing the Crisis: Mugging, the State, and Law and Order*. London: Macmillan.

Hallin, D. and Mancini, P. (2004) *Comparing Media Systems: Three Models of Media and Politics*. New York: Cambridge University Press.

Hallin, D.C. (1986) *The 'Uncensored War': The Media and Vietnam*. New York: Oxford University Press.

Hartley, J. (1992) *The Politics of Pictures*. London: Routledge.

Herman, E.S. and Chomsky, N. (1988) *Manufacturing Consent: The Political Economy of the Mass Media*. New York: Pantheon.

Howe, J. (2006) The rise of crowdsourcing, *Wired*, 14 June.

Hughes, H. (1940) *The Human Interest Story*. Chicago, IL: University of Chicago Press.

Innis, H.A. (1986) *Empire and Communications*. Victoria: Press Porcépic.

Janowitz, M. (1975) Professional models in journalism: the gatekeeper and the advocate, *Journalism Quarterly*, (Winter): 618–26, 662.

Kiernan, V. (2006) *Embargoed Science*. Urbana, IL: University of Illinois Press.

Knightley, P. (1975) *The First Casualty*. New York and London: Harcourt Brace Jovanovich.

Kovach, B. and Rosenstiel, T. (2001) *The Elements of Journalism*. London: Atlantic Books.

LaFollette, M.C. (1990) *Making Science Our Own: Public Images of Science 1910–1955*. Chicago, IL: University of Chicago Press.

Lang, K. and Lang, G.E. (1989) Collective memory and the news, *Communication*, 11: 123–39.

Lee, A.J. (1976) *The Origins of the Popular Press in England, 1855–1914*. London: Croom Helm.

Lippmann, W. (1922) *Public Opinion*. New York: Free Press.

Lordan, E. (2006) *Politics, Ink: How America's Cartoonists Skewer Politicians, From King George III to George Dubya*. Lanham, MD: Rowman and Littlefield.

Lule, J. (2001) *Daily News, Eternal Stories*. New York: Guilford Press.

Lynch, J. and McGoldrick, A. (2005) *Peace Journalism*. Gloucestershire: Hawthorne Press.

McLauchlin, R.J. (1975) What the *Detroit News* has done in broadcasting, in L.W. Lichty and M.C. Topping (eds) *American Broadcasting: A Source Book*. New York: Hastings House.

Matheson, D. and Allan, S. (2009) *Digital War Reporting*. Cambridge: Polity.

Meyer, P. (1973) *Precision Journalism*. Bloomington, IN: Indiana University Press.

Moeller, S. (1998) *Compassion Fatigue: How the Media Sell Disease, Famine, War, and Death*. New York: Routledge.

Molotch, H. and Lester, M. (1974) News as purposive behavior, *American Sociological Review*, 39 (6): 101–12.

Nerone, J. (1995) *Last Rights: Revisiting the Four Theories of the Press*. Urbana, IL: University of Illinois Press.

Park, R.E. (1940) News as a form of knowledge, *American Journal of Sociology*, 45 (5): 669–86.

Patterson, T. (1977) The 1976 horserace, *Wilson Quarterly*, 1: 73–9.

Patterson, T. (1994) *Out of Order*. New York: Vintage.

Pauly, J.J. (1990) The politics of the new journalism, in N. Sims (ed.) *Literary Journalism in the Twentieth Century*. New York: Oxford University Press.

Rosen, J. (2001) *What Are Journalists For?* New Haven, CT: Yale University Press.

Roshco, B. (1975) *Newsmaking.* Chicago, IL: University of Chicago Press.

Rowe, D. (2004) *Sport, Culture and the Media,* 2nd edn. Maidenhead and New York: Open University Press.

Scannell, P. and Cardiff, D. (1991) *A Social History of British Broadcasting: Volume One 1922–1939.* Oxford: Blackwell.

Schlesinger, P. (1977) *Putting Reality Together.* London: Constable.

Schlesinger, P. and Tumber, H. (1994) *Reporting Crime: The Media Politics of Criminal Justice.* Oxford: Clarendon.

Schoenfeld, A.C. (1980) Newspersons and the environment today, *Journalism Quarterly,* 57 (3): 456–62.

Schudson, M. (1978) *Discovering the News.* New York: Basic Books.

Schudson, M. (1992) *Watergate in American Memory.* New York: Basic Books.

Schudson, M. (1995) *The Power of News.* Cambridge, MA: Harvard University Press.

Seymour-Ure, C. (2008) Cartoons, in B. Franklin (ed.) *Pulling Newspapers Apart: Analysing Print Journalism.* London: Routledge.

Siebert, F.S., Peterson, T. and Schramm, W. (1956) *Four Theories of the Press.* Urbana, IL: University of Illinois Press.

Sigal, L. (1973) *Reporters and Officials.* Lexington, MA: D.C. Heath.

Sims, N. (2007) *True Stories: A Century of Literary Journalism.* Evanston, IL: Northwestern University Press.

Smith, A. (1978) The long road to objectivity and back again: the kinds of truth we get in journalism, in G. Boyce, J. Curran and P. Wingate (eds) *Newspaper History.* London: Constable.

Smith, A. (1979) *The Newspaper: An International History.* London: Thames and Hudson.

Sparks, C. (2000) Introduction: the panic over tabloid news, in C. Sparks and J. Tulloch (eds) *Tabloid Tales: Global Debates Over Media Standards.* Lanham, MD: Rowman and Littlefield.

Stephens, M. (1988) *A History of News: From the Drum to the Satellite.* New York: Viking.

Strupp, J. (2009) Poll finds 40 per cent of sports reporters gamble on sports, *Editor and Publisher,* 2 September.

Tuchman, G. (1972) Objectivity as strategic ritual: an examination of newsmen's notions of objectivity, *American Journal of Sociology,* 77 (4): 660–79.

Tuchman, G. (1978) *Making News.* New York: Basic Books.

Tumber, H. and Palmer, J. (2004) *Media at War: The Iraq Crisis.* London: Sage.

Tunstall, J. (1971) *Journalists at Work.* London: Constable.

Wahl-Jorgensen, K. (2007) *Journalists and the Public: Newsroom Culture, Letters to the Editor and Democracy.* Creskill, NJ: Hampton Press.

Waisbord, S. (2000) *Watchdog Journalism in South America*. New York: Columbia University Press.

White, D.M. (1950) The gate keeper: a case study in the selection of news, *Journalism Quarterly*, 27 (3): 383–90.

Wilcox, S.A. (2003) Cultural context and the conventions of science journalism: drama and contradiction in media coverage of biological ideas about sexuality, *Critical Studies in Media Communication*, 20 (3): 225–47.

Williams, R. (1978) The press and popular culture: an historical perspective, in G. Boyce, J. Curran and P. Wingate (eds) *Newspaper History*. London: Constable.

Winston, B. (1993) The CBS Evening News, 7 April 1949: creating an ineffable television form, in J. Eldridge (ed.) *Getting the Message: News, Truth and Power*. London: Routledge.

Zelizer, B. (1992) *Covering the Body: The Kennedy Assassination, the Media, and the Shaping of Collective Memory*. Chicago, IL: University of Chicago Press.

Zelizer, B. (1993) Journalists as interpretive communities, *Critical Studies in Mass Communication*, 10 (September): 219–37.

Zelizer, B. (1998) *Remembering to Forget: Holocaust Memory Through the Camera's Eye*. Chicago, IL: University of Chicago Press.

Zelizer, B. (2004) *Taking Journalism Seriously: News and the Academy*. Thousand Oaks, CA: Sage.

Zelizer, B. (2005) The Culture of Journalism, in J. Curran and M. Gurevitch (eds) *Mass Media and Society*, 4th edn. London: Edward Arnold.

Zelizer, B. (2007) 'On having been there': 'eyewitnessing' as a journalistic key word, *Critical Studies in Media Communication*, 24 (5): 408–28.

Zelizer, B. (2008) Why memory's work on journalism does not reflect journalism's work on memory, *Memory Studies*, 1(1): 75–83.

Zelizer, B. (2010). *About to Die: How News Images Move the Public*. New York: Oxford University Press.

Zelizer, B. and Allan, S. (eds) (2002) *Journalism After September 11*. London and New York: Routledge.

Zelizer, B., Park, D. and Gudelunas, D. (2002) How bias shapes the news: challenging the *New York Times'* status as a newspaper of record on the Middle East, *Journalism: Theory, Practice, and Criticism*, 3 (3): 283–308.